THE COURSE
OF RECOGNITION

Institute for Human Sciences Vienna
Lecture Series

THE COURSE
OF RECOGNITION

PAUL RICOEUR

Translated by

David Pellauer

Harvard University Press

Cambridge, Massachusetts

London, England

First Harvard University Press paperback edition, 2007

Originally published as *Parcours de la Reconnaissance;*
© Éditions Stock, 2004

Library of Congress Cataloging-in-Publication Data

Ricoeur, Paul.
[Parcours de la reconnaissance. English]
The course of recognition / Paul Ricoeur; translated by
David Pellauer.
p. cm.—(Institute for Human Sciences Vienna lecture series)
Includes bibliographical references and index.
ISBN-13 978-0-674-01925-6 (cloth: alk. paper)
ISBN-10 0-674-01925-3 (cloth: alk. paper)
ISBN-13 978-0-674-02564-6 (pbk.)
ISBN-10 0-674-02564-4 (pbk.)
1. Perception (Philosophy).   2. Phenomenology.
3. Gratitude.   I. Title.   II. Vienna lecture series.

B828.45.R5313 2005
121.3—dc22   2005040292

To Frans Vansina,
frère mineur, my oldest friend
To Charles Taylor,
so close for so long a time

Contents

Preface

This book devoted to recognition stems from three lectures I gave on this topic at the Institut für die Wissenschaften vom Menschen in Vienna, then further developed at the Husserl Archives in Freiburg. This translation is of the reworked and expanded French version of these lectures.

My investigation arose from a sense of perplexity having to do with the semantic status of the very term *recognition* on the plane of philosophical discourse. It is a fact that no theory of recognition worthy of the name exists in the way that one or more theories of knowledge exist. This surprising lacuna stands in contrast to the kind of coherence that allows the word *recognition* to appear in a dictionary as a single lexical unit, despite the multiple senses that this lexical unit embraces, of connotations attested to within at least one linguistic community, that of contemporary French.

The contrast between the apparently haphazard scattering of occurrences of the word on the plane of philosophical discourse and the kind of rule-governed polysemy that results from the lexicographer's labor constitutes the situation that gave rise to the sense of perplexity I have mentioned. Comparison of the senses of the word *recognition* attested to in the history of philosophical ideas only added to this feeling of perplexity. It was as though the heterogeneity of events that governed the emergence of new philosophical problems had contributed to a dispersion of potential philosophical meanings to the point of a reduction to mere homonymy.

This book was born of a wager, that it is possible to confer on the sequence of known philosophical occurrences of the word *recognition* the coherence of a rule-governed polysemy capable of serving as a rejoinder to that found on the lexical plane. Hence, the introduction to this book is devoted to some working hypotheses that presided over the construction of my argument—that is, to the dynamic that presides first over the promotion of recognition-identification, then over the transition from this identification of something in general to the recognition of those entities specified by ipseity, then from self-recognition to mutual recognition, and finally to the ultimate equating of recognition and gratitude, which French is one of the few languages to honor.

To put it briefly, the dynamic that guides my investigation consists in a reversal, on the very level of the grammar, of the verb *to recognize* from its use in the active voice to its use in the passive voice: I actively recognize things, persons, myself; I ask, even demand, to be recognized by others.

To conclude this argument, I would like to say that if the demand for recognition can appear as the teleological pole of the sequence of philosophical uses of the substantive term *recognition* and the verb *to recognize,* this teleological attraction works on the plane of philosophical discourse only insofar as it is at the same time resisted by a concern to give to the rule-governed polysemy considered in my three chapters on recognition its fullest play. Our initial perplexity then gives way, bit by bit, to a kind of admiration for the power of differentiation at work in language that runs contrary to the expectation of univocity that motivates the *art de dénommer.*

As for the final equation of recognition and gratitude, honored in French, it turns out to be magnified by the delaying effect that led to my decision to begin this inquiry with the identification of something in general. In this way, the question of identity is immediately introduced into the discourse on recognition. It will remain to the end, but at the price of transformations I shall discuss as we proceed. Is it not my genuine identity that demands to be recognized? And if, happily, this happens, does not my gratitude go to those who in one way or another have, in recognizing me, recognized my identity?

Have I won the wager upon which this book is based, that there can be a philosophical discourse *about* recognition that is, in fact, that *of* recognition?

By taking as my title the "course" of recognition, and not the "theory" of this discourse, I mean to acknowledge the persistence of the initial perplexity that motivated this inquiry, something that the conviction of having constructed a rule-governed polysemy halfway between homonymy and univocity does not fully remove.

THE COURSE
OF RECOGNITION

INTRODUCTION

There must be a reason that no widely recognized philosophical work of high reputation has been published with the title *Recognition*. Is it because we are here dealing with a false concept, one that leads authors seeking new insight into the pitfall of a false subject? Yet this word runs insistently through my readings, appearing sometimes like a gremlin who pops up at the wrong place, at other times as welcomed, even as looked for and anticipated. Which places are those?

Here the aid of dictionaries presents itself. So, like a good student of the philosophy of ordinary language, I have sought to spell out meanings in terms of their individual contexts of usage in everyday language. It is this work of turning from page to page, where one word explicates another, where a synonym calls for an antonym, that led me to an initial series of meanings for *recognition*, that of the lexicon of everyday language.

I am not the first person to page through lexicons in this way. Nineteenth- and twentieth-century German philosophy had already incorporated philological inquiry into the elaboration of its principal concepts. And before any of us, Greek thinkers of the classical age, as skilled lexicographers, Professor Aristotle at their head, leafed through the great book of manners and customs, seeking in the works of the poets and orators a breakthrough to the appropri-

1

ate terms, long before usage had worn away the relief of these new pieces of linguistic coin.

If frequenting lexicons is not foreign to inquiries into meaning among philosophers, it has occupied an unaccustomed place in my own recent research, owing to a semantic deficiency that will surprise any philosopher when he or she begins such an inquiry. It does seem that the word *recognition* has a lexical stability that justifies its place as an entry in the dictionary, apart from any philosophical sponsorship regarding the scope of its usages. This was the initial discovery that justified pushing my lexicographical inquiry beyond the usual sort of preface, one that itself constitutes, so to speak, the first phase of my attempt to tie things together semantically.

Yet a quick review guided by such lexicons does turn out to leave contrasting impressions. On the one hand, the obvious polysemy of the word leads to an acceptable sequential ordering that does no violence to our sense of correctness when it comes to the use of everyday words, but that also does justice to the variety of conceptual uses without extending to a dismembering that would result in the confession of mere homonymy. In this regard, we can speak of a rule-governed polysemy of the word *recognition* in its ordinary usage. On the other hand, a kind of discordance appears during the comparison of one lexicon with another, a discordance that may lead us to think that an organizing principle for this polysemy is lacking—I mean one stemming from an order other than that of ordinary usage. This lacuna, along with the controlled arbitrariness presiding over the lexicographical organization of such polysemy, reinforces the feeling of a semantic deficiency observable at the level of a properly philosophical thematic treatment of recognition. What is more, in the lexicographical treatment of the usages found in ordinary language, the passage from one meaning to another takes place by imperceptible skips. The principle of these tiny gaps lies in what is not said, the unsaid, of the prior definition, beneath which lies concealed the very generating of this ordered series of meanings, under the aegis of what I have called a rule-governed polysemy. It is this play of the gaps that drew my attention, along with the motive force of this unsaid that makes the definitions run together in such a workable way that the derivation seems to flow like a continuous stream of meanings.

In order to test out these suggestions concerning the principle governing this polysemy and what overcomes the gaps and the unsaid that bridges them, I have chosen to consult and compare two of the great works of lexicography of the French language, separated from each other by a century: the *Dictionnaire de la langue française*, composed and published by Émile Littré between 1859 and 1872, and the *Grand Robert de la langue française*, whose second edition, edited by Alain Rey, was published in 1985.[1] We might have also gone back to Antoine Furetière and his *Dictionnaire universel*, which, according to Rey in his preface to the *Grand Robert*, "is by far the best dictionary of classical French."[2] However, for our undertaking, the distance that separates the *Grand Robert* from the *Littré* relates to the respective programs proclaimed by these two types of *dictionnaires raisonnés*. The term I want to look at is the word *recognition*, which we shall examine from the exclusive points of view adopted by these two lexicographical enterprises.

That of the *Littré* is formally presented by its editor in the preface to the first volume, to which was later added the lecture of 1 March 1880 ("How I made my dictionary of the French language"), given a year before the death of this staunch, hardworking thinker, and presented under the aegis of Auguste Comte and his own inquiry into the "correct use" of French. His dictionary, Littré declares at the beginning of his preface, "embraces and combines the present and past use of the language, in order to give present usage all the fullness and soundness included within it" (116). Between archaisms and neologisms, then, present usage condenses three centuries of language use, from the sixteenth through the nineteenth centuries.

The major problems confronting the lexicographer have to do, in succession, with the "nomenclature of words"—that is, the constitution of the "corpus of the language as used" (123), along with the problems associated with delimiting a finite corpus; next, with the "classification of the meanings of words," with the question of how to order and rank the meanings listed; and finally, with the "regular and systematic citing of examples drawn from the best authors," wherein Littré sees "an innovation that seems to be in conformity with certain historical tendencies of the modern spirit" (135).

If the question of nomenclature is not a problem here, the same cannot be said for the relation between the classification of meanings and the recourse to "examples drawn from books." The order of arrangement, Littré declares, cannot be arbitrary: "It is not by accident that, in the use of a word, distinct and sometimes quite distant meanings arise from one another" (126). This filiation, he says, is "natural and consequently subject to regular conditions, having to do as much with origins as with descent" (126). The result is that "the derived meanings that become the work and creation of successive generations, no doubt distance themselves from their starting point, but do so only following procedures that, sometimes developing the proper meaning, sometimes the metaphorical one, are in no way arbitrary and disorganized" (127). Hence, Littré confidently banishes the threat of chaos: "Therefore the rule is effective everywhere from the starting point to the derivations—it is this rule that needs to be discovered" (127). My suggestion concerning a derivation of the gaps in meaning starting from the implicit unsaid of the preceding definition is grafted onto this comment of Littré's. Hence I would say, of this important phrase "it is this rule that needs to be discovered," that here lies the secret of what we shall continue to call a rule-governed polysemy, one governed by a methodical history of usage, which it is the task of the lexicographer to produce.

The "examples drawn from classical or other authors" contributes to stabilizing this sequence of derived meanings. Was it not Voltaire who said that a dictionary without citations was only a skeleton? For Littré, the point was not thereby to impose a restricted usage, that of "good use," a reproach frequently made against him, but rather to explore the senses and nuances that were not found in ordinary conversation. Thinking of his classics, he says: "In the hands of someone who imperiously manipulates it, the word points sometimes toward one meaning, sometimes toward another; and without its losing any of its proper value or true character, one sees appear properties one might not have suspected" (137). In this respect, I would say, literature is both a means of amplification and one for analyzing the resources of meaning available in the use of everyday language. This why the art of citation is tangled up with that of classifying meanings. On the one hand, it is by citing that one classifies; on the other, it is the presumption of an order of derivation that assigns a place to the examples cited. Littré could conclude, with the modestly proud tone that was his hallmark: "I claim nothing less than to give a monograph for each word, that is, an article where everything that we know about each word as regards its origin, its form, its meaning, and its use should be presented to readers. This has never been done before" (167).

What, then, of the monograph devoted to the word *recognition*, considered first from the point of view of the derivation of its meanings and then through the recourse it makes to citations?

I shall follow Littré's advice about the rule that "needs to be discovered." It lies concealed behind the succession of twenty-three (yes, twenty-three!) meanings enumerated. We have to construct it by looking in the folds of one definition for the key to the derivation of the next one, following the order of increasing separation from the previous definition.

Which meaning is taken to come first? The one that appears to be the most "natural," namely, the one that derives *recognition (reconnaître)* from *connaître*, by means of the prefix *re-*. "Recognition: 1. To bring again to mind the idea of someone or something one knows [*connaît*]. *I recognize the style. To recognize people by their voice, their bearing.*" What is unsaid lies in the force of the *re-*, taken at first sight in the temporal sense of repetition. This apparently obvious point will be challenged by the *Grand Robert*. What is more, if the definition evokes the mind's initiative ("to bring again to mind"), it leaves indistinct the *quid* of what is recognized as such. Indeed, nothing is said about the marks by which one recognizes something. This latter silence is broken in the following definition. Here we pass to the act of recognizing something one has never seen before: "2. To know by some sign, some mark, some indication, a person or a thing one has never seen before. *By her bearing, one recognizes a goddess. To recognize a plant on the basis of the description given in a book.*" This idea of a mark by which we recognize will hold a considerable place in what follows in this book. With it we pass to the idea of recognizing *as* this or that: to recognize that person in that individual. Still, the *quid* recognized is not yet distinguished by the examples that bring together plants, kings, goddesses, and God. We can also note that it is not a matter of some distinct kind under this second rubric of "making oneself recognized, to prove what one is by certain indications." This kind of initiative or attempt will call for a particular analysis on our part of "to make oneself recognized" in our zigzag course that will follow this consideration of mastery gained through lexicography. What remains unsaid here is the reliability of the sign, the mark, or the indication of recognition by which one recognizes something or someone. However, it is thanks to this intermediary idea that we pass to active knowing of something under the sign of truth: "3. To arrive at, to catch sight of, to discover the truth of something. *People recognized his innocence. One recognizes healthy water by these signs. One recognizes their bad faith,*" and so on. With the idea of truth, an aspect of value is tacitly put in place that will be thematized subsequently. As for the truth, it can be factual or normative—something that is not indifferent. What is more, the verb *to arrive at* insinuates the note of a difficulty in the form of hesitation, delay, resistance. This remark should be joined to our earlier comments about the verb "to bring again to mind." We touch here on the implicit operation by means of which a gap is both acknowledged and overcome. This point, which we might say has to do with the difficulties of recognition, becomes more precise in the following usage: "4. To recognize with negation sometimes indicates not having any regard for, not listening to. *He recognizes no law but his own will.*" The unsaid lies in the mental hesitation underlying the negative form: "recognizes only." Starting from this arduous, difficult side of recognition, the meanings that follow spread out in the direction of the discovery and exploration of what is unknown, "whether it be a matter of places, reefs, or dangers" (numbers 5, 6, and 7). Arriving at gives way to exploring. Meaning 8 can therefore be taken as the major turning point in the orderly arrangement of the meanings of our word: "8. To admit, accept as true, as incontestable. *This philosopher recognizes the existence of atoms.*" The reference to truth from sense 5 is enriched by its being linked to the difficulty in sense 6 and those which follow. *To admit* is to put an end to a hesitation concerning the truth, but also to acknowledge it. The nuance suggested by the act of admitting is made more precise in the subsequent reference to the authority of someone, implicit in the idea of admitting: "to submit to the authority of some person" (number 9). The shift from *admit* to *submit* is hardly perceptible. One could have not admitted, not submitted. Denial is not far off. By contrast, the aspect of confession in admitting something comes to the fore, something that allows us to go back to the second meaning about the signs by which one recognizes and the third meaning about the dimension of truth these marks bring to light, in the strong sense of "to recognize as," "as having such and such quality." The ideas of marks, of truth, but also of difficulty and even of reticence thus find themselves encompassed in the meaning of our word. What follows are the specialized senses of "recognize for," whether it is a question of military use (number 12), or the even more remarkable use of "to recognize" in the order of filiation: "to recognize a (natural) child." It is not just someone, but a right that is thereby recognized, underscored, by its written mark—a signature capable of being recognized as such. Beyond the religious use of a "declaration of faith" (number 10), we reach the theme of avowal: "to avow, confess" (number 15), perhaps a mistake, a debt, an error. Have we wrapped everything up? No. At the end of this list comes an unexpected guest—an uninvited one, moreover, in many languages other than French—recognition as gratitude: "16. To have appreciation for, to bear witness to one's gratitude." We can see the connection to what preceded this: the avowal of a debt to someone, an avowal addressed to him, puts us on the road to gratitude, provided that the idea of a movement in return is added, one that is spontaneous, gracious in every sense of the word, as if a debt had been forgiven.[3]

Can this table of derivation be simplified? At first glance, it may seem so. If we consult the entry for *reconnu*—hence for the *quid* of recognition—we find that only five occurrences are retained. The first one confirms the first definition of *to recognize:* "what one has brought back to mind, the image, the idea." The word *reconnu* remains in the wake of *connu,* thanks to the "one has brought back." The second sense confirms meaning number 5: "admit as true." The third one repeats the avowal of number 15, "avowed, confessed," and the pronominal forms of these verbs. In fourth position comes the expression *to recognize for,* as the past participle of the third sense of the transitive infinitive: "4. Someone who is declared to possess a certain quality." Our surprise guest—recognition-gratitude—returns in the form of a reward: He who receives signs of gratitude is "rewarded." Yet our initial impression of a reduction in scope is in fact false. It really has to do with the lesser frequency of *to recognize* in the passive form of being recognized. As the remainder of this book will demonstrate, it is exactly at this point that the principal conceptual revolution on the plane of philosophy took place, with the Hegelian theme of the struggle for recognition, where "being recognized" is its horizon. Littré did not foresee that this would take place in the reversal from active to passive, from "recognize" to "being recognized," which would bring about the major revolution that would shake the tranquil order of derivation at the level of ordinary language. Here we touch upon the gap that we shall have to account for between the mode of lexicographical derivation at the level of ordinary language usage and the reconstruction of a rule-governed polysemy in terms of philosophical concepts.

But let us remain a moment longer with Littré. We have still to take into account the use of examples in the process of derivation he presents. As Littré states in his preface and his lecture, this has to do with written language, and more precisely with the classical authors of the seventeenth and eighteenth centuries, for which it is easy to name the principal players: La Fontaine, Corneille, Racine, Molière, La Bruyère, and Mme de Sévigné, to whom are added the preachers Bossuet, Fénelon, Bourdaloue, and Sacy, plus a few Enlightenment *philosophes* dear to this disciple of Auguste Comte: Voltaire, d'Alembert, Buffon, Montesquieu, and Diderot, drawn upon principally because of their literary prestige. In this way the basic idea is confirmed that literary use of the language contributes to the sorting out of meanings either through reinforcement or accentuation or, if one may put it this way, through the analytical exaltation of the process of derivation. The effect on the polysemy of our word is both a concentration and an unfolding held within the limits of a cohabitation of different meanings by the very work of lexicography itself. Hence it is a critical, second-order reflection, armed with knowledge drawn from something other than ordinary conversation, that brings to light the tensions and contortions that linguistic usage accommodates.

When brought together, the work of derivation and that of exemplification verify in an excellent way the conception of a filiation of meanings under the aegis of one lexically distinct term. According to Littré, this filiation may be "natural" at its origin, in the sense that it is the linguistic competence of speakers, and even more that of writers, that brings into play the sort of instinct that makes us attentive to correctness in the use of words. But an enigma remains: What are we to make of the spacing between the successive definitions that the printed lexicon underscores by the conventional sign of numbering them? This space is also the one crossed in the writing of the lexicon in passing from one sense to the next one. I have suggested that it is in the folds of the previous definition that the unsaid is concealed whose reprise in the following definition assures the appearance of a slippage that makes for the cohabitation of so many different meanings under the aegis of one and the same term. The examination of this enigma will be at the heart of our investigation into the transition between lexicographical and philosophical semantics.

My announced comparison between the *Grand Robert de la langue française* and the *Littré* dictionaries brings to light the decisive innovations of a work separated by a century from its predecessor. A first difference from the *Littré* has to do with the addition of analogical considerations to the classification of the meanings of a word on the basis of its definition. The *Robert* is presented as "alphabetical and analogical." The relation of one word to other words evoked by the idea of analogy is thus added to the internal delimitation of each of the meanings that unfold its polysemy. The definition remains, it is true, "the vital center of any dictionary of a language" (I:xxxiii). And the lexicographer makes no "claim to construct the concepts and image of the world." He confines himself to reflecting the semantic organization of the language through a series of statements in ordinary language following a rhetoric that is "entirely didactic in spirit." Yet within this modest framework, each of the successive definitions is given a number based on a rigorous paraphrase "synonymous with what is defined": "the vital center of a dictionary of a language—what is essential to any terminological lexicon—remains, whatever the importance of examples, definition." These definitions are meant to cover the whole range of the word defined, while clarifying and explicating it. The *Robert* remains the heir of the *Littré* in this regard. The analogical system meant to complete the definition through recourse to the relations between words is added to this base, thereby making the dictionary an "immense network representative of the semantic relations in the lexicon of our language." Using a technical vocabulary borrowed from the semiotics of the second half of the twentieth century, we can say that to the syntagmatic relations imposed by the linguistic context are added paradigmatic relations that open the way to the elaboration of a veritable *Begriffssystem,* to which we may compare Hallig and Wartburg and, more modestly, *Le dictionnaire analogique de la langue française* of P. Boissière, which dates from 1862.[4] Yet despite this enlargement, the *Grand Robert* confines itself to finding a location for the whole little universe of discourse held to be worthy of presiding over a "pedagogy in vocabulary," the openness compensating for the exactitude obtained.

There is another innovation, common to the *Grand Robert* and to the *Trésor de la langue française (TLF):* a better articulation between the "examples of usage" and the principally literary "referenced citations."[5] In the body of the text, these examples and citations are given a distinct numbering. In this regard, the *Robert* assumes, as does the *Littré,* the "literary character of the example." But unlike its predecessor, which left out contemporaries, the *Robert* makes room for them, up to authors who immediately preceded publication of the dictionary. In this way it creates a philosophical fringe juxtaposed to the specialized vocabularies of the sciences and technology that have become commonplace and entered into ordinary usage. The *Robert* and the *TLF* can pride themselves on proposing to the public "the greatest collection of literary and dialectical citations." The *Robert* in particular aims at serving not only allegedly good use but the variety in ordinary usage, with the ambition of thereby giving a "social image" (xviii) of the worlds of everyday life.

But the most significant innovation has to do with the classification of meanings, the ticklish point of all lexicography. For the linear system of the *Littré,* which I have tried to reconstruct, the *Robert* substitutes a hierarchical architecture of uses in the form of a tree. This way of presenting things gives a greater readability to the semantic composition of a term by arranging the levels of its constitution in a hierarchy. The "mother" ideas, as the *Littré* would have put it, thereby find themselves reduced to a small number; taken together, they make up the irreducible polysemy of the term considered.

Three major senses of our term *recognition* are offered:

1. To grasp (an object) with the mind, through thought, in joining together images, perceptions having to do with it; to distinguish or identify the judgment or action, know it by memory.
2. To accept, take to be true (or take as such).
3. To bear witness through gratitude that one is indebted to someone for (something, an act).

The order in which the meanings on the second level are enumerated invites a survey that does not differ greatly from the essentially linear one proposed by the *Littré* dictionary. Nevertheless, the first pivotal definition indicates a separation of *to recognize* from *to know.* The *Littré* sticks with filiation at the level of the signifier; the *Robert* goes straight to the conceptual novelty expressed by the verbs "to grasp, link, distinguish, identify," and so on. In the comment that immediately follows, the term *know* [in the sense of *connaître*] is reintegrated into the sequence of such operations, thanks to the triad "memory, judgment, action." We cannot miss the vagueness of this primary definition, whose conceptual articulation is already quite extensive. It includes an internal ramification expressed through its careful written form: *to link* is not the same as *to distinguish,* a term separated from what precedes it by only a semicolon; no more than is *to identify,* itself separated from *to distinguish* by only an *or.* This vagueness, this looseness, says much about the difficulty in conceptualizing our term. Nevertheless, the first definition in the *Robert* does refer to a mental act, a thought, that is irreducible to the mere reiteration of an earlier experience, something seen or experienced. This is a valuable indication for later work regarding the concept. At the same time, we are not prevented from seeing in this initial displacement from one lexicon to another, after three generations, the influence of what the sociology of representations would catalog as a rationalizing ideology with overtones more Kantian or neo-Kantian than positivist. So a whole universe of thought can already be discovered in one definition supposed to account for a meaning accepted by the linguistic community.

As for the transition from the first root idea to the second, "to accept, take for true," it takes place, beneath the surface of the shift in meaning, through the intermediary idea of signs of recognition, brought to the fore by the very first definition of the substantive form of *recognition* as distinct from the verb *to recognize.* We read: "recognition: 1. the fact of recognizing (1); what serves to recognize." The latter part of this definition allows the substantive to say what the verb conceals—namely, the passage from the idea of grasping an idea with the mind, through thought, to that of taking as true, through the go-between of the idea of a sign of recognition.

As for the third root idea—less common in English and foreign to German—recognition in the sense of gratitude, it proceeds tacitly from the preceding one through the go-between of the idea of a

debt, which is like that which is unstated in the prior idea of acceptance, admission, inasmuch as the presumed truth is a value that
calls for approbation in the form of an avowal. We then have the interconnected sequence "accept, take to be true, admit, avow, be indebted, thank." But however tight the derivation is, it remains discontinuous, in a way stochastic. Here, then, lies the residual enigma
of the lexical structure of words that the dictionary makes into a
nomenclature and analyzes. Already, the alphabetical ordering is
stochastic. The internal derivation of the meaning of each word too
is stochastic in a more internal than external way.

If we now consider the species and subspecies of these meanings,
the richest arborescence comes under sense 2.

Sense 1, whose fundamental complexity we have indicated, nevertheless lends itself to an interesting dissection that places at the
head of the first series the idea of thinking (a present object) as having already been grasped by thought. This is recognition as recall,
recollection. The subordination of this principal meaning will constitute a considerable problem for conceptual semantics after Bergson. It will be much more than a question of the relation of a species
to a genus, once the something is someone and this someone is another or oneself, in the present or in the memory of the past. The citation from Bergson in this entry already makes the whole notional
apparatus tip in the direction of a conceptual problematic that lexical semantics is not able to circumscribe.

Something else is at issue with meaning 1.2, which develops
the most important implications of the generic sense: "to identify
(something) by establishing a relationship of identity between an
object, a perception, an image . . . and another by means of an already identified common characteristic; to think, judge (an object, a
concept) as comprehended in a category (species, genus) or as included in a general ideal." The analogies abound: to be acquainted
with, to identify, and also to subsume, find, verify, and so on. The
lexical examination of the parallel substantive *recognition* adds the

case of mutual identification: "the fact of recognizing oneself (1.1 and 1.2), of mutual identification, and by extension, of recognizing each other after a long separation." Within the same perimeter of meaning is introduced the sign by which one recognizes: "mark of recognition by which persons who do not know one another (or who have not seen one another for a long time) can recognize one another (1.2)." A philosophy of recognition will give this subordinate meaning an amplitude, within a much broader semantic space, whose place the lexicon limits itself to indicating. Yet we can already assign this "mark of recognition" much more than a secondary, derived role—that of implicit mediation, of being a bridge between the first root idea—to grasp in thought, etc.—and the second one—to accept, take to be true.

As I have indicated, the arborescence of root idea 2 is particularly rich. At its head comes avowal: "to admit, agree that one has committed (a blameworthy act, a fault)." A number of analogous terms follow, introduced by a double arrow: *agree, confess, assume responsibility for, accuse.* But it is by a veritable leap that we pass to sense 2.2: "to accept (a person) as leader, master"; then, by extension, to 2.3: "to recognize a God, two gods"; followed by the important analogue "to confess": "to recognize a confession, a faith, a belief." It is therefore through a kind of personalization of the vis-à-vis of the avowal that we pass from the idea of admitting to that of agreeing, in the sense of acknowledging (a person) as leader, as master. An underlying definition seems to be implied that will considerably perplex us and that remains unspoken here, the reference to some sort of superiority. This will be our burden in our reflections on authority.

Another step is taken with sense 4.1: "to admit as true after having denied, or after having doubted, to accept despite some reservations." This allusion to hesitation, or delay, will be particularly worthy of development in that it emphasizes "delay, the hesitation, the prior reservations," by means of the central connected idea of "research" (number 5), the sense of "seeking to know, determine" (number 6), with its related ideas of something unknown, of danger. Recognition in the juridical sense of recognizing a law (number 7) is more difficult to subordinate or coordinate. The derivation seems to take place through the idea of legitimacy and superiority, implicit in that of taking to be true, the truth being tacitly posited as a value whose superiority is simply moral. The conceptual clarification required here turns out to be considerable as regards this derivation that enriches the examples and cited references and makes them still more complex, beyond the analogical relations. The recognition of indebtedness, the last specification of recognition as admission, turns out to be closest to the third root idea, that of recognition as gratitude. But first appears the enigma of the concept of authority underlying recognition in the sense of "formally or juridically recognizing . . . officially admitting the juridical existence of" (number 7), whether it is a question of a government, a law, an heir, a signature. This will provide a major test for our attempt to piece together on one level the philosophemes of the *Begriffssystem* of the idea of recognition that is still inchoate on the lexicographical plane.

One question arises at the end of this brief lexicographical survey: How do we pass from the realm of the rule-governed polysemy of words from natural language to the formation of philosophical concepts worthy of figuring in a theory of recognition?

We have to renounce the at first glance seductive project of improving such lexical reflection—for example, by filling in the gaps between the partial definitions through the addition of new meanings taken as that which is not stated in the previous definition. Such an effort leads nowhere, other than to an endless rewriting of the dictionary. Philosophy does not advance by a lexical improvement dedicated to the description of ordinary language as it is commonly used. Rather, it proceeds through the emergence of properly philosophical problems that slice through the simple regulating of ordinary language in terms of its use.

Think of Socrates questioning his fellow citizens with questions in the form: What is . . . ? What is virtue, courage, piety? The break with familiar usage is complete with high-level questions such as What is being? Knowledge? Opinion? Truth? What is an object? A subject? The a priori? What is thought? The history of the formation of ideas stemming from such questions cannot be written as a history of mentalities, of representations, not even as a history of ideas. It is a philosophical history of philosophical questioning. As a result, the gap between the use values of words in natural language and the meanings engendered from them by some philosophical problematic in itself constitutes a philosophical problem. In any case, the surfacing of a problem remains unpredictable as a thought event.

The discontinuous character of these thought events augments our perplexity concerning the plausibility of our undertaking. In fact, it is to a certain dislocation in the order of lexicographical derivation that philosophical reflection seems to contribute. And this often happens in such a way that any proposed meaning that should hold together, within the same term, the most apparently distant senses seems only to raise new difficulties. This apparent dislocation, which largely explains the absence of any great unified philosophy of recognition, leaps to the eye of the least determined observer. A brief overview would summarily distinguish three philosophical approaches that seem to have nothing in common. The first one is Kantian, with the term *recognitio* in the first edition of the *Critique of Pure Reason*. Then there is the Bergsonian approach, with its recognition of memories; and finally the Hegelian one, in full flower today, with the term *Anerkennung*, dating from the period of Hegel's Jena *Realphilosophie*. The reason for this state of dislocation is clearly to be sought in the dominant problematic in each case. It is to the framework of a transcendental philosophy inquiring into the a priori conditions for the possibility of objective knowledge that we can assign the philosophical signification of the Kantian *recognitio*. Next, it is in a philosophy close to a reflexive psychology, concerned to reformulate anew the terms of the old quarrel over the relation of soul and body, that the recognition of memories becomes for Bergson a major problem, paired with that of the very survival of memories themselves. Finally, it is within a context that is no longer that of the critique of reason, but that of the "real" actualization of freedom, constituted first as an Idea, that for Hegel recognition can take its place in this process of actualization, of realization, and clothe itself in the forms that have become familiar to us as the struggle for recognition, as a demand for recognition. What relation might exist between Kantian *recognitio,* Bergsonian recognition, and Hegelian and post-Hegelian *Anerkennung,* all of which French places under the same term, *reconnaissance*? Philosophical reflection seems to have overturned the whole enterprise of aiming to produce on the philosophical plane a system of derivation of a complexity, an articulation, and a congruence comparable to those the lexicographer reconstitutes.

My working hypothesis is based on the conviction that philosophy must not renounce constituting a theory of recognition worthy of the name, a theory where the gaps in meaning engendered by what we can call considering the question are both recognized and traversed. It is the responsibility of the philosopher, educated by the discipline of the philosophical history of such problems—a history completed by the history of works and doctrines—to compose at a higher degree of complexity a chain of conceptual meanings that will take into account the gaps between those meanings governed by heterogeneous ways of stating the problem.

The philosopher can find some encouragement from the lexicographer in the search for connections—we have already spoken of the implicit, the unsaid—that ensure the transition from one definition to another. These connections both create and bridge the gaps hidden beneath the continual engendering of new meanings on the basis of the preceding ones. What we are proposing is a comparable consideration of what is implicit and unsaid on the conceptual plane, in the hope of compensating for the initial effect of dislocation produced by the raising of a philosophical problem, through a gain in cooperation among philosophical concepts made more consonant by this working-out of the transitions.

Putting this conviction to work, my working hypothesis concerning a possible derivation of meaning on the conceptual plane finds some more encouragement and support in one significant aspect of the enunciation of the verb as verb—that is, its use in the active voice: to recognize something, objects, persons, oneself, another, one another—or in the passive voice: to be recognized, to ask to be recognized. My hypothesis is that the potential philosophical uses of the verb *to recognize* can be organized along a trajectory running through its use in the active voice to its use in the passive voice. This reversal on the grammatical plane will show the traces of a reversal of the same scope on the philosophical plane. To recognize as an act expresses a pretension, a claim, to exercise an intellectual mastery over this field of meanings, of signifying assertions. At the opposite end of this trajectory, the demand for recognition expresses an expectation that can be satisfied only by mutual recognition, where this mutual recognition either remains an unfulfilled dream or requires procedures and institutions that elevate recognition to the political plane.

This reversal is so considerable that it gives rise to an inquiry bearing on the intermediary meanings concerning which we can say that they engender the gaps that they also help to bridge. This is why the three high points we briefly indicated—Kant, Bergson, and Hegel—find themselves surrounded by many peaks marking the transfer from the positive act of recognition to the demand to be recognized. This reversal has to affect the mastery of the operation designated by the verb, as stated by the lexicon without any regard for whether it relates to the active or passive voice. In this respect, uses that are not very familiar to classical philosophical reflection or that are even frankly eccentric to philosophy as it is usually taught turn out to smuggle in particularly efficacious meanings. It even turns out that questions that are apparently quite removed from the usual way of doing things philosophically have a major role in the construction of the cooperative work that would merit being called a theory of recognition.

Another implication of our working hypothesis: when this reversal from the active to the passive voice occurs, and in conjunction with the progressive predominance of the problematic of mutual recognition, recognition acquires a status more and more independent in regard to cognition as mere knowing. At the initial stage of this process, the kind of mastery belonging to the act of recognition does not differ in any decisive way from that attached to the verb *to know* in the active voice. Some features legitimizing this use of the term *recognize* in certain contexts, nevertheless, will be all the more valuable and worthy of serious examination. The case of Kant's *recognitio* will be exemplary in this respect, and before Kant the furtive appearances of the term *recognize* in the French version of Descartes's *Meditations*.

But I believe there is a supplementary reason for lingering over this first stage of our investigation. This reason has to do with a hypothesis that complements our first one, which was based on a grammatical aspect of the verbal form of enunciation. This new hypothesis has to do with the connotation of such accepted uses. It derives in the following way from our first hypothesis. Use of the verb in the active voice seems to be attached to intellectual operations that bear the stamp of some mental initiative. The lexicographer himself helps us take this step. Recall the definition of the first pivotal sense in the *Robert* dictionary: "To grasp (an object) with the mind, through thought, in joining together images, perceptions having to do with it; to distinguish or identify the judgment or action, know it by memory."

Given this suggestion, which points to the first philosophers we shall consider, I propose taking as the first philosophical use of recognition the pair *identify/distinguish*. To recognize something as the same, as identical to itself and not other than itself, implies distinguishing it from everything else. This first philosophical use verifies two semantic characteristics that we have seen connected to the use of the verb in the active voice—namely, the initiative of the mind in this mastery of meaning, and the initial quasi indistinguishableness of recognizing and knowing.

Use of the term *recognition* in the sense of identification/distinction can be taken as the first in a series of reasons leading from the most contingent to the most fundamental. In the chronological order of "thought events" that has presided over a use of the word *recognition* shaped by philosophical questioning, Kantian recognition has priority over Bergsonian recognition and Hegelian *Anerkennung*. In turn, this chronological order, which is still marked by the contingency of the advent of the problematic at issue, gives way to a priority in the thematic order as such. In fact, this *principal* meaning will not be abolished in what follows, but will accompany our journey to the end at the price of significant transformations. It will still be *identity* that will be at issue when we come to self-recognition. In its personal form, identity will constitute both what is at stake in such recognition and the bond between the problems gathered under this heading. As for our third major theme, placed under the heading of mutual recognition, we can already say that with it the question of identity will reach a kind of culminating point: it is indeed our most authentic identity, the one that makes us who we are, that demands to be recognized. There is one more supplementary reason for privileging this thematic ordering of the philosophical uses of the term recognition: progression along this axis will be marked by an increasing liberation of the concept of recognition in relation to that of knowing. At the final stage, recognition not only detaches itself from knowledge but opens the way to it.

We reach perhaps the most constraining reason for placing recognition in the sense of identification/distinction at the head of our itinerary with the following consideration. At the initial stage, the "what" to which recognition refers remains undifferentiated. Already on the lexical plane the principal definition referred to earlier speaks of grasping "an object" with the mind; in other words, some "thing." The thought operations applied by Kantian recognition will not remove this indetermination of the "what" from recognition. But it will be progressively removed over the course of our analyses. In the concluding section of the next chapter, I shall speak of the revolution in thought required in relation to a transcendental approach to the problem that is the price to pay for taking into account the "things themselves" that fall under recognition—among them persons, where the self becomes what is at stake in the second and third stages of our progression.

CHAPTER 1

RECOGNITION AS IDENTIFICATION

———

The essence of any mistake consists in not knowing.

—Blaise Pascal, *Entretien avec M. de Sacci*
sur Épictète et Montaigne, 1655

According to our working hypothesis, centered on the reversal in the use of the verb *to recognize* from the active to the passive voice, our inquiry has to begin with philosophical expressions bearing par excellence the mark of the mind's initiative.

It might seem a good idea, therefore, to turn immediately to the Kantian theory of *recognitio,* where our term appears for the first time in a philosophical glossary as endowed with a specific function in the theory presented. And does not the lexicographer himself help us take this step in the way that he defines the mother idea of recognition? Let me recall what the *Robert* says: "To grasp (an object) with the mind, through thought, in joining together images, perceptions having to do with it; to distinguish or identify the judgment or action, know it by memory." We have already noted the aspect of initiative and of resolution indicated by these verbs. Nor have we overlooked the rationalist tone, close to that of critical philosophy, in the specification of this first meaning that ends with the verb *identify,* in the sense of establishing a relationship of identity between one thing and another. It is in this direction that we are going to proceed.

But it will not be at the price of a short circuit between the lexical plane and that of philosophical discourse. The basic definition in the *Robert* also generates a variety of operations that call for a division and a supplementary work of differentiation. Definition 1.2, which brings to the fore the sense of identifying that we too have privileged, in turn is diversified into several secondary senses.

It thus seems to me that the change in linguistic status from the lexicon to critique requires a detour through several basic concepts capable of bringing about the break between our two levels of discourse. As a first approximation, the most noteworthy presupposition upon which critical philosophy of a transcendental type establishes itself lies in the concept of judgment taken in the sense both of a capacity (or faculty) and of an exercise (or operation). If this concept is in fact closest in the hierarchy of critical thought, it is certainly the Cartesian theory of judgment established in the *Discourse on Method, Meditations, Principles of Philosophy,* and Objections and Replies that needs first to be considered. This theory not only has chronological priority but presents an undeniable thematic and systematic breakthrough (even if the verb *to recognize* and the substantive form *recognition* appear only episodically in these Cartesian texts).

Yet if the background to critical theory requires a brief consideration of Descartes, it is not with the Cartesian theory of judgment that we have to stop this reverse line of questioning. A still more primitive conceptual operation is presupposed: we can detect it in Descartes's definition of the act of judging on the basis of the capacity to distinguish between the true and the false. Being able to so distinguish goes hand in hand with judging, in that the verb calls for a complement, which effectively takes on the form of an alternative: true or false. This complement, which carries this alternative, forces us to look to the thing called for by the transitive use of the verb *to recognize*. And our lexical definitions take this transitivity into account by means of a discrete parenthesis: "to grasp (an object) with the mind, through thought"—and, more precisely, "to identify" (some thing). An object, something, here is the "objective" vis-à-vis that invites us to associate *distinguish* and *identify*. So it is the determination of this some thing that constitutes what is ultimately at stake in looking back in the direction of the basic presuppositions of Kant's theory. To distinguish this "thing," be it an idea, a thing, or a person, is to *identify* it.

Two operations are thereby traced back to the same root, which is the act of judging: to distinguish and to identify. Definition 1.2 in the *Robert* prudently sets them side by side: "distinguish, identify." Philosophical reflection makes sense of this: *to identify* and *to distinguish* constitute an inseparable verbal pair. In order to identify it is necessary to distinguish, and it is in distinguishing that we identify. This requirement does not govern only a theory of recognition limited to the theoretical plane; it governs, with the same insistence, all the uses stemming from the reversal from the act of recognition to being recognized—being distinguished and identified is what the humiliated person aspires to. In this sense, the "logical" use of the operations of distinguishing and identifying will never be surpassed but will remain presupposed and included in the existential [*existentiell*] use that will be definitely enriched by this, whether we are talking about distinction or identification, as applied to persons, relative to themselves or to others, or considered in regard to their mutual relations.[1] A distinguishing, an identifying "in truth" will always be presupposed, especially when it comes to estimations or evaluations in light of the good or the just. These latter will always imply operations of identifying and distinguishing.

So if judgment, for modern thinkers, is the royal entrance that gives access to the problematic of recognition/identification, it will be worthwhile to pause before passing through this entrance, in order to take the measure of the epochal character of this event that gives judgment such a dominant position. The word *other*, already mentioned in our introduction, for an age of reflection that dates back to the pre-Socratics, was the object of a pointed dialectic to which Plato gave new breath in his metaphysical dialogues—the

Philebus, Parmenides, Theaetetus, and *Sophist.* As for us, as disconcerted, overwhelmed readers, we have no other resource than to assign this Platonic dialectic to what, following Stanislas Breton, I shall attribute to the *meta-* function of the highest level of speculation. In these dialogues, Plato proposes a second-degree ontology, one that overlaps the theory of "Forms" or "Ideas." Within this framework, he designates entities that he qualifies as "the great kinds." From this higher-order ontology come not only the notions of being and nonbeing, which torment Platonic discourse beginning with its quarrel with the Sophists, but several other "great kinds" as well, implied in the operations of "participation" among first-order kinds. It is not indifferent that the evocation of these great kinds— and first of all, those of being and nonbeing—occurs on the occasion of considerable aporias giving rise to the most pointed dialectic, that of the *Parmenides* with its sequence of formidable "hypotheses." To this same cycle of great kinds belong the ideas of the one and the many, and the same and the other, which themselves give rise to a series of operations of conjunction and disjunction underlying the slightest operation of predication, inasmuch as to predicate one term on another is to make "one idea participate in another." The *Sophist* further accentuates the reduplication of levels of discourse by proposing an order of derivation between some of these "great kinds." For example, the polarity of the same and the other turns out to overlap the dialectic of being to the extent that the *same* must be defined both "relative to itself" and "relative to something other than itself."

We are brought here to the root of the notion of identification, inasmuch as it intends the "relative to itself" of the same, conjoined with the distinction of the "relative to something other than itself."[2] In this we find ourselves far distant from the naive essentialism of the "friends of the Forms," which has all too often served as the paradigm of a self-appointed Platonism and its descendants over the centuries.

Our modern problem of judgment is in many ways the heir of this high-level speculation. The problem for Plato was, as we have seen, to reply to the prohibition against attaching an epithet *other* to a "same" subject, pronounced by Parmenides. In short, against predication. Plato responded to this challenge with the theory of a "community of kinds," also called participation, in other words, the mutual combining of kinds. It would not be an exaggeration to claim that our problem of recognition-identification is the distant heir, in another era of thinking, of this Platonic problem of a "community of kinds." Can we speak of *identifying* without recalling the inspired formula of Auguste Diès regarding the *Sophist?* What posits itself opposes itself insofar as it distinguishes itself, and nothing is itself without being other than everything else.[3]

Allow me to add that this ancient patronage constitutes a supplementary reason for placing the theme of recognition-identification at the beginning of our survey. But at the same time, this reference to another epoch of thinking contains a warning: we are invited to become aware of the equally epochal character of the problematic of judgment that we are considering. We ourselves belong to the age of the subject who is the master of meaning. Yet some encouragement also comes with this warning. Confronted with the aporias in the model of thinking issuing from the Copernican revolution, with which the Kantian recognition goes hand in hand, we are free to evoke the memory of this ancient dialectic which owes nothing to the primacy of subjectivity. We are also free, therefore, to ask ourselves whether this rediscovered memory does not conceal within its folds the possibility of responding to the Copernican revolution with a second revolution and of seeking in "things themselves" the resources for the development of a philosophy of recognition progressively removed from the tutelage of the theory of knowledge.

Setting aside this warning and encouragement for the time being, let us pass through the royal entrance of judgment.

Two philosophies of judgment, presiding over two different conceptions of identification, have to be considered: that of Descartes and that of Kant. Two different periods in the problem of recognition result from them. For the first one, identifying goes hand in hand with distinguishing, which in a way is in line with our previous comments concerning the same and the other. In relation to this Cartesian approach, Kant brings about a significant displacement by subordinating *identifying* to *connecting together*. In one sense, this displacement is warranted by the uses of ordinary language attested to by the lexicon. But the lexicon leaves the two definitions side by side, under the same heading, as we saw in the *Grand Robert*. It is up to philosophical reflection to dissociate the two uses and to refer them to thought events from which derives the displacement from one conception of identification to the other.

These thought events go to the heart of the philosophy of judgment. If it is true that we owe the break with tradition to the thematizing of method and, through this, with ordinary language use, it is still in terms of a rational psychology that the Cartesian theory of judgment is constituted. It has merit for us in that it makes a place for the movement of thinking that justifies the surreptitious recourse to the term *recognition* and its appropriate use (in ways we shall discuss).

With Kant, the passage from a rational psychology to the transcendental approach governs the exegesis of recognition, which is in some ways the target of this chapter. We can anticipate things by saying that this is a deceptive target, inasmuch as recognition will remain a secondary piece in Kant's theory of knowledge, which leaves no place for the autonomy of recognition in relation to it.

Descartes: "To Distinguish the True from the False"

Descartes was certainly not the first person to elaborate a theory of judgment, as the primary operation of thinking. But he was the first to inaugurate that analysis through a break that I would set in relation to my theme of the gap between a lexical and a properly philo-sophical treatment of the notions common to both vocabularies. Descartes gives a first, biographical version of this break in the opening part of the *Discourse on Method*, within the framework of what he calls the fable of his years of apprenticeship. Then he gives an epistemological version of it in the second part, in connection with the very idea of method. The first version concerns us insofar as it recounts in what way the break with an education shaped by memorization and literature came about. These are the same re-sources that the lexicographer makes use of, not only in the cita-tions drawn upon, but in the body of his definitions. Descartes tells us, "From my childhood I have been nourished upon letters, and because I was persuaded that by their means one could acquire a clear and certain knowledge of all that is useful in life, I was ex-tremely eager to learn them."[4] Furthermore, "conversing with those of past centuries is much the same as traveling" (113).

To be sure, Descartes will not fail to reestablish contact with or-dinary conversations, with his "provisional ethics," and again in the prefatory letters to his *The Passions of the Soul* and in the re-course he makes to the "teachings of nature" concerning the sub-stantial union of soul and body in the sixth *Meditation*. But this res-toration of usual meanings is due to an inaugural discourse that is based on a rupture.

On the epistemological plane "method" is the emblematic title for this discourse. The gesture is one of an intellectually violent rup-ture: "considering how many diverse opinions learned men may maintain on a single question—even though it is impossible for more than one to be true—I held as well-nigh false everything that was merely probable." The choice of distinguishing over defining could not be made more vehemently. To be sure, the acquisition of positive knowledge remains the goal: "it was always my most ear-nest desire to learn to distinguish the true from the false, in order to see clearly into my own actions and proceed with confidence in life"

(115). To see clearly, "with confidence," bespeaks the positive side, just as "hold as well-nigh false" bespeaks the negative side, the link between defining and distinguishing. As for the indication of initiative presiding over such an enterprise, it is expressed by a forceful verb: *to receive,* "to receive in my belief." This verb encompasses the figures of both rejection and welcome. We can see in it the matrix of recognition that makes a furtive appearance in the *Meditations.*

This active "receiving" is at the heart of the first of Descartes's four precepts in *The Discourse on Method.* It states: "never to accept anything as true if I did not have evident knowledge of its truth; that is, carefully to avoid precipitate conclusions and preconceptions, and to include nothing more in my judgments than what presented itself to my mind so clearly and so distinctly that I had no occasion to doubt it" (120). With this first text the resolute character of his project comes to light, as well as the aspect of attestation of certitude that finds grammatical expression in the use of the active voice of the verb *to recognize.* To recognize, at this stage in our investigation, is still simply to know, but this still mute term, to which later philosophers will draw our attention, conveys well the vehemence of the assertion made through this discourse. But the recourse to recognition, which we shall see makes a few furtive appearances in the *Meditations,* already appears as appropriate to discourse situations that bring to light the weakness of human understanding as summed up in the threat of error that runs through Cartesian discourse. The evocation of doubt in this first rule of his method already also alludes to a hesitation overcome. What I have called an attestation of certitude that makes recognition a confirmation and, if necessary, a reiteration of the force of knowing was already at work in the narration Descartes gives, in the first part of the *Discourse,* of the break with his education governed by memory and literature. The second part gives the epistemological version of this rupture. His method will be intellectual discipline in the service of this intrepid project to attain "the knowledge of everything within [reach of] my mental capacities" (119). As for the mark of initiative presiding over this enterprise, it is expressed by the powerful verb *to receive,* whose inscription we already discovered in the first rule of *The Discourse on Method.*

As for the contents of this receiving, their evidence is defined solely by the characteristics of the simple idea of clarity and distinctness. The connection between clarity and distinctness can be taken as equivalent to that between defining and distinguishing. We can see this in the contraries. The contrary of *clear* is *obscure,* that is, not delimited by discernible contours. The contrary of *distinct* is *confused,* the same not being distinguished from the other. Descartes's four precepts thus place ideas in a hierarchy from the simple to the complex, following an ordering rule. In this rule we see thought's mastery. A heroic accent of resolution is placed on the whole enterprise with the title "Search for a Method." It recalls the Socratic theme of *zetesis,* "research," marked by intellectual courage.

Why, nevertheless, at this stage can recognition not be distinguished from knowing? For one fundamental reason. As the remainder of this chapter will demonstrate, it is in the domain of things and their different relations to change, depending on whether they are ordinary objects, animate beings, or persons, that recognition distinguishes itself in a decisive fashion from knowing to the point of preceding it. For Descartes, from the *Discourse* to the *Meditations* to the *Principles,* "to receive as true" refers only to ideas. To be sure, the idea is the idea of something that it represents, but the differentiating of this something on the basis of the things represented does not matter as regards the representative value of the idea. The only thing that matters is the clarity and distinctness of the idea, and its place in the order from the simple to the complex.[5]

The *Meditations* will take away nothing from this aspect of resolution. In any case, the laborious character of the demonstration, limited in the first three meditations to three assertions—I am, God exists, and thought is substantially distinct from the body—break through an underlying uneasiness that justifies attaching to the idea of recognition the avowal of a resistance specific to any conquest of truth. Earlier I referred to the threat of error. It runs through the fourth *Meditation,* devoted, precisely, to judgment, that act of thinking designated as "accepting" ("not to accept anything as true that isn't"). The possibility of accepting the true as false looms like the negative shadow of this proud accepting. Whence the tone of reassurance with which the fourth *Meditation* opens. It begins with a careful summary of what has been gained through the preceding meditations. It is in the course of this brief review, at least in the French version of the *Meditations,* that the verb *recognize* comes up. Invoking the argument of the evil genius, so essential to the discovery of the first truth, the author pauses and notes: "I recognize [Latin: *agnosco*] that it is impossible that God should ever deceive me." The relevance of the translator's choice of this term seems to fit well with the function of review and recapitulation of this long *incipit.* In fact, the next step quickly follows the pause, an advance punctuated by the expression "I experience" *(experiencior)*: "Next, I experience that there is in me a faculty of judgment" (2:37). The fourth *Meditation* has found its center of gravity.

The second occurrence of the term *recognize* is no less significant. Before proceeding to the distinction between the two faculties of knowing and choosing, which are those of the understanding and the will, Descartes sets aside the suspicion that there might be a power of erring that would come from God, like that of discerning the true from the false. My argument does not allow me to linger over the pointed discussion that successively considers "a negative idea of nothingness," and the ideas of "lack" and "privation." An exit is discovered in the idea worthy of Pascal that "I am, as it were, something intermediate between God and nothingness" (2:38).

This idea provides an ontological ground for the double avowal that our power to judge correctly can indeed err—but that this error is our own fault. The remainder of the meditation explains how this can be so. It is in reviewing this argument that the translator again welcomes the word *recognize:* "Since I now know that my own nature is very weak and limited, whereas the nature of God is immense, incomprehensible and infinite, I also know without more ado [*ex hos satis etiam scio*][6] that he is capable of countless things whose cause are beyond my knowledge" (2:39). Unlike the first occurrence, this is no longer the expression of a delay in the avowal of truth in relation to its discovery, but an allusion to the hesitation that is overcome by certitude: "From these considerations I perceive that [*satis etiam scio*][7] the power of willing which I received from God is not, when considered in itself, the cause of my mistakes" (2:40).

A third occurrence of the term *recognize* is just as suggestive. The word appears in a setting of *although*s and *however*s that betrays the persistence of the fear of error: "It is true that, since my decision to doubt everything, it is so far only myself and God whose existence I have been able to know with certainty; but after considering [*animadverti*][8] the immense power of God, I cannot deny that many other things have been made by him, or at least could have been made, and hence that I may have a place in the universal scheme of things" (2:39).[9]

However, we must wait until the fourth *Meditation* to have an analysis of the act of thinking that judging constitutes. There, with no consideration for the "something" of the idea, the act of thinking that the *Discourse on Method* designated with the term *accept* is determined. And in this analysis of the constitutive elements of the act of judging, the kind of subjectivity that critical philosophy is breaking away from becomes clear, at the price of consequences we shall discuss later, having to do with the new sense given to the verb *recognize.*

I wanted to indicate a few of the occurrences of the term *recognize* in the Cartesian text. They all relate in one way or another to what we could call the hazards in the exercise of judgment. In these hazards that strengthen the threat of error I discern the preamble to the crisis in the idea of recognition that will occupy me in the chapters to come. Descartes's well-known analysis of judgment, divided between the intellect that conceives and the will that chooses (an operation common to both "affirming" and "denying"), is meant to eliminate definitively the constantly recurring suspicion of the existence of a faculty of error. The use of the faculty of the will depends on me, and on me alone. The term *recognize* then appears again: "From these considerations I perceive [*je reconnais; ex his autem percipio*] that the power of willing which I received from God is not, when considered in itself, the cause of my mistakes; for it is both extremely ample and also perfect of its kind. Nor is my power of understanding to blame; for since my understanding comes from God, everything that I understand I undoubtedly [*procul dubio*] understand correctly, and any error here is impossible" (2:40). In this way the affirmation of the impossibility of being mistaken on the plane of pure conception is underscored by an energetic *sine dubio* whose full force the French equivalent—*sans doute*—does not convey.

The kind of confirmation the verb *recognize* expresses places the seal of certitude on the whole trajectory so far completed.

I am focusing on a few features of the Cartesian philosophy of judgment, precisely those which the Kantian philosophy will eliminate along with everything else that arises from a "rational psychology," which Kant will submit to the paralogisms of a transcendental dialectic. Yet these are pertinent features of the idea of recognition on the way to its dissociation from the simple idea of knowing. The act of "accepting an idea as true" mobilizes a subject who, while not reducible to the person named Descartes, is nonetheless an "I" we can call exemplary, the very one who attests to the first truth: I am, I exist. It is, moreover, a subject who calls out to his reader. Descartes, in the first instance, adds to the publication of his *Meditations* the objections and his replies to them. Published together, these different texts constitute a philosophical apparatus no less exemplary than the resolute subject of the search for a method. Between autobiography, which is not the province of philosophy, and the numerical unity of transcendental consciousness according to Kant, there is a place for a subject responsible for its errors and hence for "accepting/recognizing as true." It is this same subject of recognition that later in our inquiry will demand to be recognized.

For myself, I am willing to take Descartes's side as regards those elements of a phenomenology of judgment that we owe to him, over against the impoverished version resulting from the elimination in transcendental philosophy of some major features of the act of judging. In this regard, the occurrences of the verb *to recognize* from the pen of the French translator of the *Meditations* are particularly important. We have noted the circumstances surrounding such use: the implicit admission of a delay in any confirmation in the discovery of truth; the allusion to the hesitation, to the doubt, to the resistance preceding the open affirmation of certitude. Does not the *Discourse on Method* place the statement of its precepts on method under the aegis of the "search for a method?" There we find the old *zetesis* of Socratic thinkers: Search in order to find. We can speak in this sense of a phenomenology of judgment that escapes the alternative of an empirical psychology or a transcendental analysis. It is one centered on the verb *receive,* and the expressions *experience, find,* and, of course, *doubt* belong to the same cycle. We owe the analyses in the fourth *Meditation* to this intimate history of a search for truth, which dramatizes the threat of error.

Perhaps we should go even further. Does not the verb *to accept,* in the expression *to accept as true,* hold in reserve descriptive resources that go beyond the simple operations of defining or distinguishing, resources governed by the higher dialectic of the same and the other? To put it briefly, the Cartesian theory of judgment, which is a tributary of a faculty psychology, keeps in reserve the concept of a transition between the two senses of *to recognize* that the *Robert* places on two different branches of its lexical tree: "to grasp (an object) with the mind, through thought" and "accept, take to be true (or take as such)." Does not what I would call the Cartesian phenomenology of judgment bring together, on the philosophical plane, what the lexicon seems to have separated on that of everyday usage? The paradox would then be that the way of stating a problem, tied to the thought event that constitutes the appearance of Cartesian philosophy, not only would have contributed to a kind of dispersion, which I attribute to the irruption of philosophical questioning into the setting of the use of natural languages, but also has had the effect of setting aside features that will be taken up only by other philosophical configurations.

It remains to be stated why a philosophy of recognition can nonetheless not be unfolded on Cartesian grounds. It is not sufficient to lay out *a parte subjecti* a distance based on doubt and uneasiness to give consistency to the distinction between knowing *(connaissance)* and recognition *(reconnaissance)*. As the remainder of our investigation shall show, it is principally *a parte objecti* that recognition establishes its credentials. To anticipate, change has to put its mark on the beings of the world, and most significantly on human beings, for there to be a hesitation, a doubt that gives recognition its dramatic character. Then it will be the possibility of *misrecognition* that will give recognition its full autonomy. Misrecognition will be an existential, worldly form for which the more theoretical form of uneasiness—misjudgment—will not exhaust the meaning.

Kant: To Connect under the Condition of Time

With the Kantian concept of recognition *(Rekognition)*, we add to the philosophical lexicon a term that in many ways has no antecedent in prior tradition. If the preeminence of judgment is acquired with Descartes, as method in the *Discourse*, then thematically in the fourth *Meditation*, it is another function of judgment that comes onstage with Kant, leading to a revolution in meaning having to do with the sense that attaches to the subjectivity to which this function belongs. For Descartes and for Kant, to recognize—whether the word is used or not—is to identify, to grasp a unified meaning through thought. But for Descartes, identifying is inseparable from distinguishing, that is, from separating the same from the other, from putting an end to obscurity. The result is the self-evidence of the idea "accepted" as true. For Kant, to identify is to join together. If we return to the lexicon of ordinary language, as something like the breeding ground for meanings found in ordinary usage, we find this meaning juxtaposed with the one we previously isolated. Let us recall definition number 1 from the *Grand Robert:* "To grasp (an object) with the mind, through thought, in joining together images, perceptions having to do with it; to distinguish or identify the judgment or action, know it by memory." Joining together has the place of honor, but it can be taken in the sense of the English-language tradition of empiricism just as well as in light of the transcendental meaning we are going to consider.

But the promotion of the connecting function, of the connection of a synthesis, is not the only thing that characterizes Kant's specific contribution to a large-scale philosophy of recognition. We need to add to it the way time is taken into account, and more generally sensibility, in the synthesis that recognition indicates in the way we are about to discuss. This manner of situating judgment at the point of intersection of two "stems of human knowledge"—namely, the capacity to receive and that of thought, the first being assigned to sensibility, the second to the understanding, according to Kant at the end of the Introduction to the *Critique of Pure Reason*—is unprecedented.[10] It bears the stamp of critical philosophy. Therefore, if we can consider the substitution of joining together for distinguishing as a displacement internal to the theory of judgment, the incorporation of time and sensibility into the problematic of judgment constitutes an unprecedented enlargement of this problematic.

At the same time, all the features of the Cartesian theory of judgment that authorize indicating a distinction between recognition and knowing are excluded, along with the apparatus of rational psychology, from the field of critical philosophy, to the point that we can affirm that recognizing is knowing. Despite its great interest, the theory of recognition will not contradict this equation.

Two theses preside over this elimination of rational psychology: first, the affirmation of the initial heterogeneity of the two "stems" of knowledge just named, an affirmation that places the theory of judgment and, with it, that of recognition at the intersection of these two sources; next, the distinction between the transcendental and the empirical points of view, which places the *a priori* outside the field of experience.

This hitherto unknown interweaving of two major distinctions, that concerning the stems of human knowledge and that concerning the levels of constitution of meaning, constitutes the foundational thought event that leads to critical philosophy. It is stated in these concluding lines to the Introduction of the *Critique of Pure Reason*: "Now, in so far as sensibility may be found to contain *a priori* representations constituting the condition under which objects are given to us, it will belong to transcendental philosophy" (A16/B34). The *now* is the sole rhetorical indication indicating the immensity of this initial and, if we may say so, this seminal decision. In this regard, the tone in which the terminological definitions, which henceforth govern Kant's discourse, is pronounced has no retort: "I term all representation *pure* (in the transcendental sense) in which there is nothing that belongs to sensation" (A20/B34). "The science of all principles of *a priori* sensibility I call *transcendental aesthetic*"

(A21/B35). "The undetermined object of an empirical intuition is entitled *appearance*" (A20/B34).

Under the Condition of Time

The priority accorded the transcendental aesthetic is affirmed from early on: "And since the conditions under which alone the objects of human knowledge are given must precede those under which they are thought, the transcendental doctrine of sensibility will constitute the first part of the science of the elements" (A16/B30). In a single breath the priority of the transcendental aesthetic over the analytic and the prevalence of the transcendental over the empirical point of view are affirmed. This dissociation of the transcendental and the empirical touches not only the theory of space, but also in an eminent way that of time, which we have already mentioned in beginning this investigation. That time is not an empirical concept, drawn from sensory experience, but an a priori representation is decided along with the status of the transcendental aesthetic. The transcendental approach, in a way, proceeds from itself. In every case of being affected by an object, it must be possible to distinguish the sensory material, given a priori, and the form that assures that "the manifold of appearance . . . allows of being ordered in certain relations" (A20/B34). The transcendental aesthetic is the science of all the a priori principles of sensibility. Kant's great innovation and also the great enigma posed in the preface to his theory of recognition is that these principles are not concepts of understanding, or discursive concepts like, for example, that of causality, but indeed principles of sensibility, without for all that stemming from experience.

The time of the transcendental aesthetic is neither the lived time of the soul, nor the time of changes in the world, but the form of an inner sense, as space is that of the external sense, and finally of both of them, inasmuch as it is the measure by which every representation passes through this inner sense: "Time is nothing but the form of inner sense, that is, of the intuition of ourselves and our inner state" ("Transcendental Aesthetic," §6b).

In positive terms, "this form of inner intuition can be represented prior to the object, and therefore *a priori*" (§6a). This formula does more than restate the negative argument. It adds an unexpected feature that gives a large stake to the argument about the inner sense. Time is the pure form not only of every inner intuition, but also of every external intuition. Whether or not they have external things as their object, all representations "belong, in themselves, as determinations of the mind, to our inner state" (§6c). As a result, time is the a priori condition of every phenomenon in general, immediately for the inner sense, mediately for the external one. Commentators have emphasized the importance of this reduction to the form of time of the inner sense, which played such a large role in the past in claiming to penetrate the secrets of the soul, its substantial reality, its freedom.

Today's reader may find it difficult to measure the magnitude of the revolution that comes from disqualifying the inner sense as revealing an ego substance, as was the case for the rational psychology of Descartes, but also for Locke, Leibniz, and Wolff. The form of time will henceforth occupy the strategic place held up to that point by this inner sense. In return, the fragility of the transcendental argument in the case of time, owing to the lack of something symmetrical and as weighty as geometry when it comes to space (dynamics?), explains why the battle in favor of the ideality of the form of time takes place at every level of critical philosophy. No longer guaranteeing the freedom of the subject, the internal sense is handed over to the antinomies of causality in the Transcendental Dialectic. But long before taking these antinomies on a cosmological scale into account, it is on the plane of the "paralogisms of rational psychology" that the operation of demolishing the dogmatism of internal sense is carried out. Time alone, not space, where everything on the plane of the transcendental aesthetic plays out, requires the assistance of a discipline committed to laying bare the *illusions* of a reason constantly tempted to overstep its bounds.

For our inquiry, the most significant feature is perhaps the fact that the demonstration concerning time copies that concerning space. Time, as a form, comes down to relations of succession and simultaneity, which make it a one-dimensional magnitude whose parts are distinguished from one another within a single, infinite time—infinite in the sense of "limitless." The recognition we are going to discuss takes place within this time. One concession, purely tactical, has to be noted: if critical thought denies any *absolute* reality to time, it does grant time an *empirical* reality, that is, an "objective validity in respect of all objects which allow of ever being given to our senses" (A35/B52). This victory is not won without resistance. In section 7, titled "Elucidation," Kant attacks those of his readers thought to be won over by the ideality of space, but recalcitrant when it comes to the ideality of time. He formulates the objection in their name. Here is how he puts it: "Alterations are real, this being proved by change of our own representations—even if all outer appearances, together with their alterations, be denied. Now alterations are possible only in time, and time is therefore something real" (A37). We might think that Kant's obstinate reply succeeds only in plugging the breach opened by the question of change: "Empirical reality has to be allowed to time, as the condition of all our experiences; on our theory, it is only its absolute reality that has to be denied. It is nothing but the form of our inner intuition. If we take away from our inner intuition the peculiar condition of our sensibility, the concept of time likewise vanishes; it does not inhere in the objects, but merely in the subject who intuits them" (A38/B54). A phenomenology still called transcendental, but one capable of thematizing something like a time of being-in-the-world with its real changes within the framework of a philosophy of the "lifeworld," beginning with Husserl, will be swallowed up into this crack in the argument.

Joining Together

It is within the framework of a transcendental logic that the coordination announced in the Introduction to the *Critique of Pure Reason* enters the plane of sensibility through which objects are given and that of the understanding by which they are thought and thematized. From the perspective of critical thought, the split between sensibility and understanding intersects with the distinction between the transcendental perspective and the empirical perspective.[11]

Despite the priority granted to the analytic of concepts that contains the whole justification of the application of the categories to experience, it is judgment that remains the principal axis of the *Critique*. The act of joining together, the unique operation from which the receptivity of sensibility and the spontaneity of understanding are composed, is fundamentally an act of judgment. Following the division into pure concepts of the very power of understanding, to which we owe the table of categories, Kant declares: "Now the only use which the understanding can make of these concepts is to judge by means of them. Since no representation, save when it is an intuition, is in immediate relation to an object, no concept is ever related to an object immediately, but to some other representation of it, be that other representation an intuition, or itself a concept. Judgment is therefore the mediate knowledge of an object, that is, the representation of a representation of it" (A68/B93). This text will serve as the polestar for what follows in our analysis. It is understood that judgment is not to confound the faculty of election with that of receiving the idea, hence of the will with the understanding as in Descartes; instead it is to place sensible intuitions under one concept—in short, that of *subsumption*.

Judgment rules everything. The well-known table of categories is one of the rules in which is concentrated the "unity of the act of bringing various representations under one common representation." A name is given to this operation, that of synthesis: "By synthesis, in its most general sense, I understand the act of putting different representations together, and of grasping what is manifold in them in one [act of] knowing. . . . Synthesis of a manifold (be it given empirically or *a priori*) is what first gives rise to knowledge" (A77/B103). With this summary term, *synthesis of a manifold,* an oxymoron, a great enigma is posed. Before proposing its resolution, Kant takes full measure of its difficulty: the question is one not of fact, but of right; it is not a question of describing how, or on what "occasion," at the cost of what "effort," the human mind comes to give order to this manifold, as the "celebrated Locke" (A86/B119) first tried to do. Drawing on the language of legal theorists, who call deduction the discipline that makes apparent the right or legitimacy of a claim, the resolution of the enigma posed by the coordination of two heterogeneous components in a synthesis on the formal plane where this enigma arises will be called a transcendental deduction.

There is an unexpected kind of mediation at issue here, as serious as the one Plato sought under the heading of the community or participation among kinds, at the price of the multiple well-known aporias that the *Parmenides* presents. Kant devoted a good number of years to the quest for a victory in this battle of giants arising from the confrontation between the receptivity of the senses and intellectual spontaneity in one and the same act of thought.

It is here that the *Critique,* in its first edition, proposes the famous triple synthesis of which recognition is the third component. For us, it is a question of the first promotion to the rank of philosophical concept of a variable concept of recognition. But this is also the stage of our investigation where recognition is indistinguishable from knowing. It is only owing to its aporias that it is capable of heralding a revolution, making possible the emancipation of the problematic of recognition in relation to that of knowledge.

Let me say what it was that caught my attention in reading this triple synthesis. It was the way in which the successive figures of synthesis—"the synthesis of apprehension in intuition," "the synthesis of reproduction in imagination," and "the synthesis of recognition in the concept"—affect the concept of time received from the Transcendental Aesthetic.

Let us first consider the synthesis of apprehension in intuition. It is as succession that time is implicated in the way the mind is affected by the manifold of impressions. The inner sense is named another time as that to which these modifications of the mind belong. The manifold, which every analysis presupposes as what the operation of synthesis applies to, presents itself as a scattering of instants, of "moments," concerning which all we can say about each of them is that it is an "absolute unity." The argument is that if consciousness is to be possible, this manifold "must first be run through, and held together" (A99). The necessity invoked here stems from the argument about form: if not, then no . . . But this necessity hardly conceals the true innovation that the words *run through* and *held together* express. When they show up in the text here, they echo the suggestion made at the end of the Introduction to the *Critique* that will be held in reserve until the wonderful chapter on the productive imagination in connection with the schematism of the understanding: if the "stems" of human knowledge are really two in number—sensibility and understanding—they "perhaps spring from a common, but to us unknown, root" (A15/B29). Do not the mediating terms on which the triple synthesis rests tell us something about this "common, but to us unknown, root"? Better yet, do they not refer to temporal properties that exceed the simple relations of succession and simultaneity? Let us hold in reserve this suggestion, which, when the time comes, we shall have to apply to the possibility of a phenomenology of recognition. Is not time, without an added synthesis, "run through and held together"? And is not the manifold, which is always presupposed as the pole symmetrical to the transcendental ego, undiscoverable?

The suggestion made here finds reinforcement in the description of the second synthesis, that of "reproduction in imagination." The *reductio* argument again is clearly used here: if appearances were so variable that one could never represent them to oneself, so that they could not be reproduced, if previous representations always escaped my thought (owing exactly to what the idea of succession allows), in short, if I were never to reproduce them in passing to the next ones, I could never represent any object as being anew the same. A new term appears at the point that joins reception and spontaneity: "reproduction." To which I pose this question: Is it something added to time-as-succession, or is not already time itself under a different aspect to which reference could be made in a Bergsonian manner in terms of recognition? But a second term is attached to *reproduction—imagination,* for which the association of ideas is the empirical counterpart. Here we are at the heart of the triple synthesis. The term *imagination* in truth covers the totality of operations of synthesis. And the suggestion made earlier comes back again: Does not this mediating operation have something to do with the "two stems of human knowledge unknown to us"? And with time itself under the auspices of another variety of recognition?

Next comes recognition properly speaking, whose name has whetted our appetite, at the cost of a disappointment already mentioned earlier in passing. The argument takes up what has preceded: the absurd hypothesis of an endless novelty of impressions and the forgetting of adjoined units. One new feature is added, in which our disappointment will be recorded. The unity that makes any representation a single representation, worthy of the title "concept," proceeds from the unity of consciousness alone. Recognition through the concept adds nothing to the way in which the preceding synthesis opens out onto the imagination. Here is where our disappointment lies. The whole of the Transcendental Deduction finds itself summed up and proclaimed here: No liaison without synthesis, but no synthesis without unity, nor unity without consciousness. The sole virtue granted recognition is that it makes apparent this unity of consciousness over the object. This is why it is spoken of as "recognition in concept." In other words, recognition consists in the fact that consciousness apprehends itself only as objectified in a representation struck with the seal of necessity and of unity. In this regard, *objectivity* is the right word, even though Kant does not explicitly use it. But he does speak of the "relation of all knowledge to its object" (A104). Consciousness, as one, recognizes itself in the "production" of this unity that constitutes the concept of an object (A105). Little is said about this production of a unity that justifies the neologism of *recognition,* apart from its connection with the idea of a rule in the treatment of a manifold of impressions (as is the case for the concept of body): "But it can be a rule for intuitions only in so far as it represents in any given appearances the necessary reproduction of their manifold, and thereby the synthetic unity of our consciousness of them. The concept of body, for instance, as the unity of the manifold which is thought through it, serves as a rule in our knowledge of outer appearances. The concept of body, in the perception of something outside us, necessitates the representation of extension, and therefore with representations of impenetrability, shape, etc." (A106). Reproduction and production are thus associated in the mediating operation between the one and the many, production adding the note of unity to reproduction defined by the notforgetting of what was previous and its retention in a cumulative representation. What is important is that the unity of consciousness produces itself in the concept in order to *recognize* itself in it.

The radical question posed in this way is, Does a full-scale philosophy of imagination announce itself under terms that are really not discussed: *run through, hold together, reproduce in imagination, produce in a concept*? Is a problem not removed in this way over the famous third "source" or "stem" of human knowing, referred to in the Introduction to the first *Critique*? Yet is the unfolding of this broader philosophy of the imagination not held back by obsession with the theme of the unity of representation through the concept on the model of the proclaimed unity of transcendental consciousness?

I shall not discuss here the reasons that led to replacing these promising pages with the second version of the transcendental deduction in §§15–24. The accusation of a Berkeley-like subjective idealism seems unbelievable in that the emphasis had already been placed on the unity of transcendental consciousness. The answer to such questions has to do with the history of the reception of the *Critique* by Kant's contemporaries. For someone who wants to work only with the published text, what imposes itself on any reading is the change in strategy from the first to the second edition. Beginning with §15, the new version of the transcendental deduction, synthesis is exclusively the fruit of this higher-order unity placed above any of the intermediary operations of "holding together" or "synthesis." They proceed from the primary synthetic unity of apperception that is warranted only by itself (§16). As for the requirements of a deduction that proceeds from above to below, the mediating concepts used in the first edition reappear at the end of the Deduction only as "the application of the categories to objects of the senses in general" (§24). Imagination still holds the place of honor, however, under the heading of the transcendental synthesis of the productive imagination, in order to distinguish it from the reproductive imagination, which applies only to empirical experience, following the law of association. But what is it "to produce"?

It is in the second edition that we read the famous declaration concerning the imagination: "Synthesis in general, as we shall hereafter see, is the mere result of the power of imagination, a blind but indispensable function of the soul, without which we should have no knowledge whatsoever, but of which we are scarcely ever conscious" (B103). In what way is it blind? Scarcely ever accessible to consciousness? A function of the soul? This assertion is all the more astonishing in that the new Deduction pays no attention to these apparently psychologizing operations, in order to concentrate on the deduction of every synthesis in the object starting from the identity of apperception for the self, whose radical subjectivity is underscored by the capacity of the "I think" to accompany all of our representations, as is affirmed at the start of §16, "The Original Synthetic Unity of Apperception."

Nevertheless, the final word has not yet been spoken. In truth, the productive imagination need not be invoked within the framework of the Analytic of Concepts, the heart of which is the Transcendental Deduction, but only in the Analytic of Principles, which takes charge of the effective application of the concepts of experience, in what we could call a concrete logic, in order to distinguish it from the abstract logic centered on the categories. In this sense, it is only within this analytic of principles that the effective operation of subsumption, which is judgment, is brought to its conclusion.

Here is where the theme of schematism comes up, at the most vulnerable point of the Kantian system, where all attention is brought to bear on the troublesome problem of the mediation between the two poles of sensibility and the understanding.

This passage from one analytic to the other takes place under the heading "Application." The point of greatest importance for us is that the operation of relating, which for Kant specifies the idea of identification by which we have characterized the first figure of recognition—however indiscernible it may be from knowing—is really achieved only in the Analytic of Principles, in which the schematism is the most noteworthy aspect. What is more, since this operation of holding together only occurs under the condition of time, we shall also have to be attentive, as we move forward, to an enrichment of the notion of time.

One word stands out, against every obstacle: the word *homogeneous,* which points both to the problem and to its solution. In order to be able to say that "an object is contained under a concept" (A137/B176)—which is precisely what subsumption signifies—application requires the mediation of a third term that will be homogeneous on the one hand with the category, on the other with the phenomenon: "This mediating representation must be pure, that is, void of all empirical content, and yet at the same time, while it must in one respect be *intellectual,* it must in another be *sensible.* Such a representation is the *transcendental schema*" (A138/B177).

In order to grasp the full force and amplitude of this theory of the schematism, we have to couple the chapter on schematism with the one that follows it in the Principles and thus becomes what is finally at stake in the whole undertaking. This coupling imposes itself as soon as we pass from a general theory of the schematism to the enumeration of schemas in tandem with that of the categories. And on this occasion clarifications are proposed about time that significantly enrich the considerations drawn from the Aesthetic. The theory of the schema and the schematism is therefore not complete in the striking pages of the first chapter of the Analytic of Principles, titled "The Schematism of the Pure Concepts of Understanding."

The theory starts with the distinction between schema and schematism. The mixed figure that restrains the concept in its use is called a schema, and the schematism is "the procedure of understanding in these schemata" (A140/B179). With the schema, the imagination comes back onstage. The schema is said to be what is produced, but this schema is not the image, in that the image is particular in each case. The schema is instead a method for giving images to a concept. In this respect, it signifies only as a procedure of the understanding—the schema is a schematism of the understanding.

It is with this clarification that the extraordinary sentence appears which echoes a comparable assertion, already mentioned: "This schematism of our understanding, in its application to appearances and their mere form, is an art concealed in the depths of the human soul, whose real modes of activity nature is hardly likely ever to allow us to discover, and to have open to our gaze" (A141/B180–181).[12]

We must take the full measure of this paradox which makes the third term a hybrid of discursiveness and intuition. Does it not point us in the direction of that "common root" mentioned in the Introduction to the first *Critique*? All the words of this enigmatic sentence resonate in a strange way: "hidden art," "depths of the human soul," "secret nature," "uprooting," almost as if, from a far-distant past, the adage that "nature loves to conceal itself" has returned. It is striking and worth emphasizing that Kant passes over the avowals that this enigma might lead to, and instead employs himself in working out a painstaking typology of schemata and schematism. The reader is forced to go back and forth between the table of major schemata and their actual use in the following chapter, titled "System of All Principles of Pure Understanding." These principles are, in effect, propositions governing the use of the categories under the guidance of the schemata. Thus we have to deal with two parallel and complementary classifications, the schemata and the principles.

The table of categories, the centerpiece of the Analytic of Concepts, offers a guideline for laying out one after the other a table of schemata and a table of principles that amount to the proper development of its application. The analytic of concepts divides the categories into four groups, in conformity with the table of judgments: quantity, quality, order, modality. The enumeration of major schemata is poured into this mold.

This analysis is carried out broadly speaking in the chapter on the schematism, but its detailed examination has to be sought in the following chapter, devoted to the principles. For example, the axioms of intuition correspond to the schema of quantity; the anticipations of perception, to that of quality; the analogies of experience, whose treatment will decide the fate of reason in its claim to surpass the limits of sensible experience, to that of relation. Finally, to the schema of modality correspond the postulates of empirical thought in general.

I shall not take up this complex architecture here. I want to concentrate on just one point: the development of the transcendental concept of time over this course.

Time is first mentioned as a magnitude under the heading of quantity. It is shown to be homogeneous with the schema of quantity that is number. This schema is moreover homogeneous with quantity as "a representation which comprises the successive addition of homogeneous units" (B182). It is this congruence between the discursive aspect belonging to the additive operation and what we can call the cumulative feature of time that needs to be emphasized. This feature had been first glimpsed with regard to the synthesis of apprehension, the first of the three "subjective" syntheses considered earlier. It is not surprising that the same expression reappears in this new context: "I produce time itself in the apprehension of intuition" (A143/B182). In other words, I produce time in counting. This cumulative aspect of time is reaffirmed in the examination of the Axioms of Intuition that unfolds in the next chapter in accordance with the resources of concrete synthesis contained in the schema of number, where it is said that "all intuitions are extensive magnitudes." An extensive time is presupposed here—that is, a time made up not only of moments run through, but of accumulated ones.

Another aspect of time is highlighted by the schema of quality. It has to do with existence in time depending on whether it is filled or empty, something not conveyed by mere succession. The anticipations of perception offer a valuable complement here by introducing the idea of intensive magnitude—that is, the idea of degree. The opposition between empty and filled time takes first place in the anticipations of perception: "It is remarkable that of magnitudes in general we can know *a priori* only a single *quality,* namely, that of continuity, and that in all quality (the real appearances) we can know *a priori* nothing save [in regard to] their intensive *quantity,* namely that they have degree. Everything else has to be left to experience" (A176/B218).

Moving on to the schematism of relation, Kant first considers its initial form, substance. Time is once again invoked. The schema of substance presents itself, in effect, as the permanence of the real in time, having as its corollary the opposition between what remains and what changes. In this way is revealed the character of time as being itself "immutable and fixed," while everything flows within it. This "residing" of time in no way seems implied by the idea of succession. This feature is essential, however, as regards the discussion carried out within the framework of the first analogy of experience. We are surprised to read there that the three modes of time are permanence, succession, and simultaneity (A176/B219). It is the first of these three, mentioned for the first time, it seems, that is at issue in the discussion about the idea of substance, treated as a relation between what changes and what does not change. The feature of the permanence of time comes in as reinforcement. Nothing could be simultaneous or successive if there were not "an underlying ground which exists *at all times,* that is, something *abiding* and *permanent*" (A182/B225). Therefore, it is the schema of substance that led to this rereading of the Aesthetic on the point of the relation of permanence, succession, and simultaneity. The phenomenon of the immutable in existence, that is, substance, corresponds to this "endurance" of time.

The second subcategory of relation, causality, presents itself in the discussion of cosmological problems stemming from a "logic of illusion." The Transcendental Dialectic thus has a privileged relation with time through its schema of relation: law-governed succession. Something important about time is then said, as developed in the second Analogy: "All alterations take place in conformity with the law of the connection of cause and effect" (A189/B232). The synthetic power of the imagination, it is said, "determines inner sense in respect of the time-relation." The one-after-the-other of succession cannot be anarchical—that something happens cannot proceed from nothing, and, in this sense, there is no absolute beginning: "appearances follow one another" (A189/B233). The fact that something happens is a call to seek the cause of the event.

The requirement for order that weighs in this way on pure succession is so pregnant that Kant is forced to counterpose the objective succession of phenomena to the "*subjective succession* of apprehension.*" The former is arbitrary. The latter "will therefore consist in that order of the manifold of appearance according to which, *in conformity with a rule,* the apprehension of that which happens follows upon that which precedes" (A193/B236). This warning against the seduction of the ideas of event, birth, order, origin at the same time indicates Kant's distancing himself from the threefold synthesis discussed earlier. If the first edition of the Transcendental Deduction could be suspected of subjective idealism, it was in part owing to this absence of any distinction between subjective and objective succession. What is important about an event is not that it occur, but that it be preceded. Consequently, succession alone does not suffice to characterize time, for apprehension alone can give rise to "a play of representations, relating to no object; that is to say, it would not be possible through our perception to distinguish one appearance from another as regards relations of time" (A194/B239). For Kant, we could say, time, expecting order, hates the event.

In the Analytic of Principles a remarkable schema corresponds to the third subcategory of relation, defined in the Transcendental Analytic as community, or reciprocal action between the agent and the patient: "the reciprocal causality of substances in respect of their accidents" (A144/B183). This schema, and its development in the Principles, reveal a new aspect of time having to do with the simultaneity at work here between multiple realities or, in Kant's terms, between "rule-governed determinations." In the third Analogy, which corresponds to community, the emphasis is on the simultaneity in space in which "thoroughgoing reciprocity" (A211/B256) consists. What makes sense here is not just the reciprocity in action, an idea whose fortune will be considerable in other philosophical contexts discussed later, but the universal import of the idea of a reciprocal action, so marvelously illustrated by the Newtonian system. This universality completes the objectivity of the causal relation, at the expense once again of the merely subjective apprehension of the "at the same time," characteristic of simple simultaneity. To think of two things at the same time is not to set in place a "thoroughgoing community of mutual interaction" (A213/B260). Kant is aware that he has not exhausted all the resources of the word *Gemeinschaft,* equivalent to the Latin *communio* or *commercium.* Existing in the same place does not suffice. Only a real communion of substances satisfies the principle of reciprocal action. As for time, which is presupposed here, it offers the possibility of a compromise between succession and simultaneity expressed by the ideas of mutuality and reciprocity—notions whose career is interrupted here at the same time that it is begun. The remainder of our investigation will give ample play to this idea of reciprocal action in the form of mutual recognition.

There still remain the three schemata relative to the categories of modality, which, it will be recalled, add nothing to the content represented. This is why nothing of importance in the chapter on the Principles corresponds to them. Nevertheless, important ideas concerning time do correspond to the modulations of modality with regard to possibility, existence, and necessity, namely, the ideas of existence at "some time" (possibility), "at all times" (necessity), and at a "specific time" (reality). But the objectivity of the phenomenon is in no way affected by all this.

From this rapid overview of the system of schemata and principles, Kant retains their impact on the very conception of time considered successively from the point of view of the "time-series" (quantity), the "time-content" (quality), the "order of time" (relation), and finally "the scope of time" (modality) (A145/B184–185). This enrichment of the problematic of time establishes the inner sense as the bearer of the unity of apperception. Homogeneity has to prevail between these two poles. In the end, it is not in the section devoted to recognition that the fate of the idea of identification understood as a connection in time plays out, but in the Application, stemming from the Analytic of Principles, thanks to which the identification of any object whatsoever takes place. For us, this is perhaps the most important result of this exegesis of identification understood as placing into relation under the condition of time. It has given us the opportunity to follow Kant's heroic struggle on the two fronts of the absolute gap between the transcendental and the empirical points of view, on the one hand, and the originary heterogeneity of the two sources of human knowledge: sensibility and understanding, on the other. In this regard, Kant gives us the example of a battle with no concessions.

The Ruin of Representation

The question of moving beyond Kant is a difficult one. There are two paths that lead nowhere: discussion of fragments of Kant and a general revision of the whole system. In the first case, it is not this or that argument that needs to be fixed, even if one holds on to superb analyses like those of the threefold synthesis and of the schematism, or the Refutation of Idealism and the addition of *Selbstreflexion* in the second edition, for use in a different manner. These pieces are too much a part of the central argument to be simply detached from it. In the second case, revision, whether in the sense of positivism or in that of neo-Kantianism, reduces transcendental philosophy to epistemology and thus amputates the paradoxes and enigmas that make it so great, having to do with the thing-in-itself, the noumenal self, and more fundamentally the irreducibility of the gulf between *Denken* and *Erkennen* that makes possible the unfolding of the three critiques.

We must leave transcendental idealism with a single step, just as one enters it with a single step. To do this it is necessary to discern the threshold, in order to be able to say just what it is that one is breaking with, and how radical this break may be. I will say that it is at the level of *Vorstellung,* "representation," which we have mentioned several times but never made explicit. In truth, Kant does not justify it either. He assumes it, in order to be able to formulate the two presuppositions that we have placed foremost in our analyses: the dissociation of the transcendental from the empirical point of view, and the initial heterogeneity of the two sources of human knowledge, receptivity and spontaneity. The problem of the a priori synthesis, we have seen, is caught up at the intersection of these two *requisita* and gives rise to the *questio juris* developed by the transcendental deduction. We have to move beyond these two presuppositions to thematize this litigious concept of *Vorstellung.*[13]

The canonical text in this regard is the preface *(Vorrede)* to the second edition of the *Critique of Pure Reason,* published in 1787. Here is where the transcendental point of view is introduced all at once as a revolution on the philosophical plane comparable to that of Copernicus in cosmology. Here we witness the irruption of a veritable thought event. The tone is no less decided or imperious than that of Descartes in the *Discourse.* We experience the same disappointment at the spectacle of a fragmented metaphysics. And then, suddenly, there is the demand that we "accept" the reversal that constitutes the founding act of critical philosophy: "Hitherto it has been assumed that all our knowledge must conform to objects. But all attempts to extend our knowledge of objects by establishing something in regard to them *a priori,* by means of concepts, have, on this assumption, ended in failure" (B xvi). Then comes the recalling of the Copernican reversal of the relations between the earth and the sun: "A similar experiment can be tried in metaphysics, as regards the *intuition* of objects." The word *Vorstellung,* representation, comes onstage in this context as the emblematic term for the philosophical gesture that announces itself first of all as "acceptance," then as an "attempt." The alternative opened up by this revolutionary hypothesis is knowing whether the object "must conform to the constitution of our faculty of intuition." Here, then, is how the word *representation* makes its first appearance: "Since I cannot rest in these intuitions if they are to become known, but must relate them as representations to something as their object, and determine this latter through them" (B xvii). The term *Vorstellung* becomes in this way the emblem of "our new method of thought," which Kant sums up in the following formula: that we can "know *a priori* of things only what we ourselves put into them" (B xviii). And a bit farther on: "This attempt to alter the procedure which has hitherto prevailed in metaphysics, by completely revolutionizing it in accordance with the example set by the geometers and physicists, forms indeed the main purpose of this critique of pure speculative reason" (B xxii).

It is in the wake of this gesture that the term *representation* takes the throne. The condemnation of reason's claim to know the unconditioned is the obligatory corollary of this reversal, and the word *representation* is placed like a seal on this gesture of elimination that decides the fate of dogmatism: "If, then, on the supposition that our empirical knowledge conforms to objects as things in themselves, we find that the unconditioned *cannot be thought without contradiction,* and that when, on the other hand, we suppose that our representation of things, as they are given to us, does not conform to these things as they are in themselves, but that these objects, as appearances, conform to our mode of representation, *the contradiction vanishes.*" In a single move, with the disappearance of the contradiction, the hypothesis gets changed to a thesis: "We are justified in concluding that what we at first assumed for the purposes of experiment is now definitely confirmed." Henceforth, it is within the great circle outlined by representation that all the relations play to which we devoted our analyses of the understanding and sensibility, and all the operations of synthesis for which the productive imagination figures as the third term. What we have just called the circle of representation is nothing other than the graphic figuration of the Copernican reversal that makes "objects as appearances be governed by our mode of representation" (B xx).

To move beyond Kant, therefore, is by the same gesture to refuse the Copernican reversal and to move out of this magic circle of representation. Through this gesture the fundamental experience of being-in-the-world is posited as the ultimate reference of every particular experience capable of standing out against this background.

This gesture shares one feature with Kant's, through its abrupt character. It is first of all a proposition that one is asked to accept, a test, an attempt, a hypothesis. The *Annahme und Versuch* are justified only by the research program that they open. But unlike in the case of Kant, whose model is the a priori character of scientific knowledge and its ambition for systematic demonstration, a philosophy of being-in-the-world can only be problematic, not just for reasons having to do with its thematic focus, but for reasons having to do with the commitment of the philosopher who professes it and who assumes the risks of a controversy inseparable from its nonscientific character. Besides being problematic, this philosophy will also be, for the same reasons, fragmentary and nontotalizable. Its practitioners will never be able to write, as Kant does, "We are justified in concluding that what we at first assumed for the purposes of experiment is now definitely confirmed." Having begun as a test, this philosophy will always remain one.

Before outlining the initial contours of a distinct philosophy of recognition, I want to refer to several texts where we can read about the founding of the philosophical gesture opposed to the one that takes representation for its emblematic theme.

Rather than leaping precipitately into Heidegger's fundamental ontology, I looked for my first handhold in Husserl's *Krisis*.[14] He still claims the authority of a transcendental philosophy where the ego is the bearer of a project of constitution in which the fundamental act of *Sinngebung* unfolds; yet confronted with the "crisis of European sciences," he characterizes his philosophy from the start as "the expression of a radical crisis in the life of European humanity." It is only in part three that he directly takes on Kant and his fundamental choice. This part is titled: "The Way into Phenomenological Transcendental Philosophy by Inquiring Back [*Rückfrage*] from the Pregiven Lifeworld." He places his break with Kant under the heading of this questioning back. "But Kant, for his part, has no idea that in his philosophizing he stands on unquestioned presuppositions and that the undoubtedly great discoveries in his theories are there only in concealment" (103). Husserl calls this overlooked ground "the everyday world of life . . . presupposed as existing— the surrounding world in which all of us (even I who am now philosophizing) consciously have our existence; here also are the sciences, as cultural facts in this world, with their scientists and theories" (104). It is within this context that he elaborates the concepts of *Leiblichkeit,* with the distinction between *Leib* and *Körper*— flesh or living body and physical body—*Lebenswelt,* and *Zusammenleben* (107).

We can say, as Levinas did, in an article published on the occasion of the centenary of Husserl's birth in 1959, that in Husserl's last philosophy is proclaimed the "ruin of representation"—this is the title of Levinas's essay, reprinted in his *Discovering Existence with Husserl,* whose first edition dates back to 1969.[15] It is from within the major theme of Husserlian phenomenology, that of intentionality, that Levinas catches hold of the nascent theme that announces the ruin of representation. This theme is that of the implicit, the unperceived potential, of what escapes toward unmastered horizons, including even perception understood as presence to things. This implicit meaning and this horizon structure mean that every "cogito as consciousness, is, in a very broad sense 'the mean-ing' of the thing it intends, but that 'meaning' *exceeds,* at each in-stant, that which at that very instant, is given as 'explicitly in-tended'" (115).[16] This "exceeding of the intention in the intention itself" ruins the idea of a relation between subject and object such that that object would be at every instant exactly what the subject is currently thinking. Thus, it is in terms of the very structures of pure logic that "Husserl puts into question the sovereignty of representa-tion"—in other words, the pure forms of "something in general," where feeling plays no part and nothing is offered to the will, and yet which do not reveal their truth "when set back into their hori-zon" (116). The break with the Kantian hypothesis is consummated the moment this gesture "exceeding the intention in the intention it-self" (117) emerges. We must also move from the idea of horizon implied in intentionality to that of the situation of the subject and of the subject in situation. At the very least, "the way is open for the philosophy of the lived body, in which intentionality reveals its true nature, for its movement toward the represented is rooted there in all the implicit—nonrepresented—horizons of incarnate existence" (117).

This Husserlian moment is extremely valuable, even if some think that only Heideggerian ontology can deploy all its resources. I confess with the Levinas of 1959 that "the wavering between the disengagement of transcendental idealism and the engagement in a world, for which Husserl was reproached, is not his weakness but his strength." The persistent idealism of *Sinngebung* had to yield ground, so as to be able to proclaim that "the world is not only con-stituted, but also constituting" (118). The vocabulary of constitu-tion is preserved, but its ruin is announced in the aftermath of the ruin of representation.

As for Heidegger, he launches a frontal attack on the idea of rep-resentation and that of the world as representation in his famous Kant book.[17] He does not limit himself to substituting the point of view of fundamental ontology for that of critical philosophy but reinterprets the problem of the synthesis of the sensible and the intelligible starting from the third term, schema, schematism, transcendental imagination. I am drawing on the section titled "The Transcendental Power of Imagination as Root of Both Stems" (§§28–31). There Heidegger does not turn to either of the two operations I have indicated as futile: correcting Kant's text in places, or totally improving on it. He starts from the enigmas and aporias of the *Critique,* restoring to them their inaugural value by reinserting them into a perspective that announced itself as "laying the ground for metaphysics" (see the title of Heidegger's §3).[18]

Recognition Put to the Test by the Unrecognizable

I want to draw the initial consequences for a philosophy of recognition from this reversal that marks the ruin of representation. This new cycle of analyses will verify the comment made earlier that research placed under the heading of being-in-the-world, no longer being measured by the standard of scientific knowledge, agrees to remain problematic and fragmentary. I want to place the emphasis on this latter feature. It is a question not of rewriting the *Crisis,* or *Being and Time,* but more modestly of bringing together in a kind of test some of the most significant experiences that testify to the gap between recognizing and knowing, without as yet abandoning the way the idea of recognition is made more specific by that of identity.

It is as ways of being-in-the-world that these experiences are significant, and that means that the gap between recognizing and knowing is not to be sought first in the subject of judgment, as the furtive appearance of the verb *to recognize* at certain strategic points in Cartesian discourse might lead one to believe, but rather in the "things themselves." It will be recalled that neither Descartes nor Kant really makes specific the "something" identified either by procedures of distinction or by procedures for placing things into relation. For Descartes, the only thing that counts is that representative value which confers a kind of being on the idea, the objective being of the idea. But this holds just as much for scientific entities, for objects of perception, for persons, and finally, at the highest degree, for God. For Kant, only mathematical and physical entities satisfy the criteria of objectivity delimited by the transcendental point of view, the distinct status of persons in relation to things being set aside for practical philosophy. For a philosophy of being-in-the-world, on the contrary, it is the variety of modes of being of the things in the world that is important.

The one common feature that these modes of being must share to give rise to operations of recognition, it seems to me, is *change*. This apparently simple, quiet affirmation marks a decisive reversal as regards the theses of the Transcendental Aesthetic concerning time. The formal character of time as the subjective condition for the reception of intuitions, whether of outer or inner sense, implies, as we have observed, the primacy of time over change. This latter falls into the categories of relation only if it first satisfies the subjective condition of the form of time stemming from the Aesthetic. The reversal that restores to change its primacy in relation to time implies a "deformalization" of time that frees it from the a priori criteria reduced to succession and simultaneity. Henceforth, varieties of temporalization will accompany varieties of change, and it is these varieties of change and temporalization that will constitute the occasions for identification and recognition.

These varieties of temporalization present degrees of dramatization, depending on whether recognition passes through increasing degrees of misrecognition to the point of nonrecognition. A philosophy of being-in-the-world requires that this gradation first be taken into consideration *a parte objecti*. The question can then be formulated in these terms: What is it, in the way things change, that can at the limit make them unrecognizable?

Therefore, it is with the unrecognizable as the limit case of mis-recognition that recognition will henceforth be confronted.

Remaining, here at the beginning of our investigation, within the sphere of judgments about perception, we rediscover familiar examples dealt with in the phenomenology of perception—in particular, by Merleau-Ponty in the second part of his *Phenomenology of Perception,* devoted to the perceived world, and there, in particular, in the chapter titled "The Thing and the Natural World."[19] The first phenomenon that draws his attention is that of the stability of the characteristics or properties of the thing perceived. This latter appears from varying perspectives that we do not attribute to the object. We recall the example of the cube, where we never see all the sides at once. Husserl speaks about this in terms of profiles, sketches. But we do not speak yet of recognition, so long as the deformations of perspective do not threaten the quasi-instantaneous process of identification at work at the pre-predicative level of perceiving. Not only do the presentation of the object and the orientation of our gaze concur in this identification, but that of our body as a whole caught up in an active-passive exploration of the world. Identification rests then upon perceptual constants having to do not only with form and size, but with all the sensorial registers, from color to sound, from taste to tactile aspects, from mass to movement.[20] Identification takes place so long as deformations do not render it problematic. We can speak of an "originary faith" in regard to this set of experiences, in order to indicate this confidence in the stability of things. "The natural world," Merleau-Ponty also says, "is the schema of inter-sensory type-relations" (327). But it is necessary to add immediately that in this relation of familiarity with things there really is little place to speak of recognition. The possibility of a mistake begins to become clearer: Should I call this sequence of profiles by the same name? It is only after a moment of hesitation, as one of Descartes's texts suggested, that we say that we recognize it. What we recognize then is a style, the ground of the constancy of things. Unease can also come about from the presumption of uncertain, even disturbing, surroundings. This unease relates to the structure of the horizon of perception. Here is where time comes into play. But this is not abstract time that does not pass. Speaking of the synthesis of horizons to which the exploration of these surroundings gives rise, Merleau-Ponty declares it to be an essentially temporal synthesis: "Which means, not that it is subject to time, nor that it is passive in relation to time, nor that it has to prevail over time, but that it merges with the very movement whereby time passes" (330).

This latter remark leads to situations of perception and recognition where change goes hand in hand with time that passes. The paradigmatic example in what we earlier called perceptual faith is caught up in the dialectic of the appearing, disappearing, and reappearing of the same presumed object. An object, an animal, a person belonging to our environment enters our field of vision, suddenly leaves it, and, after a lapse of time, reappears. We say, It is the same one—yes, it is the same one. The comings and goings of animate beings are the ordinary occasion for this familiar experience. But in relation to earlier experiences, the role of time has changed. Succession is no longer enclosed within the sequence of profiles appearing to an uninterrupted gaze that holds before itself the object that our fingers turn. The sudden disappearance of the object makes it exit our field of visual perception and introduces a phase of absence that the perceiving subject does not control. A threat looms. What if the object, the animal, the person does not reappear? To lose a cat, as the young Balthus deplores in pathetic drawings that delighted Rainer Maria Rilke,[21] can symbolize all these losses, including those of persons who do not return, persons who have disappeared through flight, who have run away, those who have died. The shadow of death hangs over all disappearances. The simple coming and going of living beings spares us in varying degrees from the pangs of anxiety of a possible nonreturn, of a definitive disappearance. There is something like a grace of things that "wants" to make them return. But there is also a whimsicality about things that disappear and reappear on their own: the keys to the house or the car, for example. In the most favorable case, that of familiar—often familial—comings and goings, the chain of appearing, disappearing, and reappearing is so well forged that it gives to perceptual identity an aspect of assurance, even of reassurance, as regards perceptual faith. The temporal distance that disappearance stretches and distends is integrated into such identity through the very grace of otherness. Something escaping the continuity of our gaze for a time makes the reappearance of the same a small miracle.

I will take as an example of a more complex temporal experience the case in which the phase of disappearance leads to changes such that in the appearance of the thing that reappears we can speak of alteration. It is on such occasions that we begin advisedly to employ the word *recognition,* which might seem inappropriate to the preceding perceptual situations. Kant was not wrong in section 7 of the Transcendental Aesthetic, in the part on time, when he took into account the objection against the ideality of time drawn from the phenomenon of change. He thought he could get rid of this objection by granting the empirical reality of time, without giving up anything essential: that is, things change in time, which itself does not change. But lived experience proposes an example of the threatening aspect that attaches both to change and to time that passes. It is this aspect that gives recognition an emotional dimension that literature explores and that is not overlooked in our dictionaries.

In this regard, the recognition of persons clearly distinguishes itself from that of things, in this way cutting through the indetermination of the "something" through which Descartes and Kant designate the object of the operations of thought. For things, to recognize them is in large part to identify them through their generic or specific features. But certain familiar objects have a kind of personality for us, which means that to recognize them is to feel a relation to them not only of confidence but of complicity. People, on the other hand, recognize one another principally by their individual features. It is with people that the length of the time of separation reveals that destructive power which ancient wisdom grants to time and that Aristotle did not fail to note.[22] In this regard, growing old has emblematic value.

We owe to Proust's *Time Regained* pages of a cruel beauty, devoted to the hazards of recognition in circumstances that the narrator recounts with a calculated precision. He is torn from his meditation, in the solitude of the library of the Prince de Guermantes, on the first glimmerings of his projected book, and finds himself suddenly thrown into the spectacle of a dinner where all the guests who had earlier peopled his solitude and evening outings reappear, struck by decrepitude under the blows dealt by old age. The narrative of this dinner would suffice to nourish a small treatise on recognition.

Straight off, the emphasis falls on hesitation in "recognizing the master of the house and the guests."[23] Each of them seemed to have changed completely and to have "put on a disguise—in most cases a powdered wig." The work of recognition must struggle with the threat of the "unrecognizable." It is as though the protagonists had disguised themselves to hoodwink one another. One "had got himself up with a white beard and dragged his feet along the ground as though they were weighted with soles of lead, so that he gave the impression of trying to impersonate one of the 'Ages of Man.'" It is as though age gave a kind of visibility to Time (for which Proust reserves a capital *T*). The faces were like "puppets which exteriorized Time, Time which by habit is made invisible and to become visible seeks bodies, which, wherever it finds them, it seizes upon, to display its magic lantern upon them" (342). In these conditions, recognition requires "a process of logical deduction, by inferring from the mere resemblance of certain features the identity of the figure" before one (337). This kind of reasoning must proceed through the successive states of a face. Thus, the alteration that makes a woman's cheeks "unrecognizable" (343) produces reasoning that has to find its resolution in the contradiction between two states of the same being. In one of the many wise assertions that abound at the end of Proust's novel, he risks a generalization: "To 'recognize' someone, and, *a fortiori,* to learn someone's identity after having failed to recognize him, is to predicate two contradictory things of a single subject, it is to admit that what was here, the person whom one remembers, no longer exists, and that what is now here is a person whom one did not know to exist; and to do this we have to apprehend a mystery almost as disturbing as death, of which it is, indeed, as it were the preface and the harbinger" (365–366). The final word, however, is not left to reasoning. It only mirrors the work of time. Time, on which age confers visibility, is revealed to be a double agent, both of lack of recognition and of recognition. The page on "Time the artist" is well known: "'Instead of your own straight and handsome nose, it has given you your father's crooked nose, which I have never seen on you.' And yet this was what had happened: the nose was new, but it was a family nose. If this was a portrait-gallery, Time, the artist, had made all the sitters portraits that were recognizable, yet they were not likenesses, and this was not because he had flattered them but because he had aged them. He was an artist, moreover, who worked very slowly" (360–361). How can the reader not be as "intrigued" as is the narrator himself by the spectacle of the disguises worn by faces ravaged by age? Has recognition reached its apex, at least as identification, when it has to be won from the "unrecognizable"? The common little dialectic of appearing, disappearing, and reappearing then, upon reflection, takes a turn almost as disturbing as the death for which old age is "as it were the preface and the harbinger."

We are not left speechless by this evocation of mystery, however. Proust's narrative opens another horizon than that of such disconsolate meditation. If we return to just before the dinner scene narrative, this well-known scene is announced by the narrator, speaking in the first person, as a "spectacular and dramatic effect which threatened to raise against my enterprise the gravest of all objections" (336).

What enterprise? That of the work still to be written, whose meaning has just revealed itself, thanks to a kind of illumination that has taken place in the prince's library. And this revelation was itself placed under the sign of recognition—but of a different sort of recognition, not that of such protagonists in a narrative as we have been considering, but of the reader himself, summoned to become, in reading, "the reader of his own self." Indeed, "the writer's work is merely a kind of optical instrument which he offers to the reader to enable him to discern what, without this book, he would perhaps never have perceived in himself. And the recognition by the reader in his own self of what the book says is the proof of its veracity, the contrary also being true, at least to a certain extent, for the difference between the two texts may sometimes be imputed less to the author than to the reader" (322). This is the enterprise to which the coup de théâtre of the dinner was going to raise "the gravest of all objections."

What objection? How does this excruciating scene add up to an objection to the writing project the narrator offers the reader, so that in the end he will recognize himself in it? In this, that the spectacle of the ravages of age that have rendered "unrecognizable" the guests carries the sense of a metaphor for death. For us, readers of the book finally written, the scene where each of the guests seems to "have put on a disguise" works no longer as an objection to an enterprise effectively brought to term but, in my interpretation, as a limit experience of the recognition of the unrecognizable, in a sense close to what Karl Jaspers calls limit-situations (such as death, suffering, war, guilt) in his philosophy of existence. Saved by writing, this scene has to do from now on with that other recognition announced in the illumination that happened in the library: "the reader's recognition within himself of what the book says."

The following chapter will attempt to do justice to this recognition "within oneself," something like reading a life.

CHAPTER 2

RECOGNIZING ONESELF

Je me sui reconnu poète.

—Arthur Rimbaud, in a letter to Georges Izambard, 13 May 1871

The road to recognition is long, for the "acting and suffering" human being, that leads to the recognition that he or she is in truth a person "capable" of different accomplishments. What is more, this self-recognition requires, at each step, the help of others, in the absence of that mutual, fully reciprocal recognition that will make each of those involved a "recognized being," as will be shown in my next chapter. The self-recognition at issue in the current chapter will remain not only incomplete, as in truth mutual recognition will, but also more mutilated, owing to the persistent dissymmetry of the relation to others on the model of helping, but also as a real hindrance.

The Greek Background: Action and Its Agent

I have chosen ancient Greece as my starting point. Not because I am thinking in terms of progress that would underscore that the Greeks were behind us, principally when it comes to the self-designation grammatically noted by the reflexive pronoun "self-," but, on the contrary, because of an underlying kinship on the plane of what Bernard Williams does not hesitate to call "Recognizing Responsibility" in the second chapter of his *Shame and Necessity*.[1] Following him, I want to refer to "some unacknowledged similarities" having to do with "the concepts that we use in interpreting our own and other people's feelings and actions" (2). The ancient Greeks "are among our cultural ancestors, and our view of them is intimately connected with our view of ourselves" (3). At issue precisely are "ideas of responsible action, justice, and the motivations that lead people to do things that are admired and respected" (4). This "liberation of Antiquity" (the title of Williams's first chapter) from a prejudice our philosopher calls progressive, far from inclining us to minimize the novelty of some concepts stemming from self-recognition that we owe to Augustine, Locke, and Bergson, invites us to accept these concepts as innovations tied to thought events that come along on the same thematic trajectory as do the ethical ideas of the Greeks to which Williams's book is devoted. It is this trajectory that I have risked characterizing, in these opening remarks of this chapter, through the recognition by the acting and suffering human being that he or she is someone capable of certain accomplishments. Like Williams, we can, without anachronism, place this recognition under the heading of "recognizing responsibility" (50–74).

If we take the Homeric world as the terminus a quo of the trajectory that traces the curve of the recognition of responsibility in the Greek setting, this is because it can be demonstrated that a threshold has already been crossed there in the direction of a reflection centered on the notion of deliberation, as will be the case with Aristotle. I borrow the following comment from Williams concerning Homer's characters: they "are constantly wondering what to do, coming to some conclusion, and acting" (22). This capacity presupposes a minimum of personal consistency in these characters that allows them to be identified as veritable "centers of agency" (the title of Williams's second chapter). Ulysses asks himself whether

he should leave Nausicaa, who regrets his departure; Hector medi-
tates on death, Achilles ponders his anger. The words *thymos* and
noos bear witness in the texts to this apprehending, which we could
call pretheoretical, of the central categories of human action. Were
someone to object that the innumerable references to divine intervention prevent the constituting of autonomous entities, at least in
our sense, this is true, but what is striking is that "the question that
the god helps to answer is a question asked by an agent deciding for
reasons" (30–31).[2] One might also say that psychological categories important to us are lacking. But let us say, more modestly, that
"at the beginning of Western literature, [Homer] had the basic
terms that we need, and he lacked several things that we do not
need, in particular the illusion that the basic powers of the mind are
inherently constituted in terms of an ethical order" (46). It remains
to be said that the heroes' decisions are narrated as those of characters designated by their name, awaiting, the modern reader will say,
their appropriate theory. Yes, but that will be a homogeneous development. In book 3 of his *Nichomachean Ethics* Aristotle will give
the theory for deliberation as practiced by Homeric characters.

It is not sufficient just to grant that these characters behave as
"centers of agency" but lack the concept, for the heroes talk about
and give names to the movements of their heart that punctuate their
actions. In the case of Agamemnon, Ajax, and others, they end by
designating themselves in the first person as *aition,* a word that has
something to do with the idea of a cause, and by characterizing
their action by adverbial epithets: *hekōn* (deliberately) and *aekōn*
(reluctantly). Even more important, the same character can take
himself to be *aition* yet think he acted against his will, as though
a god had ravished his reason. Nevertheless, the character holds
himself responsible for an action that he does not dissociate from
himself. An implicit theory of action as part of "some universal ba-
nalities" (55) had already found these words, which we have no difficulty translating as cause, intention, normal or abnormal state, ne-

cessity to make up for (blame, punishment, compensation). They are, I will say, following Williams, "universal materials" (56). That an agent should be the cause, merely through the fact that a new state of affairs comes about as a result of his action; that we can blame him and demand reparation from him for it; that he may have acted, however, in an abnormal state, on account of a curse, taint, some supernatural cause—all this complicates the state of affairs, without the agent's ceasing to be *aition*. It will be up to philosophy to articulate the question of intention as a distinct problem, determined to give it the depth that the problem of evil will subsequently impose upon it, as will the connected problem of freedom of will.[3]

Ulysses Makes Himself Recognized

The famous story of the return of Ulysses to Ithaca is incontestably a narrative of recognition in which the hero is both the protagonist and the beneficiary.[4] It is right to say that he causes himself to be recognized by other partners, following a carefully orchestrated climax and an art of delay often commented upon by critics. Why could such a narrative not serve as an opening to our later reflections on mutual recognition? For several reasons. In the first place, despite the distribution of roles among a number of characters, there exists just one among them who is the object of recognition, Ulysses come home to Ithaca. To be sure, the other protagonists satisfy the criteria for "recognizing responsibility" referred to earlier. But their presumed identity is not at issue. It is not a narrative of mutual recognition. However, there is another more decisive reason that keeps this narrative from crossing the threshold of reciprocity: the recognition scenes stake out the reconquest of his household by an inflexible master, at the expense of the usurpers in the posture of pretenders to possession of the legitimate wife. This aspect of violence means that a history of recognition finds itself inextricably entwined with one of vengeance. The rhythm of this sec-

ond story governs that of recognition, to the point that the degrees
of recognition are stages along the path of vengeance that ends with
a massacre of pitiless cruelty. A spouse will be recognized, but in
that thrust a master will be reestablished in the fullness of his rule.

Still, the delayed progression in the recognizing of Ulysses by his
people is rich in lessons for our investigation. It is no indifferent
matter that the first recognition should be by the son and, if we put
our trust in the scholiasts, that the last one should be by the father,
even if the dramatic peak is attained in the scene of the wife's recognition, where the dissymmetry mentioned earlier comes close to
yielding to something like a mutual recognition. Nor is it a matter
of indifference that thanks to the strategy of delay characteristic of
Homeric narration, the other protagonists together make up the
whole configuration of the household with its different roles.

Not wishing to get caught up in the picturesque aspect of these
encounters, I shall focus on three features capable of enriching our
inquiry: the verbal formulas of recognition, the role of the marks of
recognition, and that of disguises.

In book 16 of *The Odyssey*, the encounter between father and
son opens the game in the presence of the swineherd and barking
dogs. Ulysses is received as a "stranger," yet welcomed as a "guest."
Clothed in new garments by his son, rejuvenated in appearance by
the goddess, he is at first taken for a god. Then comes Ulysses' exclamation: "No, I am not a god. . . . No, I am your father." To make
oneself recognized is first to give rise to a mistake, then to correct it.
Here it is the result of cunning. It should be noted that my French
translators say "recognize" where the Greek has several verbs at its
disposal: *idesthai, agnoein* (17:265, 273). It is the latter term that
the poet uses to sum up in a single word the direct recognition
of Ulysses by his faithful dog, Argos: "He recognized [*enoēsen*]
Ulysses in the man who was approaching and, wagging his tail, he
laid back his ears. He lacked the strength to approach his master"
(17:301). Satisfied at last, the animal dies shortly thereafter: "But
Argos was no more; the shadows of death had shrouded his eyes,

which had just seen Ulysses again after twenty years" (326). Disguised as a beggar, Ulysses enters his mansion besieged by the pretenders, soon submitted to the test of the bow, which Ulysses wins. The first recognitions will have served as signposts along the path of vengeance. Thus it is from the scar of his wound that the old servant, washing the stranger's feet, recognizes her master (19). "Ulysses, it's you!" "Nurse, it's you!" Now taking the initiative in the presence of his servants, Ulysses declares: "But wait, if you need a sure mark [sēma], your hearts will no doubt be able to recognize me." "With these words, removing his rags, he showed his large scar to the herdsman" (222). The symbolism here is strong; the sign of the scar runs in counterpoint to the disguise. The sign is a mark in the flesh, the disguise an opportune covering. It is only after the great slaughter—"the work was accomplished" (23:479)—that the poet sets forth the great game of seduction carried out by Penelope at the beginning of what will become the recognition scene between husband and wife. She has recognized [esideken] him by his features; she can allow herself to pretend not to know him, for confidence arms her heart: "If it is really Ulysses who returns to his household, we will recognize each other without trying [gnōsometh'allēlōn kai lōion], for between us there are secret marks [sēmata] unknown to all others" (23:109–10). Indeed, the "mark" will be more secret than the "large scar." It will be the marriage bed. Penelope gives the order to ready the bed as a test for the hero. For Ulysses knows about the bed; he made it of an olive tree rooted in the soil. Admirable sign of a shared secret: "The making of this bed was my great secret" (23:187).

Has the cycle of recognition come full circle? A shadow passes over the night of love: "O woman, do not believe you are at the end of your trials! I still have someday to brave a complicated, dangerous, boundless labor [ponos]" (23:249). Penelope has only a weak reply: "If for our old age the gods have truly reserved happiness, let us hope we shall escape our trials at last" (286).

The scholiasts have added to this cycle of recognition a final scene, to which they give the technical name *anagnōrismon* (which will be the word Aristotle will use in the *Poetics* for the sudden episode in which lack of recognition turns into recognition: *anagnōrisis*). This will be the recognition of Ulysses by his father, Laertes. Was not the first recognition that of the father by the son? The cycle of recognition opened by that of the father by the son loops back together with that of filiation, by way of the conjugal relation. And once again it is by a mark [*sēma*] that father and son recognize each other: through the description of the thirteen pear trees, forty fig trees, and ten apple trees offered once long ago as a gift and a promise: "But Laertes, at these words, felt his knees and heart buckle. He had recognized [*anagnontos*] the truth of the signs [*sēmata*] Ulysses gave him" (24:345).

What shall we retain from all this for our inquiry? The Homeric characters who, we have granted, behave as "centers of agency" and "recognize themselves as responsible" are also capable of a recognition that passes through others, but which we cannot yet call mutual, because it is still focused on a single protagonist and limited to the role that tradition assigns to those who stand in the entourage of a master. For this master, to be recognized is to recover his mastery once it has been threatened. This limit to the message left by Homer is attested to by the interweaving of the story of recognition with that of vengeance, which is still far from what in the following chapter I shall call the struggle for recognition. At least we can hold in reserve the valuable insights concerning the role of "disguise" and its opposite, "marks," in the story of recognition.

At Colonus, Oedipus Retracts

My second example is drawn from the corpus of Greek tragedies.[5] For what is of interest to our inquiry, the difference on the dramatic level between epic and tragedy is not essential. That an action should be recounted by another or "acted out" before our eyes does not affect the mimetic character of either as regards the action represented or especially the configuring role assigned to the plot, as it applies to either actions or characters. More significant is the difference between the delaying effect in epic, which the story of Ulysses illustrates, and the tension belonging to tragedy noted by Goethe and Schiller in an exchange of letters in April 1797.

I have chosen *Oedipus at Colonus* as my example because the tension there results from a reversal that occurs in this second of the Oedipus tragedies on the plane of the recognition of responsibility that had already occurred in the first one, *Oedipus the King*. This reversal from one tragedy to the next is equivalent to a retraction by one and the same character of the accusation brought against him twenty years earlier. From the dramatic point of view, the relation of one tragedy to the other is of the same nature as that which the plot is supposed to bring about within a single tragedy, and which Aristotle in the *Poetics* points to with the two linked categories of *peripeteia*, in the sense of a reversal in the action as regards knowing, and recognition *(anagnōrisis)*, defined as a transition from ignorance to knowledge, leading to the shift from enmity to friendship, or conversely, in "characters destined for good or ill fortune" (1452a31). And it turns out that Aristotle uses precisely the tragedy of Oedipus as his example: "The finest form of discovery is one attended by reversal, like that in *Oedipus*" (1452a33). *Oedipus at Colonus* also brings about this double effect produced by the plot within one tragedy in another sense. This new recognition, in the dramatic sense of the term, taking place not within just one tragedy but between two of them, has the significance of a retraction at the level of the recognition of responsibility that is our theme here. And it is the tension arising from this shift that lends the coloration to the fear and pity, which every tragedy gives rise to, that the denouement of *Oedipus at Colonus* imprints on these tragic passions.

If *Oedipus at Colonus* demonstrates one thing, it is that the tragic character, however overwhelmed he may be by the feeling of the irresistible character of the supernatural forces that govern human destiny, remains the author of that innermost action consisting of his evaluating his acts, particularly retrospectively. If misfortune is the dominant note in *Oedipus at Colonus,* to the point of refuting the ancient guilt, this misfortune becomes a dimension of the action itself, in the sense of being endured in a responsible manner. Across this trajectory of endurance, the play builds a progression from misfortune undergone to misfortune assumed. It is the reversal from accusation to exculpation that gives a rhythm to this inner progression in endurance. The old, blind, impoverished Oedipus, supported by his daughter, Antigone, soon to be joined by her sister Ismene, is first confronted with the test of exile and grief: "O stranger, I am an exile" (207). But "signs" (94) allow him to "recognize" (96) the sacred place where his wanderings have led him, there to "wrap up" his life (104). For "knowledge" *(mathein)* is necessary in order to be able to act with prudence. This *mathein* will turn suffering into an action (116). Yes, these are "the actions that were imposed on him," proclaims Antigone, anticipating the paternal denial. And that denial soon follows: "My actions, which inspire such terror on your part, I did not carry out voluntarily [*dedrakota*], I underwent [*peponthota*] them" (267)—and we rediscover the expression *akōn* already encountered in Homer. And "if I had acted in full awareness [*phronōn*], even then I would not have been guilty [*kakos*]" (271). "Holy, innocent"—that is how the old penitent will bring blessings to the inhabitants of this country.

Will someone object that the Greeks were unaware of self-consciousness? In its reflexive, speculative form, yes, but not spontaneously: "Does one not," the old man says, in effect, "have reason to think of oneself" [*hauto philos*] (309)?

What is there about his past for Oedipus to challenge? First, his anger [*mochthos*] and the heated words [*thymos*], whose excess led him to poke out his eyes, the violence to which the last verses of

Oedipus the King gave a terrifying eloquence. But more radically, it is the fault itself, earlier accepted, that had led to this excess punishment. Addressing the leader of the chorus, he says: "I am charged with a crime, stranger; yes, I am so charged in spite of myself [*hekōn*]; let the gods know, I wanted nothing of this" (421–422). And again: "a fatal marriage, an accursed union, the city bound me to this, and I knew nothing about it" (326). And here is the connection between misfortune undergone and fault, untied in a single gesture: Oedipus: "I have borne unforgettable misfortunes." "You . . ." (Oedipus): "I did nothing." And a bit farther on: "I have killed, I have taken a life, but without knowing [*anous*] what I was doing. According to the law, I am innocent. I was unaware of my crime in committing it" (546). Creon, himself become old, receives this protestation from the old blind man: "Your mouth reproaches me for murders, injustices, misfortunes that I have supported, unfortunate that I am, against my will [*akōn*]." The same word— *akōn*—appears again, redoubled, regarding the incest: "There is however one thing of which I am well aware: willingly you recall these horrors against me and against her, whereas I, who married her against my will [*akōn*], it is also against my will [*akōn*] that I speak of it. But never shall I be proclaimed guilty either for this marriage or for the murder of my father, for which you are still accusing me, bitterly insulting me." Oedipus is able from that point on to discharge himself of his crime on the Furies: "Above all, I blame your curse, and what is more I hear the soothsayers telling me that it is right to do so" (1295–1302). And again: "The gods brought about everything" (998).

What then about "recognizing responsibility"? Like Bernard Williams, I believe that this accusation, which takes on the value of an excuse, is inscribed in the same space of human action as ordinary human deliberations. It complicates the avowal but does not abolish personal initiative. In this sense, the disavowal in *Oedipus at Colonus* does not abolish the avowal in *Oedipus the King*: "No other hand than my own struck," we read in *Oedipus the King* (1331). The reversal from action to suffering takes place within the field of meaning of acting: "I underwent my acts; I did not commit them" (*Oedipe à Colone*, 437). Still, it remains true that it was *he who did that,* whatever may be said about archaic beliefs applying to blood crimes. As Bernard Williams says, "we understand it because we know that in the story of one's life there is an authority exercised by what one has done, and not merely by what one has intentionally done" (69). Do we express this in terms of regret? What the old Oedipus is able to experience is a regret that the "agent demands of himself" (68). Because of this he can endure his unhappiness until he dies serenely: "My children, the end of my life has come and I can no longer hold it off" (1472–1473). The plot structure is able to add a touch of the miraculous to this ending: Oedipus withdraws from our sight. What remains is the word of love left to his daughters by the guilty-innocent man: "No one could have loved you more than this father you are about to be deprived of for the rest of your lives" (1615–1619).

Oedipus leaves behind him, as the story goes, only the fratricidal hatred between Eteocles and Polynices.

But *Oedipus at Colonus* leaves this message: it is the same suffering human being who recognizes himself as agent.

Aristotle: The Decision

There exists a strong thematic continuity from Homer to the tragic writers and Aristotle that runs even to the words used: *aition, akōn, hekōn, phronein.* The philosopher, like the epic poet and the tragic poet, but also like the orator using rhetoric in public speech, speaks of characters who, in Williams's terms, are "centers of agency" and beings capable of "recognizing responsibility." The break with the poets and the orators does not, therefore, occur principally on the plane of what is at issue but, according to an expression now familiar to us, on that of thought events that inaugurate a new way of asking questions. The thought event brought about by Aristotle finds its mark in the title of his great work, which we will now turn to: *Ethics*, where the adjective can be joined either to the neuter *biblia* or to the feminine *theōria*.[6] In this respect, Aristotle can be taken as the creator of the expression and the concept of a moral theory, as a discipline distinct from metaphysics, physics, the treatise on the soul, or even the one on politics, despite the proximity between ethics and politics, and a certain inclusion of the first within the second.

In the preliminary remarks to the *Nichomachean Ethics* three distinguishing criteria are proposed: in relation to the object, to the type of reasoning, and to the audience—all precautions for which the poet has no use. As for the quick definition of the object, it is common opinions that first give rise to the search for the concept. To begin, a first characterization of the object is proposed close to that of common sense: "Every art and every inquiry, and similarly every action and choice is thought to aim at some good as its end" (1094a1). As for method, "it is the mark of an educated man to require in each field only the rigor that fits the nature of the subject" (1094b23). As for the audience, a judge is not just anyone who wants to be, but rather "he who is learned in this field." In this way, the philosopher requires an appropriate audience, concerned not about theoretical knowledge but about action.

The philosopher of action does not make a direct move toward the structures of what we can call rational action. He does so only in book 3, after having taken a position on two major questions regarding which he has to indicate his way between current opinions and existing attempts at conceptualization, including those of Plato and his students. These two disputed questions are those of the definition of the good in its relation to happiness, and that of moral virtue as the obligatory pathway in the pursuit of happiness.

What, then, is this good concerning which we are told in the opening remarks that all knowledge and every intention aspire toward it in some way? More precisely, what is the highest good of all goods that can be the ends of human action? It would be premature to take up the structures of human action if one did not know how to situate them on this long trajectory leading to the highest good. We agree, along with most people, that this highest good has a name: happiness. But regarding just what it is, there is controversy. It is a matter for the *sophoi,* the clear thinkers. In order to orient himself in this dispute, Aristotle takes up the list of "kinds of life"— the life of pleasure, the life devoted to politics, the contemplative life. It is the interpretation of the last of these three that constrains him to take a stand between those who leave the preferred goods in no clear order, without the seal of the highest good, and those who make of the highest good a something-in-itself unrelated to us. Next comes the declaration that directly has to do with our inquiry into the structure of action. For human beings, it is said, there is something above and beyond every particular task, a task proper to them, an *ergon,* which is to live a "fulfilled" life (1098a16). To this as yet undetermined idea of a specific task—a task specific to human existence—is grafted the question of virtues, so many guiding excellences capable of indicating, determining, and structuring both the aim of happiness and the fitting task for human existence. Therefore, we can say that "human good will be an activity of the soul according to virtue and, if there are several virtues, according to the best, the most complete one." With this, the idea that happiness comes only through divine favor or luck is excluded. Happiness has its source in us, in our activities. Here lies the most primitive condition of what we call self-recognition. Its deepest-lying possibility is its anchorage in the goal of happiness in those activities that make up the human task as such, our task.

It is therefore as components of happiness that the virtues are considered. "Since happiness is an activity of the soul depending on virtue attained, we must now deal with virtue. Is this not the best way to come in the end to know what happiness itself is?" (1102a5–6). Once again it is repeated that it is human virtue that will be considered. "For the good we are seeking is human good, and the happiness we seek is human happiness" (1112a13–15). A long detour will then be necessary, passing through the study of the structure of the soul, with a view to isolating that irrational part which "has one rule"—namely, that desiring part which participates in some way in the rule, "insofar as it submits to it and obeys it" (1102b28). The virtues come from this part of ourselves. And it is in terms of the vocabulary of praise that their demand makes itself known: "However, we praise the philosopher, him too, for the philosophy he possesses as a habitual state; these praiseworthy habitual states we call the virtues" (1103a13). The practical rather than theoretical aim of this study of virtue is also affirmed: "Our present inquiry, unlike all the others, does not have as its aim a speculative end. If we undertake this inquiry, it is not in order to know what virtue is—for our study would then have no use—but in order to become good. We must therefore necessarily turn our examination to the domain of our actions, and seek in what way we ought to carry them out. Is it not they, as we have said, that are the decisive element capable of determining the very quality of the habitual states of our character?" (1103b26–30).

It is not surprising, therefore, that in the detailed examination of the idea of virtue in chapters 4 and 5 of book 2 of the *Nichomachean Ethics,* the major concept of the Aristotelian theory of action should now be anticipated. "Virtues are in some way intentional decisions or, more exactly, they do not occur without some intentional decision [*prohairesis*]" (1106a2). The human *ergon,* inseparable from the idea of virtue, is also recalled, a few lines later: "Human virtue will also be (just as vision makes the eye good) a state that makes the person good and allows him to guide his work to a successful conclusion" (1106a22). Considerations follow regarding the golden mean in each virtue between excess and deficiency. But this is meant to lead back to the heart of the discussion concerning the definition of virtue. This definition, more than the preceding drafts, mobilizes the structures of action that we are about to discuss. "From what we have said, virtue is a habitual state that directs decision making [*hexis prohairetikē*] which consists in a golden mean relative to us, one whose norm is the moral rule; that is, the one that would be given by the wise man [*phronimos*]" (1106b36–38). In this crucial text, it is not only the connection between habit *(hexis)* and decision *(prohairesis)* that is remarkable, but also the referring of the norm to the wise man as the bearer of this wisdom of judgment, to which book 6 will be devoted, under the heading of *phronēsis*. The *phronimos* is the sole agent of that intellectual virtue which springs up at the turning point of the distinction between the so-called virtues of character, to which the following books are devoted, and the intellectual virtues, which are the object of book 6. Already named in book 2, the *phronimos* will be the anticipated figure of the reflexive self implied by the recognition of responsibility. It is not stated that he designates himself. But the complete definition of virtue does designate him as the living measure of excess and deficiency, the dividing line that marks out the mean that is characteristic of all virtue.

The description of the structures of rational action stands out against the vast backdrop of these definitions, upon which the ethical project as a whole is presented. This description finds its key point in the notion of decision, with which we translate the Greek *prohairesis*—and additionally in that of wishing. Recognition of responsibility, whose outline we have caught sight of in epic and tragedy, finds its guiding concept in that of decision. It is what was named by way of anticipation in the definition of virtue cited earlier. It stands now at the heart of book 3 of the *Nichomachean Ethics*.

Aristotle does not approach the concept of *prohairesis* head-on; instead, he places it in a broader circle, that of the "willingly" *(hekōn)* and the "in spite of oneself" *(akōn)*, two notions already familiar to us from our discussion of Homer and Greek tragedy. Aristotle elevates these notions to a philosophical level through a confrontation with the Socratic adage that "No one does evil willingly." No, Aristotle protests. The bad person is so willingly. Socrates' case of an evildoer, if we can put it this way, requires one to begin with the "in spite of oneself." This turns out to involve different excuses that the wrongdoer can draw from situations of constraint or ignorance. Cases of constraint are the occasion for opposing the external character (in relation to the agent) of the principle *(archē)*, also called the cause *(aitia)*, of the action carried out because one was forced to. In contrast, action carried out willingly is that "whose principle is internal to the subject and, moreover, in the subject's power to carry it out or not to" (1110a16). What interests me is this connection at the level of vocabulary between the *en hautōi* (internal to the subject) and *ep' hautōi* (in the power of the subject). What will be designated in our subsequent vocabulary as "self" finds itself prefigured here by the *hauto* joined to its two prepositions in the Aristotelian definition of "willingly": the principle (or cause) is within the agent and depends on him. After the excuse of constraint, that of ignorance in these mixed cases still needs to be removed. For someone to do something legitimately in spite of himself, something that he does out of ignorance (where ignorance can apply either to the factual conditions or to the rule), after the fact one has to be able to feel regret. Having set aside these two excuses, the definition of *hekōn* given earlier easily imposes itself.

Once the ground has been cleared, the notion, dearer to Aristotle, of *prohairesis*, decision—or if we prefer to stay closer to the Greek, preferential choice—is given the place of honor. With it, we come to the innermost nature of our intentions, which, more than our external acts, make it possible to judge character *(ethos)*. After saying what it is not (appetite, impulsiveness [*thymos*], wishing), what it is has to be stated: a type of willing specified by prior deliberation. The *pro-* of *prohairesis* is found again in that of the *pre-* in *predeliberated*. We have reached the heart of what we have, from the beginning of this chapter, placed under the heading of recognizing responsibility. I will not take up the discussion of what matters most in evaluating Aristotle's theory, to know what we don't ponder (the eternal, the unchanging, or regular and frequently occurring things), and what we do ponder: that is, we are told in the context of book 3, the means rather than the ends. There is a huge argument among interpreters concerning this distinction, which I shall not take up. What is sufficient for me is the definition: "Man seems . . . to be the principle of his actions; for deliberation bears on what can be an object of action for him, and actions are carried out for ends other than themselves. Let us conclude, therefore, that the object of deliberations will be the means, not the end" (1112b32–33).

The description of the components of rational action would be incomplete if one did not make a place for that complement of decision constituted by wishing *(boulesis)*. Aristotle brings it up in the wake of his definition of deciding: "As a result, since the 'decided' is the 'desired thing deliberated upon,' it being understood that it is a question of something that is in our power, the decision itself will be a deliberated-upon desire for things that are in our power. For, as soon as we have judged, following deliberation, we desire, by virtue of the wish" (1113a9–11). This connection is expected once we admit that one deliberates over means and not ends. The wish is, if we may put it this way, in charge of the ends, as we have known since Plato's *Gorgias*. The description of the "deliberated-upon desire" would be incomplete, then, without this reference to wishing. What is more, if the wished-for object were reduced to what seems good to us, the wish would fall outside the field of a rational ethics. We shall have simply turned our back on Plato and his plea for the absolute good, but to no further end. This conclusion can be avoided insofar as right judgment is exercised, as in every branch of moral activity, by a virtuous human being, that is, the one who was designated earlier as the personal instance of the delimiting of the "mean" for the case of each of the virtues examined in books 4 and 5. The measure in each case is not merely the person, it is the virtuous person. What is anticipated here is the doctrine of *phronēsis*, of practical wisdom, or, as it is traditionally translated, of prudence. This practical wisdom will remain a major topic for the remainder of our book.

With *phronēsis*, therefore, we shall end our borrowings from the Aristotelian conception of moral action under the heading of recognizing responsibility. Its appearance had been anticipated with the definition of virtue: "a habitual state that directs decision making [*hexis prohairetikē*], which consists in a mean relative to us, one whose norm is the moral rule; that is, the one that would be given by the wise man [*phronimos*]" (1106b36–38). To deal with *phronēsis* thematically, however, a change of planes is necessary that will take us from the so-called moral virtues or virtues of character to the intellectual virtues. This change is important inasmuch as with it the analysis is raised to what we can already call the reflexive level. It is worth noting that the object of this virtue cannot be defined separately from its subject, the wise man. The question of the mean—of evaluation—assures the transition in this argument between the two kinds of virtues. If the mean for the moral virtues is determined by the correct rule *(orthos logos)*, also called the norm *(horos)*, this is the work of practical reason.

Another connection with the treatise on virtues in book 2 is ensured by the reference to the task *(ergon)* of human beings as human beings. The argument here proceeds from genus to specific difference. The genus is the habitual state *(hexis)*, and the specific difference is precisely this notion of a task. As Jolif notes in his commentary, "intellectual virtue, like moral virtue, must allow the subject to carry out his task well" (443). So on the plane of the intellectual virtues, clarifying the aim of truth holds the same place as does the notion of the mean on the plane of the virtues of character. The decision is henceforth anchored by the act of judgment in the dynamism of the practical intellect. What desire pursues and thought articulates, that is, the end, are one and the same. Aristotle, Jolif goes on to say, "teaches here that desire is virtuous when the thought is true, that is, when what thought says is the end is truly the end, and the desire upright, that is, when what desire pursues is precisely this end stated truthfully by thinking. Thinking's affirmation and the pursuit of desire then overlap exactly" (447). There is no longer any grounds, therefore, for opposing book 6 and book 2 on the question whether deliberation has to do only with means. The center of gravity is displaced with the question, What does it mean to act according to the correct rule [*orthos logos*] in determining the mean (1138b18)? The determination of the norm *(horos)* implicit to this correct rule requires the combined play of that part of reason called calculating and desire in its habitual state. This yields the practical thinking that expresses the idea of a deliberated-upon desire. This practical thinking has felicitous action as its stakes; the rectitude of the desire joins forces with the question of practical truth on the plane of thought.

The aspect of wisdom that is of the greatest interest to our investigation has to do with the implication of the *phronimos* in his *phronēsis*. "The best way to grasp what wisdom is, is to consider the quality that language attributes to the *phronimos*" (1140a24). A declaration like this one constitutes an important step in our inquiry into the emergence of the point of view of the subject in the description of rational action. Aristotle proceeds in his demonstration by interrogating language. And not simply language, but the testimony of several exemplary individuals; for example, Pericles. The philosopher will only give the barest outline of the practical syllogism to his argument, which proceeds from the idea of the "excellent deliberator" as the major premise, and as the minor premise the idea of situations marked by uncertainty, to conclude with the definition of wisdom as the "true, rational [*meta logou*] habitual state that directs action and has as its object things that are good and bad for human beings" (1140b4–6). In this way the practical judgment gives a rich content to the idea of the human *ergon*. In this regard, practical wisdom has a greater affinity with politics than with speculative philosophy, as the example of Pericles confirms.

Aristotle will return one last time to the definition of *phronēsis* constructed in terms of the theme of the excellent deliberator *(euboulos)*.[7] He does so in order to add one feature to it that has to be of interest to us. To direct action, practical wisdom must proceed from universal knowledge to knowledge of the particular. I see in this crucial observation the anticipation of what today we qualify as suitable action. Practical wisdom is this discernment, this quick glance, in a situation of incertitude, in the direction of the suitable action. This is inseparable from an agent of action who we can say is prudent. If he happens to be "wise," this is because, as concerns things that matter to him, he is an expert in evaluating "his own interest" (1141b33), or as Tricot prefers to translate here: "in knowing the good that befits oneself."[8] Of course, Aristotle does not allow this self-reflexive wisdom to occupy all the space, at the expense of the political. But how could the wise man be "wise" beyond his own sphere if he did not know how "to govern himself" (1142a10—Tricot's translation)?

Here I shall call a halt to my borrowings from the Greeks, from Homer to Aristotle. Can anyone persist in proclaiming that the Greeks lacked our concepts of the voluntary, of free will, of self-awareness? Yes, they did lack them in terms of the categories that have become our own, but they also established between us and them an affinity on the plane of understanding manners and customs that frames an insightful analysis of social action. In this regard, Aristotle's discourse on the virtues of character and the intellectual virtues itself stems from that *phronēsis* that constitutes both one of the named virtues and the implicit principle of continuity for the discourse undertaken first as epic, then as tragedy, and finally as moral philosophy. The philosopher is the *phronimos* of this second-order phronetic discourse about rational action—action for which its author acknowledges himself to be responsible—that retraces the path taken by the Greeks, from Homer to Aristotle.

A Phenomenology of the Capable Human Being

If there is one point where modern thought has moved beyond the Greeks concerning self-recognition, it is not principally on the thematic plane, that of recognition of responsibility, but rather on the plane of the reflexive consciousness of oneself implied in this recognition. Let us give a name to this reflexive self, that of *ipseity*, the equivalent in French to the English words *self* and *selfhood*. To be sure, the Greeks had known—as the numerous examples we have given show—the use of the reflexive pronoun *hauto/heauto*. But this was a spontaneous aspect of ordinary language, just as it continues to be today. For reasons having to do with the ontological and cosmological turn of their philosophy, they did not elaborate a theory of reflection where the emphasis would be shifted from action, its structures, and its virtues to its agent, as the theory of *phronēsis* might have led to, and in which we may be tempted today to discern retrospectively a hint of such a reflexive philosophy.

There is no doubt that we owe the decisive impulse in the direction of what I propose calling a hermeneutics of selfhood to the Cartesian philosophy of the *cogito* and Locke's theory of reflection. In this respect, the advent of the Cartesian *cogito* constitutes the major thought event after which we think in a different way, and after which reflection on the self finds itself elevated to an unprecedented thematic status. It is true that it is within the theoretical field that this reflexive inflection first finds expression, as we began to realize in our earlier chapter on recognition-identification. Following

Descartes, the transcendental philosophies of Kant and Fichte had the effect of making the "I" and its self-reflection the cornerstone of theoretical philosophy. Our second debt to them has to do with the extension of the problematic of the reflexive to the practical field. We owe this especially to the split in Kant's *Critiques* between theoretical and practical reason. But it was not to the benefit of the theory of action that this split was imposed, but to that of moral philosophy and the philosophy of right. These two vast developments centered on the idea of obligation and right left little space for the theme of self-recognition as a distinct instance of discourse, despite the explicit reference to the self in the notion of autonomy so forcefully demanded by Kantian ethics in opposition to the idea of heteronomy. But the self of this autonomy was not characterized there by its capacity for self-designation, but as a synonym of the will that in the synthetic judgment underlying the idea of autonomy combines with the idea of law. The *auto-* in *autonomy* makes sense only in this a priori synthesis, without ever being thematized for itself. It figures then as the *ratio essendi* of the law, while the law becomes the *ratio cognoscendi* of the will. This is why it was not emphasized as a "self" on the occasion of this correlation.

How can we explain this effacement of ipseity in the treatment of moral autonomy? I would say: as a result of the absence of a thematization of action as the practical field placed under the rule of norms. I find confirmation of this deficit in Kant's examination of the categorical imperative. As is well known, the criterion of its categorical character lies in its universality, and this in turn lies in the capacity of the maxims of our action to pass the test of universality. But we are not told where these maxims come from. Yet this is where we would expect a theory of action.

My problem starts here: How can we give a continuation to the Aristotelian analysis of action, with its notion of rational desire, within the setting of the reflexive philosophy inaugurated by Descartes and Locke, then extended to the practical dimension by

Kant's second *Critique* and brought by Fichte to its highest transcendental power?

I will try to answer this challenge through a reflection on those capacities which together sketch the portrait of the capable human being. Such reflection will be both neo-Aristotelian and post-Kantian, not to say post-Hegelian, as I shall admit in my next chapter. The sequence of the most noteworthy figures of the "I can" constitutes for me the backbone of a reflective analysis where the "I can" considered in its many uses gives the fullest amplitude to the idea of action first thematized by the Greeks.

That the inclusion of an analysis of those capacities constitutes a legitimate enrichment of the notion of self-recognition finds a justification in the semantic kinship between, on the one hand, the epistemic mode of the kind of certitude and confidence that attach to the assertion typical of the modal expression *I can* in all its forms and, on the other, one of the accepted lexical meanings of the verb *to recognize*, which the *Robert* places first in a series of variants: *to avow, confess, approve,* and so on. In an earlier chapter we have already come across this transition in meaning from recognition-identification to recognition-avowal, thanks to the Cartesian expression *receive as credible,* where the verb *to receive* constitutes the link that holds together the chain of meanings. In *Oneself as Another,* I adopted the term *attestation* to characterize the epistemic mode of assertions having to do with capacities. It perfectly expresses the kind of belief attached to expressions of the type *I believe that I can,* distinguishing it from belief as a weak form of theoretical knowledge. The assurance that attaches to assertions introduced by the modal form *I can* has as its contrary not doubt, but suspicion, which can be refuted only by a reassurance of the same epistemic tenor as the contested certitude.

My thesis on this level is that there is a close semantic kinship between attestation and self-recognition, in line with the "recognizing responsibility" attributed to the agents of action by the Greeks, from Homer and Sophocles to Aristotle. In recognizing that they have done something, these agents implicitly attest that they were capable of doing it. The great difference between the ancient thinkers and us is that we have brought to the reflexive stage the juncture between attestation and recognition in the sense of "taking as true."

There remains a gap in meaning, however, between *attesting* and *recognizing*, having to do with their belonging to different lexical families. *Attesting* belongs to the same family as does *testifying*, which branches off into a number of connotations, running from the use of the term in ordinary conversation to its use in historiography and the law court and, beyond these, to its use in the religious sphere, where the value of testimony attaches to those contingent signs that the Absolute gives of itself in history, to use an expression of Jean Nabert's, in his posthumously published *Le désir de Dieu*.[9] We then speak of "witnesses of the absolute," with testimony becoming the existential complement of a "criteriology of the divine" that takes a critical slant, as the word indicates. For its part, self-recognition belongs to the semantic field where it is related to recognition-identification and recognition-*Anerkennung*. In intersecting in the certitude and assurance of the "I can," the two semantic fields of attestation and self-recognition bring to bear their respective harmonics, in this way lending richness and density to what I propose to call recognition-attestation. From this mixture comes the certitude of assertions introduced by the modal phrase *I can*.

The following analysis, which deals with the capacities so attested to and recognized, owes several original features to its reflexive turn, starting from the amplitude and variety of forms stemming from the idea of action thematized for the first time by the Greeks.

But the novelty of this analysis in relation to the Greeks is not limited to the scope and ordered character of the survey of types of the "I can." It also consists, secondarily, in the indirect, mediate aspect that seems to me to characterize a hermeneutical approach within the constellation of reflexive philosophies. In this regard, I am indebted to Jean Nabert for having attended to the detour through the "object" side of experiences considered from the point of view of the capacities employed. This detour through the "what" and the "how," before returning to the "who," seems to me explicitly required by the reflexive character of the self, which, in the moment of self-designation, recognizes *itself*.

To these first two features of a hermeneutic of the self—taking into account the capacities to be found in the mode of the "I can," and the detour through the object, in order to give a reflexive value to the self—a third can be added, constituted by the dialectic between identity and otherness. This last consideration is of the highest importance as regards the ambitions proclaimed by the philosophy of recognition I am advocating. Self-recognition, by virtue of this last dialectic, and along the trajectory of the sovereign act of recognition-identification considered in the first chapter, puts us on the way toward the problematic of being recognized, implied by the request for mutual recognition that we will take up in the next chapter. In this sense, recognizing oneself occupies the midpoint of this long trajectory, thanks precisely to those features of otherness at the heart of the self-designation of the subject of capacities indicated by the grammar of the "I can," which combines with the two other features I have stressed: the characterization of action in terms of those capacities which constitute its actualization, and the detour by reflection through the object side of the experiences considered.

To Be Able to Say

Contrary to what the reader might expect, I shall not proceed directly to considering capacities relative to action as the ability to intervene in the course of the world, in direct succession with the examples drawn from the Greek legacy. Instead, I want to move back behind this ability to act to those capacities implied by the use of speech. This way of enlarging the field of the "I can," and in that sense that of action, draws on what I call the analogy of action, which ensures the affinity in meaning among the diverse types of ability to act that I shall undertake to enumerate and analyze. Acknowledgment of this priority of the "I can speak," "I can say," is justified in two ways. First, the acting and suffering agents of epic, of tragedy, and of the Aristotelian theory of action are speaking subjects. The characters in Homer and, even more so, the tragic heroes all speak continually of their action. And they name themselves when they make themselves known; they call upon themselves when they disavow their actions. And when we turn to the subject of decision and wishing, it is designated as the "cause" and the "principle" of what they do. Aristotle, the philosopher, has them speak of their action. But there is also another reason that only the modern pragmatics of discourse can bring to light. It is the fact that to speak, following the well-known saying of J. L. Austin, is "to do things with words."[10] By launching the idea of capacity by way of that of being able to say things, we confer on the notion of human action the extension that justifies the characterization of the self as the capable human being recognizing himself in his capabilities. Acting will then be the most appropriate concept at the level of the philosophical anthropology that characterizes my approach. At the same time, it will be a prolongation of Aristotle's famous assertion, concerning the notion of being on the plane of fundamental ontology, that being is spoken of in many ways, including being as potentiality *(dynamis)* and as act *(energeia)*. On the level of fundamental anthropology, the concept of acting is situated in terms of the meaning stemming from the most primitive polysemy, that of the notion of being. When set within the ambit of this undeniable patronage, the treatment of being able to speak as the eminent capacity of the capable human being is assured of a priority that is reinforced by the contemporary analysis of the pragmatics of discourse.

More than other ways of exercising the "I can," the ability to speak appears obliquely, as is fitting a reflexive approach, on the basis of a strictly semantic approach whose major concept is that of the statement, whose meaning in the case of ambiguity is submitted to the arbitration of particular contexts where such speaking occurs. By proceeding in a regressive fashion from the orientation of the statement to the act of stating and the utterer of the statement, pragmatics offers reflexive philosophy a valuable analytical tool. This reflexive approach is based on the referential one, by way of the theory of speech acts, which ever since Austin and Searle has figured among the classics of the discipline. At first reserved for performative utterances, so named in order to distinguish them from constative ones, this theory was extended to the illocutionary aspect of every statement, including those implied in constatives themselves in the form "I affirm that. . ." In this way, the second feature of a hermeneutics of the capable human being is verified: the detour through the question *what* by means of a semantics of statements, in order to get to the *who* of the question, Who is speaking? The utterer of the utterance still needs to be made more explicit. He or she is designated by means of deictics, tools of language that are limited to "showing" singularities, which escape any generic specification. Personal pronouns, adverbs of time and space, verb forms, and definite descriptions in ordinary language are means of designation from which the self-designation of the speaking subject follows. In the expression *I say that* the "I" does not figure as a lexical term in the linguistic system, but as a self-referential expression by means of which the one speaking designates him- or herself as the one who makes use of the first-person singular. As such, this person is not substitutable.

The third distinctive feature by means of which reflection on the speaking subject attaches to a phenomenology of the capable human being is of particular interest to our inquiry into recognition. The self-designation of the speaking subject is produced in interlocutory situations where the reflexivity is combined with otherness. The speech pronounced by someone is a speech act addressed to someone else. What is more, it often is a response to a call from others. The structure of question and answer thus constitutes the basic structure of discourse, in implicating the speaker and the interlocutor. In this regard, the theory of speech acts is incomplete if it does not put into correlation the illocutionary aspect of these acts with their interlocutory character. The illocutionary character of a simple constative in the form "I affirm that" is grounded on a tacit request for approbation that can serve to reinforce its self-assurance. Self-designation receives more than a strengthening of its illocutionary force from this call to others. This plays a founding role, in the sense that the attribution of a proper name, following the conventional rules that govern the distribution of first and family names, as well as the pronouns in any given culture, constitutes a veritable founding of a speaking subject capable of saying, "Me, my name is Paul Ricoeur."

I Can

The second major use of the modal form *I can* has to do with action itself in the limit sense of the term that designates the capacity of the acting subject to make events happen in the physical and social environment. In this "making something happen," the subject can recognize him- or herself as the "cause," in a declaration of the form: "I did it." This is something the Homeric and tragic heroes were capable of affirming. For us, as modern thinkers, this appropriation has lost its innocence. It has to be reconquered from operations of objectification that align the events one intentionally makes happen with those that simply happen. We recall Kant's formula in the Second Analogy of Experience (in the Analytic of Judgment):

"All alterations take place in conformity with the law of cause and effect." That something happens which did not previously exist can signify only that one thing succeeds another according to a rule. No objective difference distinguishes *happen* from *make happen*.

To this alignment of "make happen" with the mere happening of the event we can oppose in the first place a semantic analysis of action sentences whose open-ended structure differs from that of the closed attributive proposition (for example, "A is B"). We can write, "Brutus stabbed Caesar on the Ides of March in the Forum with a dagger," and so on. On the basis of this semantics of action sentences, we can oppose two meanings attached to the answer *because* in response to the question *why.* The first designates a cause in the sense of a rule-governed succession; the second a reason for acting, an intention. In her *Intentions,* G. E. M. Anscombe notes that "a man who knows how to do things has practical knowledge."[11] A motive, unlike a cause, is as such a motive for action. It is logically implied in the notion of an action carried out or to be carried out, as the grammar of *wanting* verifies. Furthermore, the open-ended structure of the action sentence invites an interpretation of gestures as a function of the broadest possible context of circumstances, rules, and norms belonging to a culture.

But this first opposition between intentionally making happen and happening as a result of cause and effect can be weakened by an ontology of events like that proposed by Donald Davidson, who puts the logical break between the class of events and that of substances or states of things in the sense of fixed objects. In this case, actions fall into the first class. What remains is the adverbial use of intention, as in the expression "done intentionally." This way of interpreting things tends to make explanation in terms of reasons a kind of causal explanation on the basis of an ontology of the event. The primary reason for an action will then be "its cause."[12]

This reduction is inevitable if we do not get behind the objectifying process that separated the pair *What* and *Because* in action sentences from the relation of both of them to the question *who*. The meaning of an intention adheres no less to its declarative side than to its descriptive one. Attribution to a person, which has been called ascription, is part of the meaning of intentional action. In this regard, the logical analysis of action sentences, centered on the connection between the what and the how, does not expunge the reference to the agent as the *possessor* of his or her action. Ascription of the action to an agent is part of the meaning of *action* as making something happen.

Here the contemporary discussion links back up with the Aristotelian theory that in its explanation of action joins the criterion of the dependence of the action on its agent to that of the inwardness of its principle. The contemporary grammar of ascription bears this analysis to the level imposed by discussion on the linguistic plane, which remains close to both ordinary and more rhetorical literary use. The term *ascription* points to the specific character of attribution when this has to do with the connection between action and its agent, of which we say that he or she *possesses* it, that it is "his," "hers," that he or she *appropriates* it. In the vocabulary that is still that of the pragmatics of discourse, ascription is directed to the agent's capacity to designate him- or herself as someone who does or who has done this. It binds the what and the how to the who. This "hegemonic" tie, which was only metaphorical for the Greeks—the pilot, the father, the master of the house—seems to reflect a primitive fact. In the *Phaedo,* Plato did not hesitate to split the idea of cause when he explained why Socrates remained seated in his cell rather than flee. And before the Stoics, Aristotle had said that there are things that depend on us, and there are others that stem from causes traditionally placed under the headings of nature, necessity, or chance: "But we deliberate about what is in our power to do, that is, about those things which can be objects of action" (*Nichomachean Ethics,* 1112a33–34). It remained for Kant, in the well-known Third Antinomy of Dialectical Reason, all innocence having been lost, to place the allegedly free cause on the same cosmological plane with physical causality. What calls for thought, therefore, is the "capacity to begin by oneself" (*von selbst* [A448/B478]) a series of phenomena that will unfold according to the laws of nature. For us, the difficulty is not to let this "spontaneity of causes" become absorbed into the moral phenomenon of imputation, for which the ability to do something constitutes a radical precondition. This ability to do something comes down to an ability to begin encompassing a series of fragmentary actions, upon which this ability confers a kind of wholeness, which later will find the rule governing its configuration in narrative. In the absence of such a configuring operation, the efficacy of the beginning may seem unlimited, as when we ask about the import of a decision. Historians and jurists are well aware of the paradoxes that can follow from this. A similar problem is posed by the interweaving of one person's actions with those of others. Within such a complex of interactions, how are we to mark off the share belonging to each person? We have then to rely on the acting subject's avowal, in which he or she takes upon him- or herself and assumes the initiative in which is actualized the power to act of which he or she feels capable.

Being Able to Narrate and to Narrate Oneself

In the third position of this phenomenology of the capable human being I put the problematic of personal identity tied to the act of narrating. In the reflexive form of talking about oneself narratively [*se raconter*] this personal identity is projected as a narrative identity.

The three features by which I have characterized the problematic of the capable human being stand out in the narrative phase of this course initiated with reflection on the speaking human being and continued with reflection on the acting human being.

Beyond the privilege granted any capacity in relation to its actualization, the detour through the "outside" is indicated in the narrative order by the passage through a regional semiotics, that of narratology. Here I want to emphasize not so much the originality of this semiotics of narrative as its profound kinship with the schema of Aristotle's *Poetics*. It was in terms of epic and tragedy that Aristotle elaborated his notion of "emplotment" *(muthos)* aimed at the "representation" *(mimēsis)* of action. Emplotment confers an intelligible configuration on a heterogeneous collection composed of intentions, causes, and contingencies. The unity of meaning that results rests on the dynamic equilibrium between a demand for concordance and the admission of discordances that, up to the close of the narrative, put in peril this identity of a unique kind. The unifying power applied to the episodic dispersion of narrative is nothing other than "poetry" itself. An important implication of this configuring operation for us is that emplotment applies no less to the "characters" than to the actions. A character is someone who *carries out* the action in the narrative. The category of character is therefore also a narrative category, and its role in the story stems from the same narrative understanding as does the plot itself. The character, we can say, is him- or herself emplotted.

Contemporary narratology, which we can trace back to Vladimir Propp's *Morphology of the Folktale,* is built on this remarkable correlation.[13] Propp set out to dissociate the "functions," that is, the recurring segments of action, from the characters, in order to define the folktale merely by the concatenation of these functions. In relation to them, a typology of roles, relative to their spheres of action, can be attempted. This undertaking, along with those which followed, up to Greimas and his actantial model,[14] verify the intuitive hypothesis that the plot governs the mutual genesis between the development of a character and that of the story told.

A phenomenology of the capable human being will retain from this long detour through narratology that it comes down to the reader of plots and narratives to undertake to refigure his or her own expectations as a function of the models of configuration offered by plots engendered by the imagination on the plane of fiction. An "aesthetic of reception" like that of Hans Robert Jauss added a new chapter to narrative theory as a function of the pair made up of writing and reading.[15] For example, a reader can declare that she recognizes herself in some character in some plot. To which we must add that this appropriation can take on a multitude of forms, from the pitfall of servile imitation, as with Emma Bovary, to all the stages of fascination, to suspicion, to rejection, to the search for a just distance with regard to such models of identification and their power of seduction. Learning to "narrate oneself" may be the benefit of such critical appropriation. Learning to narrate oneself is also learning how to narrate oneself in other ways.

In saying "in other ways," we set a whole problematic in motion, that of the personal identity associated with the ability to narrate and to narrate oneself. I have proposed the term *narrative identity* to characterize both this problem and its solution.

The problem is that of the temporal dimension both of the self and of the action, a dimension that could be neglected in the preceding analyses. The reference of the statement to the speaker, and that of the ability to act to the agent, can apparently be characterized without taking into account the fact that the speaker and the agent have a history, are their own history.

It is in this way that personal identity, considered as enduring over time, can be defined as a narrative identity, at the intersection of the coherence conferred by emplotment and the discordance arising from the peripeteia within the narrated action. In turn, the idea of narrative identity gives access to a new approach to the concept of ipseity, which, without the reference to narrative identity, is incapable of unfolding its specific dialectic, that of the relation between two sorts of identity, the immutable identity of the *idem,* the same, and the changing identity of the *ipse,* the self, with its historical condition. It is within the framework of narrative theory that the concrete dialectic of sameness and ipseity can initially blossom, in expectation of its culmination in the theory of promises.

Our previous discussion, which dealt with the relation between recognition and identification, knew only *idem* identity, taken in the sense of the numeric identity of a thing held to be the same in the diversity of its occurrences. At the time, we noted the dialectic of appearing, disappearing, and reappearing by means of which reidentification, which then served as a criterion, could give rise to hesitation, doubt, contestation. An extreme resemblance between two or several occurrences can then be invoked as an indirect criterion of qualitative identity, to reinforce the presumption of numeric identity. Lacking this, the uninterrupted continuity between the first and the last stage in the development of what we take to be the same individual can conjure up doubt and mitigate the threat contained in the moving experience of the unrecognizable, which we referred to with Proust and his famous dinner of disguised faces so cruelly recounted toward the end of *Time Regained*. But in so doing, we had not left behind the sphere of *idem* identity.

Now, narrative identity does not eliminate this kind of identity. It places it in dialectical relation with *ipse* identity. We can assign to character this first kind of identity in the sense of all the features of permanence in time, from biological identity grounded in the genetic code, and picked up in fingerprints, to which we can add physiognomy, voice, and gait, moving on to stable, or, as we say, acquired, habits, and finally to those accidental marks by which an individual can be recognized, such as Ulysses' scar. As for *ipse* identity, fiction produces a multitude of imaginative variations, thanks to which the transformations of a character tend to render problematic the identification of the same. There are even extreme cases where the question of personal identity becomes so confused, so indecipherable, that the question of personal identity takes refuge in the naked question, Who am I? At the limit, the nonidentifiable becomes the unnameable with the loss of a proper name, reduced to an initial. Ipseity totally disappears only if the character escapes any problematic of ethical identity, in the sense of a capacity to hold oneself accountable for one's acts. At this level, ipseity finds in the capacity to make promises the criterion of its ultimate difference from identity as sameness. Ordinary experience, urged on by narrative models coming not so much from fiction or history as from everyday practice, oscillates between these two poles of sameness and ipseity. Alistair MacIntyre, in looking at all the levels of narrativization of daily life, ranging from short-term actions to professional practices, skills, games, and life plans, proposes the notion of a "narrative unity of life." He says that the idea of bringing together life in the form of a narrative is the only way to give a handhold to the aim of a "good life," the keystone of his ethics, as it is of my own. How, indeed, can a subject of action give his life an ethical qualification if this life cannot be brought together in the form of a narrative? The difference from fiction has to do with the scope of this story, regarding the obscurity of any life's beginnings and the uncertainty regarding not only its end, but its very continuation. Neither birth, having already occurred, nor death as anticipated, whether feared or accepted, constitutes a narrative opening or ending. As for the vicissitudes of life, they remain in search of narrative configuration. This is why, below, I shall entrust to promise making the burden of bearing the destiny of ipseity, in defiance of circumstances that threaten to ruin the identity of the same. The proud assertion "I will do it" expresses in language the risky posture of ipseity, as self-constancy that goes beyond the safety of mere sameness.

We can complete this panoramic survey of the problem of narrative identity by referring to another dialectic than that of the *idem* and the *ipse,* the dialectic of identity confronted by otherness. The question of identity in this sense has two sides, one public, one private. The story of a life includes interactions with others. One author, Wilhelm Schapp, goes so far as to say in his book *In Ge-*

schichten Verstrickt that our being caught up in interwoven stories, far from constituting a secondary complication, must be taken as the principal experience in such matters.[16] Before any question of narrative identity or any other kind, we are caught up in stories. In trying to take this book into account, I shall undertake to give as much weight to the dialectic between self-identity and the identity of others as to the dialectic of *idem* and *ipse,* both on the plane of characters and on that of actions.

This interweaving can be observed as much on the individual as on the collective level of identity. We need to anticipate here what I shall say later about the status of collective memory with regard to individual memory. If we admit, as I propose, attributing the capacity to remember to all the subjects that find lexical expression in one or the other of the personal pronouns, every collectivity is qualified to say "we" on the occasion of particular operations of remembering. In the test of confronting others, whether an individual or a collectivity, narrative identity reveals its fragility. These are not illusory threats. It is worth noting that ideologies of power undertake, all too successfully, unfortunately, to manipulate these fragile identities through symbolic mediations of action, and principally thanks to the resources for variation offered by the work of narrative configuration, given that it is always possible, as said above, to narrate differently. These resources of reconfiguration then become resources for manipulation. The temptation regarding identity that lies in the withdrawal of *ipse*-identity to *idem*-identity thrives on this slippery slope.

Imputability

The fragility of narrative identity brings us to the threshold of the final cycle of considerations relating to the capable human being. The series of questions, Who speaks? Who acts? Who tells? finds a continuation in the question, Who is capable of imputation?

This notion brings us to the heart of the problematic that we have placed, beginning with the evocation of Homeric epic, under the heading of recognizing responsibility. It is at this point that there is the greatest affinity between us and the Greeks concerning the conception of action. It is also at this point that the conceptual advance we claim over them is most manifest. The concept of imputation itself could be articulated only in a culture that, on the one hand, had pushed the causal explanation of natural phenomena as far as possible, up to and including the human sciences, and that, on the other hand, had elaborated a moral and juridical doctrine where responsibility is framed by well-worked-out codes, balancing offenses and punishments on the scales of justice. It is up to a phenomenology of the capable human being to isolate the capacity that finds its most appropriate expression in imputability. The very word suggests the idea of an account, which makes the subjects accountable for their acts, to the point of being able to impute them to themselves. What does this idea add to that of ascription as the attribution of a particular genus of action to its agent? It adds the idea of being able to bear the consequences of one's acts, in particular of those taken as faults, wrongs, in which another is reputed to have been the victim. We saw the ancient Greeks join praise and blame in the evaluation of actions stemming from the category of a preferential, a predeliberated choice. In this sense, praise and blame belong to the broader set of reparations called for to compensate for a wrong inflicted on others.

A threshold is thereby crossed—that leading to the subject of rights, of the law. A specific manner of designating oneself as the subject who is capable of such things is added to the capacities susceptible of objective description.

Let us start from the predicates assigned to action itself under the rubric of imputability. These are ethico-moral predicates connected either with the idea of the good or with that of obligation, which allow us to judge and evaluate the actions considered good or bad, permitted or prohibited. When these predicates are applied reflexively to the agents themselves, these agents are said to be capable of imputation. Thus, with imputability the notion of a capable subject reaches its highest meaning, and the form of self-designation it implies includes and in a way recapitulates the preceding forms of self-reference.

In a strictly juridical sense, imputation presupposes a set of obligations negatively delimited by the precise enumeration of infractions of a written law, to which corresponds the obligation in civil law to offer reparation for a tort committed, and in criminal law to undergo punishment. The subject placed under obligation to make reparation for harm done or to suffer punishment is said to be imputable.

A semantic analysis brings to the fore the metaphor of an account—assigning the action, so to speak, to someone's account. This metaphor suggests the idea of an obscure moral accountability of merits and faults, as in a double-entry bookkeeping system of credits and debits, with a view to a kind of positive or negative balance sheet. This metaphor of a moral record underlies the apparently banal idea of rendering an account and the apparently still more banal one of giving an account in the sense of reporting, telling, at the end of a "reading" of this odd record or balance sheet. What is of interest to us here is the juridical sense of this metaphor. The *Robert* dictionary cites in this respect an important text from the 1771 edition of the *Dictionnaire de Trévoux:* "to impute an action to someone is to attribute it to him as its actual author, to put it, so to speak, on his account and make him responsible for it." Let us leave aside for the moment the question of the passage from the idea of imputation to the broader one of responsibility and focus on the idea of attributing an action to someone as its actual author. Here we rediscover our concept of ascription, in the sense of attributing a specific physical and mental predicate to someone, but we now find it moralized and juridized. It now is a question of attributing a blamable action to someone as its actual author.

This juridization does not hide the aporetic character of such an attribution on the plane of its articulation, as both cosmological and ethical, whose depths ancient thinkers could not perceive. It was Kant who formulated the antinomy resulting from the conflict between two antithetical uses of causality. In the Observation that follows the statement of the thesis of a free causality, we read: "The transcendental idea of freedom does not by any means constitute the content of the psychological concept of that name, which is merely empirical. The transcendental idea stands only for the absolute spontaneity of an action, as the proper ground of its imputability. This, however, is, for philosophy, the real stumbling-block, for there are insurmountable difficulties in the way of admitting any such type of unconditioned causality" (A448/B476). The Doctrine of Right says the same thing: "An Action [*Tat*] is called a deed insofar as it comes under obligatory laws and hence insofar as the subject, in doing it, is considered in terms of the freedom of his choice. By such an action the agent is regarded as the author [*Urheber*] of its effect, and this, together with the action itself, can be imputed to him, if one is previously acquainted with the law by virtue of which an obligation rests on these. A person is a subject whose actions can be imputed to him. . . . A thing is that to which nothing can be imputed."[17] This juridized version of imputability ends up concealing beneath the features of retribution the enigma of attribution to the moral agent of this unconditioned causality designated as "spontaneity of action" on the cosmological plane.[18]

It is left to phenomenological and hermeneutic philosophy to take up the question left hanging in this way about the self-designation attaching to the idea of imputability as an aptitude for imputation. The passage from the classical idea of imputability to the more recent one of responsibility opens new horizons. The resistance that this idea offers to the eliminating or at least the limiting of the idea of a fault through those of risk analysis, insurance, prevention is very revealing. The idea of responsibility shields that of imputability from its purely juridical reduction. Its first virtue is to place the accent on the alterity implied in the idea of harm or tort. Here I mean not that the concept of imputability is foreign to this concern, but that the idea of an infraction tends to counterpose to the offender only the law that was violated. The theory of punishment that we read in Kant's Theory of Right, under the heading "On the Right to Punish and to Grant Clemency" (104), recognizes only the wrong done to the law and defines punishment in terms of retribution, the guilty person meriting the punishment solely by reason of his crime as an attack on the law. From this results the elimination as parasitic of any taking into account of either rehabilitation of the condemned person or the protection of his fellow citizens. Reparation in the form of indemnification or some other penalty is part of the punishment, for which one criterion is to make the guilty party suffer because of his fault. This imposed suffering in response to the infraction tends to cover over the first suffering, which was that of the victim. But it is toward this suffering that the idea of responsibility reorients that of imputability. Imputability thus finds its other in the real or potential victims of a violent act.

One of the aspects of this reorientation has to do with the sphere of responsibilities beyond the harm with which the actors and the victims are held to be contemporary. In introducing the idea of harmful effects, linked to the extending in space and time of human power over the environment, Hans Jonas's "principle of responsibility" is equivalent to a decisive remoralizing of the idea of imputability in its strictly juridical sense.[19] On the juridical plane, we declare the author responsible for the known or foreseeable effects of his action, among them the harm done to the agent's immediate entourage. On the moral plane, it is the other person, others, for whom one is held responsible. As a result of this change in emphasis, the idea of vulnerable others tends to replace that of damage done as the object of responsibility. This transfer is facilitated by the adjacent idea of an assigned charge. It is for the other who is in my charge that I am responsible. This expansion makes what is vulnerable or fragile, as an entity assigned to the agent's care, the ultimate object of his responsibility. This extension to the vulnerable other involves, it is true, its own difficulties, having to do with the scope of responsibility as it applies to the future vulnerability of human beings and their environment. However far our power extends, that far extend our capacities for harmful effects, and that far extends our responsibility for damage done. Here is where the idea of imputability regains its moderating role, thanks to recalling one acquisition of penal law, that of individualizing the penalty. Imputation also has its own kind of wisdom. An unlimited responsibility would amount to indifference, by overthrowing the "mineness" of my action. Between flight from responsibility and its consequences and the inflation into infinite responsibility, we must find a just measure and not allow the principle of responsibility to get too far from the initial concept of imputability and its obligation to make reparation or undergo punishment, within the limits of a relation of spatial and temporal proximity between the circumstances of an action and its eventual harmful effects.

Memory and Promises

In memory and promises, the problematic of self-recognition reaches two high points simultaneously. The one is turned toward the past, the other toward the future. But they need to be considered together within the living present of self-recognition, thanks to several features that they have in common.

In the first place, they are inscribed in an original way within the cycle of capacities of the capable human being. True, we speak of the abilities to remember and to promise just as we speak of other abilities. But in each case real problems arise when the emphasis is placed on the moment of actualization. Now I remember; now I promise. This first feature in common justifies a distinct treatment from what we granted to the preceding capacities.

Another remarkable feature: at the moment of actualization, memory and promising get placed differently in the dialectic between sameness and ipseity, the two values constitutive of personal identity. With memory, the principal emphasis falls on sameness, without the characteristic of identity by ipseity being totally absent; in promising, the prevalence of ipseity is so great that the promise can easily be referred to as the paradigm case of ipseity.

Finally, and this is not the least of their features, both are affected by the threat of something negative that is constitutive of their meaningfulness: forgetting for memory, betrayal for promises. We thought we were justified in treating the different modes of doing things, the ability to speak and act, the ability to recount, up to and including imputability, without giving an equal weight to the inabilities that correspond to them—something that would be open to criticism if we had to take into account the psychological, the sociological, and especially the pedagogical dimension in the effective exercise of these capacities. But we cannot allow such a deadlock in the cases of memory and promises. Their opposite is part of their meaning: to remember is to not forget; to keep one's promise is not to break it. This shadow of the negative will accompany us in both registers of the following analysis.

What Do I Remember?

It is remarkable that it is with memory that the terms *recognition* and *recognize,* so rich in ramifications on the plane of lexicography, and so poorly represented on that of philosophical semantics, accede in a new way to the dignity of a real philosophical concept, with the question of recognition of images from the past. In the Introduction, I spoke of the Bergsonian moment of recognition, following the Kantian moment of *Rekognition* discussed in the preceding section, and before the Hegelian moment of *Anerkennung.* It is under the aegis of Bergson and his theme of the "recognition of images" that we shall place this section. With Bergson, the Greek notion of *anamnēsis* comes back in force, in all its glory and with all its pitfalls. In the course I propose, the Bergsonian moment will cap a series of analyses starting from the question *what*—What do I remember?—and the question *how*—How does recalling a memory confirm the dynamic of remembering? It is with the question, Who remembers? that recognition of a memory comes to equal recognition of oneself. The Bergsonian moment will seal this alliance.

The priority of the question *what* has become familiar to us from the preceding analyses placed under the heading of the capable human being, where the detour through the external regularly precedes the return to the self. This order goes well with the phenomenological approach in general, thanks to the principle of intentionality that remains its great discovery. Applied to mnemonic phenomena, this detour through the external brings to the fore the recalled memory as the "object" side of memory.

In this way phenomenology links up with a distinction familiar in Greek between *mnēmē* and *anamnēsis* dealt with in one of Aristotle's shorter treatises, known to us through its Latin title, *De Memoria et Reminiscentia*.[20] *Mnēmē-memoria* designates the mere presence to the mind of an image of a passed past. An image of the past comes to mind for me. In this sense, it is a passive moment—a *pathos*—opposed to the active side of remembering that will come to occupy a central place for us. Nonetheless, the *mnēmē-memoria* of Aristotle's treatise requires our lingering over it because of the paradox that its analysis brings to light, the enigma of the presence in an image of an absent thing that this image represents. What is at issue here is the epistemic status of this *eikōn* that is present yet stands for something else that it signifies. This iconic constitution of the memory image will not disappear from the horizon of our reflections. In the *Theatetus* Plato attempted to resolve the aporia by conferring an explanatory force on the idea of an imprint—the *typos*—in spite of its clearly metaphorical character.[21] For centuries, the idea of an imprint left in wax by a seal ring would remain the model of the idea of a trace, whose fortune is well known thanks to the echo of those ramifications to which I shall refer here, in distinguishing three kinds of traces: cortical traces as dealt with in the neural sciences; mental traces of sense impressions and of our being affected by striking, not to say traumatic, events; and finally the documentary traces conserved in private or public archives. I shall set aside here the problem posed by the diversity of traces; I retain only the redoubling of the enigma of the presence in an image of a passed past that produces the idea of a trace. Every trace, in effect, is in the present. And the trace will always depend on the thought that interprets it, that takes it as a trace *of*—of the "impact" of the seal in the wax; in other words, the trace bears the paradoxical character of being the effect of some initial impulse, of which it will be at the same time a sign; an effect that is a sign of its cause—this is the enigma of the trace.

It is here that the problem of forgetting unexpectedly springs up. In effect, the deciphering of traces presupposes that they were, as we say, left behind. This simple phrase evokes their fugitive, vulnerable, revocable character. In short, it belongs to the idea of a trace that it can be wiped out. With this unsettling idea of the threat of effacement comes that of the threat of forgetting. To be sure, there are many forms of forgetting that do not stem from the wiping away of traces, but from deceit or a bad conscience. And there are many kinds of effacement that serve only to conceal something that remains ineffaceable in remembered experience. Still, there remains the threat of an irremediable, definitive forgetting that gives the work of memory its dramatic character. Yes, forgetting is indeed the enemy of memory, and memory is a sometimes desperate attempt to pull some flotsam from the great shipwreck of forgetting. This haunting sense of forgetting was not overlooked in Augustine's *Confessions*, to which we shall return below.

Anamnesis

This rapid evocation of forgetting as bordering on the moment of passivity in simple memory seems to me to be the obligatory transition from *mnēmē-memoria* to *anamnēsis-reminiscentia,* dealt with in the second chapter of Aristotle's treatise. The struggle against forgetting is not the only raison d'être for this active moment of remembering. We need to add to it the effect of a distancing in time that gives recall (or recollection) the aspect of crossing a distance, leading to questions of the form "Since when?" and expressions such as *recently, once, formerly, it's been a long time.* These are all expressions that convey the pastness of the past, its distance from the present. Speaking of this temporal distance has its own paradoxical character reflected in our grammar: the past is both what no longer is and what has been.

As regards the operations of thinking required for this reconquest of an abolished past, Aristotle was the first to describe their dynamics: the possibility of crossing the gap in both directions, with any point in time taken as a starting point; the predominance of associative procedures, to which British empiricism will give particular weight; and the calculation of the lapse of time involved. But Aristotle does not tell us how we obtain the assurance that our quest, in the most favorable case, has been crowned with success. This assurance is connected with the core experience of *recognition* for which Bergson will be the herald. Still less does Aristotle show any interest in a question that could be born only in the context of a philosophy of the subject like that of our own: In what way does recognition of the past contribute to self-recognition? This will be the great advance that the Bergsonian moment of recognition will constitute.

Before coming to this radical question, the study of recalling things knew three great moments: with associationism in the epoch of British empiricism; with psychoanalysis considered in its practice and its theory; and finally with Husserlian phenomenology. It is interesting that something like associationism should have found an echo in post-Cartesian philosophy, with its tendency to deal with the phenomena of memory in the wake of the imagination, itself treated with suspicion. For example, we read in Proposition 18 of part 2 of Spinoza's *Ethics:* "If the human body has once been affected by two or more bodies at the same time, when the Mind subsequently imagines any of them, it will immediately recollect the others also."[22] This short circuit between memory and imagination is placed under the sign of the association of ideas. If two affects are connected by contiguity, to evoke one—therefore, to imagine it—is to evoke the other—therefore, to remember it. Memory, reduced to recall, thus works in the wake of the imagination. And imagination, taken in itself, is situated at the bottom of the scale of modes of knowledge, under the heading of affects submitted to the rules connecting things external to the human body, as the scholia that follows makes clear: "This association arises according to the order and association of the modifications of the human body, in order to distinguish it from that association of ideas, which arises from the order of the intellect" (466). This statement is all the more noteworthy in that we read in Spinoza a magnificent definition of time, or rather of enduring, as "the continuation of existence." It is striking that memory should not be set in relation with this apprehension of time.

Spinoza's assertion, which reflects dependence on a kind of mechanism, finds its counterpart in the more dynamic approaches for which the Aristotelian analyses of *anamnēsis* reserved a place. Here is the place for me to recognize my debt to psychoanalysis, first at the level of its practice, then at that of its theory. Starting from practice, we observe that the recourse to dreams, so characteristic of Freudian therapy, implies the recalling of diurnal memories of the nocturnal dream, at the price of all the reworkings that this transposition presupposes. The assignment that is part of the therapeutic contract to "say everything" works as a form of discipline in the exercise of recall, which the person undergoing analysis is told to let flow freely, so that to it may be grafted the operations of free association, to which in turn the work of interpretation will be applied. It is the resistances encountered by this technique that gave psychoanalytic theory a decisive handhold. The obstacle encountered along the way to recall is attributed to the resistances of repression that lead to the compulsion to repetition, responsible for stagnation in the whole course of the cure. I shall not say anything here about the role of transference in the tactics of making an end run around those resistances. I will attend instead to the reformulation that Freud proposes of the whole phenomenon of remembering in terms of a kind of work. For example, he speaks of the work of remembering as operating as a counterweight to the compulsion toward repetition.

These proposals of Freudian doctrine have everything to do with our reflection on the relation between memory and forgetting. Forgetting, we have said, accompanies each phase of our reflection on memory. And we first referred to forgetting on the occasion of the effacement of traces. In this definitive form, it is irremediable. But psychoanalysis confronts us with a wholly different situation, that of apparent forgetting, forgetting that at the level of consciousness reveals itself to be the work of repression. This active forgetting, which makes remembering a chore, is henceforth inseparable from the theory of the unconscious for which it becomes a corollary. Surprising paradoxes are then proposed, such as, "The unconscious is unaware of time," "The unconscious is indestructible." At the level of consciousness, these approaches to forgetting by psychoanalysis are welcomed, but uneasily. Is the conscious subject therefore no longer master of himself? How can he still be responsible for his actions? But also with confidence. In the end, we forget less than we might fear. In this way, the old pair, *anamnēsis* and *lēthē*, reminiscence and forgetting, is rejuvenated.

It is also to the phase of recall that I would link the best-known works of Husserl on memory, even though the admirable posthumous text titled *Phantasie, Bildbewusstsein, Erinnerung,* now published as volume 23 of the *Husserliana* series, has more to do with the object of memory than with remembering.[23] The remembered memory *(Erinnerung)* is distinguished with infinite care and patience from all sorts of images (in the popular sense of the word) that share with it the character of "presentification" *(Vergegenwärtigung),* distinct from simple perceptual presentation. This work of distinguishing things is quite involved. It is one thing to "depict" a real but absent being in a portrait, another to "feign" presence through fiction, another to make a subjective image of the world as in the Kantian *Vorstellung,* and still another to "figure" the past to oneself in images. For me, this text constitutes the very model of purely phenomenological description.

The same cannot be said about Husserl's 1905 *On the Phenomenology of the Consciousness of Internal Time.*[24] There, it is not memory that is at issue but the constitution of time in and through consciousness, itself subtracted from the natural world by the transcendental "reduction," or *epochē*. It was within the framework of this transcendental phenomenology with an idealistic accent, however, that the valuable distinction between retention or primary memory and reproduction or secondary memory was elaborated. I will isolate these pages from the rest of this work devoted to the "degrees of constitution" of the innermost consciousness of internal time, where the "object" aspect is progressively effaced to the benefit of the self-constitution of the flow of consciousness.

The constitution on a first level at which I shall stop for a moment is that of a thing that endures, on the model of a tone that continues to sound, then of a melody that one remembers after the fact. The *epochē* lays bare these pure experiences, those "of time," but does so on the basis of the experience of something that endures. The question is thereby posed of the persistence whereby "what we perceive remains present to us for a time, but not without undergoing modification" (§3, 11). What does it mean for a thing that endures to remain? From the perception of the remaining of something, the analysis will finally turn to the examination of the enduring of perception itself, setting aside its "object" side, to the benefit of an apprehending of a nonobjectifiable enduring.

It is with regard to this displacement of emphasis that the noteworthy distinction between retention and remembering takes on meaning. Retention remains within the orbit of the present. It is constituted by the experience of the beginning, continuing, and ending of one and the same object before it "sinks" into the passed past. There is "retention" in the sense that something maintains itself on the edge of perception, a little like the tail of a comet. There is nothing imaginary about this retention. It continues to participate in perception that can no longer be identified with the simply passing moment. Thus Husserl can speak of a "modification" internal to perception even to say that one thing, the same thing, begins, continues, and ends. And following from this, we have a retention of retentions (§11). But first, the "just passed" past gives a temporal extension to perception, which thus envelops within itself the distinction between the "impression" and "retention," and therefore carries a negative note, to which "reproduction" replies in the case of secondary memory. Therefore, we can speak of remembering, while excluding any possible confusion with imagining. It is from this point of view that the analyses in *Husserliana* 23 strengthen those to be found in the earlier, better-known lectures.

"Who" Remembers?

The question *who* has not been emphasized in analyses bearing on memory as the *what* of remembering, both on the anamnesis of the Greeks and on recollection by modern philosophers as constitutive of the "how" of memory. We need therefore to thematize this "who" of memory with an eye to the Bergsonian moment that makes self-recognition coincide with the recognition of images.

This attending to the subject of memory can be traced back to Augustine's *Confessions:* "Ego sum, qui memini, ego animus" (X.xvi.25).[25] This reference to the "I" is not unexpected in a book built on a first-person narrative of conversion: How did I become a Christian? The reflections on memory in books 10 and 11 stand out against the background of a discourse of avowal, for which confession in the liturgical sense does not completely exhaust the meaning. In the typology of speech acts, avowal constitutes a category *sui generis,* as lexicography confirms. For example, the *Robert* connects avowal with the second large group of senses of the word *recognize,* the group defined in terms of "taking to be true."

Book 10 opens with a hymn to memory. It is through the well-known metaphor of the "vast palaces of memory" that this book is best known. This metaphor gives inwardness a specific spatial aspect, that of a familiar place. Everything is "deposited" there; "memory's huge cavern, with its mysterious, secret, and indescribable nooks and crannies, receives all these perceptions, to be recalled when needed and reconsidered" (X.viii.13). Everything that I recall in my memory attests that it is within *(intus)* that I accomplish these acts, in this vast palace of memories. The treasure that memory is supposed to "contain" is indeed immense: perceptual images, memories of passions, but also abstract notions, intelligible entities, and finally the memory of myself as experiencing and acting. The power of memory is great, to the point that I can remember myself as having remembered. In short, "we call the memory itself the mind" (X.xiv.21).

Is memory a happy fact, then? Of course. And yet forgetting never stops haunting this praise of memory and its power—forgetting, that thief of time, forgetfulness that "destroys what we remember" (X.xvi.25). This reference to forgetting is the occasion for a spontaneous occurrence of the verb *recognize*: "If I had forgotten what the force of the sound was, I would be incapable of recognizing it" (X.xvi.24). Indeed, what is a lost thing—the lost coin of the Gospel parable—if not something in a way that one holds in memory? Here, discovering is rediscovering, and rediscovering is recognizing, and recognizing is approving—hence judging that the rediscovered thing is indeed the same as the one sought—and therefore taken after the fact as having been forgotten: "The object was lost to the eyes, but held in the memory" (X.xviii.27). Augustine dares to take up the paradox: "Unless we could recall forgetfulness, we could never hear the word and recognize the thing which the word signifies. Therefore memory retains forgetfulness" (X.xvi.24). In effect, it is memory at the moment of recognition of the forgotten object that testifies to the forgetting. Is this a sophism? Maybe. "Yet in some way, though incomprehensible, and inexplicable, I am certain that I remember forgetfulness itself, and yet forgetfulness destroys what we remember" (X.xvi.25). Does forgetting finally triumph, even at the level of our words?

Book 11 confirms this confession of the inwardness of memory by granting it what Aristotle refused it, the direct measuring by memory of time that has passed, without the detour through the physics of movement, for which, according to Aristotle, time would be a variable. A long time, a short time? It is our soul that measures this: "We measure periods of time as they are passing" (XI.xxi.27). Then it is within this interior space of the soul that the well-known dialectic between *distentio* and *intentio* unfolds—distension between the three orientations of the same present: the present of the past in memory, the present of the future in anticipation, and the present of the present in intuition (or as I prefer to say, initiative). But also intention that runs through the phases of reciting a loved poem. The soul, like time itself, is a passage from the future toward the past through the present.

Some may doubt whether Augustine really succeeded in getting around the difficulties taken up by Aristotle when he toiled to graft the distinction between instants and the evaluation of intervals onto the continuity of movement. This is not the place to discuss that. Augustine did not mean to resolve the enigma of time, at the risk of locking it into the threefold present. On the contrary, he sought to open the moment toward heaven, in the direction of the *nunc stans* of divine eternity. Hence, it is not to some artifice of composition that we should attribute the passage from the theory of memory and time in books 10 and 11 to the long commentary on the book of Genesis and creation starting in book 12. The verticality of eternity intersects the horizontal flow of time, which is also that of narrative, in the present.

This being Augustine's major preoccupation in the *Confessions,* we ought not to expect from this admirable bard of avowal an explicit reflection on the character of the "mineness" of memory that is spoken of in the first person. It will suffice to have evoked with Augustine, and under the sign of confession, the birth of the tradition that I shall call that of the inner gaze, following Charles Taylor, when he speaks of inwardness in his *Sources of the Self.*[26]

With John Locke the aura of confession yields to that of reflection. And it is within the domain of such reflection that memory is interrogated. We owe the advancement of the problematic of identity, which was not the major concern for Augustine, to this shift in emphasis and interest. The occasion is thereby given for returning to the dialectic of sameness and ipseity that earlier found its privileged place in the concept of narrative identity. Locke, of course, is unaware of this concept of narrative identity, which gives us the privilege of a distanced reading in relation to the text of this brilliant advocate of identity as sameness.

Locke is the inventor of the sequence comprising the three notions of identity, consciousness, and the self.

The terms *consciousness* and *self* are in fact his invention drawing on the concept of identity. For Descartes, the *cogito* was not a self, nor even a consciousness. And it is remarkable that in both the title and the whole of Locke's argument in the key chapter of the *Essay* "identity" should be opposed to "diversity" in the sense of difference. The affirmation of identity results from the comparison of one thing with another, but this is done for the purpose of emphasizing a thing's identity with itself, through the very negation of its alterity. In formal terms, and abstracting the scale of identities that will be considered, a thing is identical to itself in the sense that "it is that very thing, and not another."[27] The expression "and not another" consecrates the equation: *identical* equals *same as itself*. One could not affirm more strongly the solidarity between identity and sameness. Or, to put it another way, for Locke there is no shadow of difference between *idem* and *ipse,* for the self is the same as itself. The important break in the scale of identities considered, from simple particles to trees, animals, and ultimately human beings, resides in "consciousness," with no reference whatsoever to some underlying substance. Consciousness alone is what makes each person a self. And here is where memory comes into play as a result of the temporal extension of reflection: "As far as this consciousness can be extended backwards to any past action or thought, so far reaches the identity of that person; it is the same self now it was then; and it is by the same self with this present one that now reflects on it, that the action was done" (1:449). Personal identity is a temporal identity. The equation between consciousness, self, and memory is thus a complete one, at the price of all the paradoxes arising from the fact of forgetting, of sleep, of the tension in memory between imagination and reality, even of the imagining of substituting one memory for another in the same body. (Locke is in this regard the inventor of the "puzzling cases" that flourish in contemporary analytic philosophy, in particular in Derrick Parfit's brilliant book *Reasons and Persons*.)[28] The only thing that matters to Locke is the getting rid of the idea of substance. Consciousness and its memory suffice by themselves. And the category of sameness governs everything. According to this category, the diversity linked to the plurality of acts or states of consciousness is easily encompassed within reflexive identity. Even the passing of time, which so tormented Augustine, gives rise to no irreducible diachrony. The same thing may be said about concepts of a juridical origin, such as imputation, which make the self "accountable," and of the assignment by virtue of which the self "appropriates" its acts as affirms them as its own. These are only synonyms for the *same* borrowed from juridical language.

Thus it is surprising that the concept of diversity should be evoked only to be revoked immediately by the formula that opens this chapter in the *Essay:* The same "is that very thing, and not another." The result is that for Locke the self is not an *ipse* opposable to an *idem.* The self is a "same" and even a "selfsame," at the peak of the pyramid of identity-as-sameness. The only diversity that might have disturbed a political thinker of Locke's caliber would have been that arising out of human plurality, so strongly present in his two Treatises on Government when he is dealing with the problems posed by property and power. The *Essay concerning Human Understanding* makes room only for a concept of reflection such as the one found in the tradition of the inward gaze. No footbridge is constructed between the inwardness established by reflection and the plurality presupposed by political philosophy. The political thinker is like another man, of whom the philosopher is unaware. We shall call this tacit presupposition into question in the next chapter.

The dialectic of the same and the *ipse* cannot be unfolded, therefore, except on the basis of considerations foreign to Locke. We have given a first outline of them in the notion of the narrative identity that installs diversity at the very heart of every plot of life. The sameness of reflection and of memory finds its actual opposite only in the promise, the paradigm of an ipseity irreducible to sameness. Along with the internal diversity arising from the heart's intermittences, the ipseity belonging to the promise, owing to its intersubjective dimension, will be confronted with another kind of diversity, an external diversity, if I can put it that way, made up of human plurality.

The Bergsonian Moment: Recognizing Images

It is with Bergson that I have chosen to end this inquiry into the contribution of memory to self-recognition in quest of its counterpart in the promise. With him, the word *recognition* is welcomed into the very selective family of accepted philosophical uses, between Kantian recognition, which found its place in the previous chapter, and Hegelian *Anerkennung,* which will serve as the backbone of the next chapter.

The two central chapters of *Matter and Memory* are titled "Of the Recognition of Images: Memory and Brain" and "Of the Survival of Images: Memory and Mind."[29] Two concepts are thus paired: recognition and survival. We shall also treat them as a pair. What is more, it is not indifferent that it should be within a reworking of the classical problem of the relation between soul and body— Bergson prefers to speak of the "union" of soul and body (180)— that the pairing of the recognition of images and their survival is projected into the center of this work. The revolution brought about on the conceptual plane can be set within the continuation of our proposals concerning the idea of the trace, where we distinguished three kinds of traces: the cortical trace belonging to the sciences that study the brain; the mental trace, which for Bergson becomes the trace par excellence; and the documentary trace, which interests the historian in the archives. For Bergson, everything turns on the conjunction of the first and second kinds of trace. The central thesis of *Matter and Memory* in this regard is that the mental trace is not to be explained by the cortical trace, the brain being the organ of action, not of representation. When so freed from its cortical reference, the mental trace become a problem unto itself. And it is this problem that finds its appropriate formulation in the idea of survival. The one way remaining open that could give meaning to the idea of survival, then, was to develop it in tandem with the concept of recognition. In this way, this latter concept is dignified as a major philosophical concept.

What Bergson puts in the place of honor is the ancient concept of *anamnēsis* or *reminiscentia,* taken up in different ways by the psychology of recall, of recollection, and of remembering. But it is asked to provide the key to what a contemporary philosophy sees as the "mortal question," namely, the old problem of the union of soul and body, the union of the soul to the body.

Bergson himself had initially set his analysis of the recognition of images in a continuation of the classical psychology of recall, in an essay titled "Intellectual Effort" in *Mind-Energy,* in which "the effort of remembering" is a special case.[30] The recalling of a memory as "hard work" belongs to the broad set of mental phenomena characterized by the distinction between two attitudes, one of tension, the other of relaxation. The tension, in the case of memory, is connected with the traversing of a "series of different levels of consciousness," from "pure memory," not yet translated into distinct images, to this same memory actualized in nascent sensations and the beginnings of movements. In this movement through the levels of consciousness, the work of remembering is guided by what Bergson calls a "dynamic schema," whose function is to indicate a certain "direction of effort." The "effort of memory appears to have as its essence the evolving of a scheme, if not simple at least concentrated, into an image with distinct elements more or less independent of one another" (201). We are not far from what Freud will call the work of memory.

We come closer to what I like to call the small miracle of recognition if we discern in it the solution of the oldest enigma of the problematic of memory—that is, the present representation of something absent. Recognition is the effective resolution of this enigma of the presence of an absence, thanks to the certitude that accompanies it: "It's the one—yes, it is!" This is what makes recognition the mnemonic act par excellence. But is not the enigma in this way made even more impenetrable on the speculative plane? If we say that the originating impression-affect remains and if we add that it is what makes the recognition possible because it remains, how do we know this? The answer lies in saying that we are dealing here with a wholly retrospective presupposition. We must therefore proceed in the opposite direction, from recognition as experienced to the presumed persistence. The argument then runs as follows: Something had to remain of the first impression for me to remember it now. If a memory returns, it is because I have not lost it. If, in spite of everything, I rediscover and recognize it, it is because its image has survived.

Therefore, we must take up the problem again, in *Matter and Memory,* at the point where the examination of the effort of recall left it. We postulated the existence of a "pure" memory, like some virtual state of the representation of the past, prior to its coming to be an image. We must now assign this to "pure" memory, beyond its virtuality, and beyond the fact that it is not conscious, an existence comparable to that which we attribute to external things when we do not perceive them. The distinction between past and present is given in the very recognition where events return "with their outline, their color, and their place in time" (88). In short, the "concrete process by which we grasp the past in the present is *recognition*" (90). Furthermore, our memory, Bergson notes, "remains attached to the past by its deepest roots, and, if, when once realized, it did not retain something of its original virtuality, if, being a present state, it were not also something which stands out distinct from the present, we should never know it for a memory" (134). Here the enigma of the presence of the absent, which appears several times in this essay, is reaffirmed: occurring *in* the present, recognized *as* a memory.

We still have to move back from the fact of recognition to the presumption of survival. To recognize a memory is to rediscover it. And to rediscover it is to presume it as available in principle, even if not accessible. It thus belongs to the experience of recognition to refer to a latent state of the memory of a first impression whose image must have been constituted at the time of the original experience. For how can any present become past unless it was constituted as such at the same time as it was present? This is the most profound paradox of memory. The past is "contemporaneous" with the present that it *has been*. Hence, we do not perceive this survival, but we presuppose it and believe in it. This is the latent and unconscious aspect of memories preserved from the past. It is also the profound truth of the Greek *anamnēsis*. To seek is to discover, and to rediscover is to recognize what one once—previously—learned. As Aristotle puts it well in speaking of *anamnēsis*, "memory is of the past." Nor will Freud contradict Bergson concerning the indestructibility of the past. Bergson himself recognized all this: "Even my idea of integral conservation of the past has more and more found its empirical verification in the vast collection of experiments instituted by the disciples of Freud."[31] We must therefore go so far as the extreme paradox that this presumption of an indestructible past prolonging itself in the present dispenses us from having to seek out the place where this memory is preserved. "They preserve themselves" (74). This self-preservation is what Bergson calls duration. Undoubtedly we would have to suspend what he calls attention to life, giving ourselves over to a kind of dreamlike thinking to get close to the truth of this paradox. "A human being who should *dream* his life instead of living it would no doubt keep before his eyes at each moment the infinite multitude of details of his past history."[32] We might even speak here of a meditating memory, in the sense of the German *Gedächtnis*, distinct from *Erinnerung*.

Recognition of images of the past and self-recognition coincide in this meditating memory.

Promises

Let us review the reasons that led us to pair memory and promises in dealing with the problematic of self-recognition.

First, it is clear that the one, turned toward the past, is retrospective; the other, turned toward the future, is prospective. Together, and thanks to the interactions between them that we are about to discuss, their opposition and complementarity give temporal breadth to self-recognition, founded on both a life history and commitments about the long-term future. It is a recovered part of the Augustinian conception of time, whose distension proceeds from the inner divergence of the present, divided among the present of the past or memory, the present of the future or expectation, and the present of the present, which, unlike Augustine, I will place under the heading of initiative rather than of presence.

The treatment of memory assigns second place to the different solution brought to the issue of identity by these two instances: memory tipping toward identity as sameness; the promise serving as a paradigmatic example of ipseity. In this regard, the phenomenology of promises links up with that of narrative identity where this dialectic found its initial expression.

I would put the relation to the negative case, considered earlier in third place, quite high in the order of importance. Both memory and promises confront contraries that for each of them are what we can call a mortal enemy—forgetting for memory, betrayal for promises—with all their ramifications and ruses. The power not to keep one's word is an integral part of the ability to make promises and leads to a second-degree reflection on the internal limits of attestation of ipseity, and thus of self-recognition.

Special mention must be made of the alterity that seems to pertain to promising, unlike memory, which is more strongly marked by "mineness," which underscores that nothing can substitute for it. The relation to the other is so strong in the case of promises that this feature can serve to mark the transition between the present chapter and the one that will follow, on mutual recognition.

I shall begin the phenomenology of promises with another common feature already emphasized regarding memory. It has to do with the relation between a capacity and its actual use. To be sure, it is legitimate to speak of the ability to make promises, in such terms as Nietzsche uses in a text I shall come to below. In this respect, the ability to promise is in line with the abilities of the capable human being that I have already enumerated. In this way, promises are both a new dimension of the idea of capacity and a recapitulation of these earlier abilities. We shall have occasion to observe that the ability to promise presupposes the ability to speak, to act on the world, to recount and form the idea of the narrative unity of a life, and finally to impute to oneself the origin of one's acts. But the phenomenology of promises must focus on the act by which the self actually commits itself.

This phenomenology unfolds in two phases. In the first of these it is the linguistic dimension of the act of promising, as a speech act, that is emphasized; in the second, which stems from the former, it is the moral characteristic of promises that comes to the fore.

The linguistic level is a good place for us to recall that illocutionary acts are "the principal units of literal meaning in the use and comprehension of natural languages."[33] Thanks to Austin and Searle, we know that the truth conditions of declarative statements, in line with the logic founded by Frege and Russell, do not exhaust the entire meaning of sentences in our discourse. It is in accomplishing illocutionary acts, such as assertions, questions, statements, demands, promises, thanksgiving, offers, and refusals, that complete meanings are communicated through such utterances to one's interlocutors, the illocutionary force being grafted to the propositional content. Here meaning and use cannot be dissociated.

Promises belong to those performative acts signaled by easily recognized verbs from the lexicon. If we hear these verbs, we understand that they "do" what they say, as is the case with making a promise. When someone says, "I promise," the speaker effectively commits himself to some future action. To make a promise is to commit oneself to "do" what the proposition says.[34] What I want to retain for the next step is the double characterization of promises: the speaker does not simply limit himself to "placing himself under a certain obligation to do what he says." This relation is merely from himself to himself. But the commitment is first of all to the other to whom the promise is made. It is a commitment to "do" or "give" something held to be good for him or her. In other words, the promise has not simply a receiver, but a beneficiary of the promise. It is through this "goodness" clause that linguistic analysis calls for moral reflection. But first, one more remark about the definition we are proposing. What the speaker commits himself to is to do or give something, not to experience feelings, passions, or emotions. As Nietzsche notes in one of his texts concerning promises, "one can promise actions but not feelings; for the latter are involuntary."[35] In this sense, one cannot promise to love. To the question, What can one promise? the analysis of the illocutionary act brings a limited answer: To do or give something.

The moral reference arises from the very idea of *force* implied by the preceding analysis. Whence does the maker of a promise draw the force so to commit himself? From a more fundamental promise, that of keeping one's word in all circumstances. We can speak here of "the promise that precedes any promise making." It is what gives every promise its aspect of commitment, commitment toward and commitment to. And it is to this commitment that the character of ipseity of the promise attaches, which finds support in some languages in pronominal forms of the verb—as, for example, when in French one says, "Je m'engage à." This ipseity, unlike the sameness typical of the biological identity and fundamental character of an individual, consists in a will to self-constancy, to remaining true to form, which seals the story of a life confronted with changes in circumstances and changes of heart. It is an identity that is preserved in spite of . . . , in spite of everything that might incline one to break one's word. This preservation of self-constancy goes beyond the unpleasant trait of being obstinate, when it becomes a habitual, modest, unspoken disposition to respect one's given word. It is what we call fidelity when speaking of friendship. I shall speak below of the kind of pathology that can affect what presents itself as a virtue, in the sense of an excellent quality of a habitual disposition, one generative of what Aristotle would call rational desire.

But we need first to celebrate the greatness of promises, just as Augustine did for memory and its vast reaches.

This greatness lies in its reliability. More precisely, it is from the habitual reliability attached to the promise before any promise making that each specific promise draws its credibility in relation to the beneficiary and witness of that promise. This dimension of reliability prolongs, on the moral plane, the linguistic analysis of the illocutionary force that conjoins commitment *toward* the other person or persons interlocutor and the commitment *to* do something through which the one making the promise places himself under a binding obligation.

This aspect of trustworthiness is common both to the promise and to testimony, which, in one of its phases, includes a moment of promise. This cousin of promising holds an important place in ordinary conversation, in the courtroom, and in the historian's inquiries. Whereas in the promise the speaker commits himself to do something for the one to whom the promise is made, testimony, in its illocutionary force, belongs to the type "assertion," whose list is long.[36] Testimony is a kind of declaration, of certification, with the perlocutionary intention of convincing the other, that is, that one is "certain." In testimony two sides are articulated in terms of each other: on the one hand, the utterance is an assertion of the factual reality of the reported event; on the other, it includes the certification or warranting of this declaration by the witness through his ordinary behavior, what we called his reliability in the case of the promise. The specificity of testimony lies in the fact that the assertion of a reality at which the witness says he was present is paired with the self-designation of the testifying subject. And this is part of a dialogical relation. The witness attests before someone to the reality of what is reported. This dialogical structure of testimony immediately brings out its dimension of trustworthiness. The witness asks to be believed. If he is an eyewitness, he does not confine himself to saying, "I was there"; he adds, "Believe me." The certifying of testimony is not complete until it is not only received but accepted and eventually recorded. Then it is not only certified, but accredited. One question thereby arises: To what point is testimony reliable? This question weighs the respective merits of confidence and suspicion. Here is where the ordinary reliability of the witness as a promise maker comes into play, waiting for the confirmation or disconfirmation that proceeds from the confronting of one testimony with another. Promises do not rest on a declarative element. The test is whether they are carried out or not, whether one keeps his word. However different in structure, testimony eventually has recourse to the promise if the witness is asked to give his deposition again. The witness is then the one who promises to testify again.

This dimension having to do with the reliability common to both testimony and the promise extends far beyond the circumstances in which they are exercised. Through its habitual character, confidence in testimony, like that in the promise, strengthens the general institution of language, whose customary practice encompasses a tacit clause of sincerity and, if we may put it this way, of charity: I want to believe that you mean what you say.

Hannah Arendt has pushed the praise of promises so far as to make it carry a good part of the weight of the general credibility of human institutions, with due regard to the weaknesses that affect human affairs in their relation with temporality.[37] The promise, coupled with pardon, allows human action to "continue." In "absolving," pardon is the retort to the irreversibility that threatens to destroy the capacity to respond in a responsible way to the consequences of action. Pardon is what makes possible reparation. By "binding," the promise offers a response to the unpredictability that threatens confidence in some expected course of action, in grounding itself in the reliability of human action. The relation we are establishing between memory and promises echoes, in one sense, the one Arendt makes between pardon and promise, inasmuch as pardon turns an uneasy memory into a memory assuaged, a happy memory.

The moment has come to turn to the dark side of promises. To forgetting when it comes to memory, we have suggested, corresponds betrayal when it comes to promises. To be able to promise is also to be able to break one's word. This ability to keep or not to keep one's word is so banal and taken for granted that it invites us to move beyond the indignation and reprobation it arouses, to articulate a second-order reflection on some of the kinds of suspicion likely to unmask the secret weaknesses of this ability to make promises, which, we have seen, is charged with remedying some of the weaknesses inherent in the conduct of human affairs.

The suspicion of a trap behind talk of maintaining self-constancy, remaining true to form, goes along with the moral examination of promises, as Nietzsche's ambiguous praise of promise making attests, when he attempts to turn it subtly into denunciation, at the beginning of the second essay of his *On the Genealogy of Morals*. "To breed an animal with the right to make promises—is not this the paradoxical task that nature has set itself in the case of man? Is it not the real problem regarding man?"[38] But if the act of promise making defines what is most human in human beings, all suspicion as regards it can engender only devastating effects on the scale of the overall human moral condition. Nietzsche's suspicion is aroused as soon as a force more deeply rooted in life is evoked, for whose effects the ability to promise can compensate—that is, the "strength to forget." A worrisome play of forces is set up. To forgetting, the token of robust health, is opposed "an opposing force, memory, with the aid of which forgetfulness is abrogated in certain cases—namely in those cases where promises are made" (57). We may not have expected the promise, which our analysis situated in contrast to memory, should reappear in the domain of memory, but that of a different kind of memory, the memory of willing, of "a desire for the continuance of something desired once." In fact, it is not the phenomenology of memory that is appealed to here but that of the will in its obtuse and obstinate form. This is not the will that mobilizes the promise of promising with its features of constancy, so long as it is indiscernible from genuine self-constancy. But Nietzsche pushes the point of his probe even further: Is it not memory of the will that makes a man "*calculable, regular, necessary,* even in his own image of himself, if he is to be able to stand security for *his own future,* which is what the one who promises does!" (58). The apparent initial praise loses any ambiguity once the whole panorama of moral horrors is uncovered: fault, bad conscience, and all that resembles them.

Like others of Nietzsche's assertions, this one is to be taken as a warning and a caution. The kind of self-mastery that the glory of ipseity seems to proclaim turns out to be a snare, one that risks conferring on promise making the same kind of claim to mastering meaning, which recognition-identification as applied to something in general nourished in our previous chapter.

This is why it is urgent that we seek in the exercising of promises the reasons for such an internal limitation, one that will put self-recognition on the road to mutual recognition.

To end this section, I propose listing quickly a few remedies for this secret pathology of the ability to make promises.

First, we should attempt not to presume on its power, not to promise too much. In his own life and narrative identity, the promise maker can find counsel that would put him under the protection of the old Greek adage: Nothing in excess!

Next, thinking of Gabriel Marcel and his plea for a "creative fidelity," we need to place as much distance as possible between self-constancy and the constancy of an obstinate will, at the price of a benevolent patience with regard to others and to oneself.

But above all, we need to reverse the order of priority between the one who promises and his beneficiary. First of all, another is counting on me and on the reliability of my word; and I must answer his expectation. Here I return to my comments about the relation of responsibility to that which is fragile in general, as something placed in my care.

Finally, we need to place the promises for which I am the author back within the setting of promises made to me of which I was and am the beneficiary. It is a matter not only of those founding promises, for which the promise made to Abraham is paradigmatic, but of the sequence of promises into which whole cultures and particular ages have projected their ambitions and dreams, many of which promises were not kept. For them too, I am the indebted continuer.

Capacities and Social Practices

In the final section of this chapter a bridge will be constructed between the individual forms of human capacities and their social forms capable of serving as a transition between self-recognition and mutual recognition. In an expanded sense, the capacities in question are no longer attested to solely by individuals; they are claimed by collectivities and submitted to public evaluation and approval.

That what is fundamentally at issue is the power to act, in the sense of *agency* in English, is what binds together everything we have said in the preceding sections. Now, it is the modes of recognition that are profoundly transformed. With the terms *evaluation* and *approval,* recognition-attestation yields to forms of ethical-juridical justification that bring into play the idea of social justice, as we shall see with the most advanced idea of "capabilities" that I owe to the economist Amartya Sen, which he pairs directly with the idea of rights in the complex expression "rights and capabilities" (or sometimes "rights and agency"). This noteworthy conceptual pair will constitute the most fully developed form of social capacities discussed in this section. At the same time, it will offer the most appropriate transition in our next chapter from self-recognition to mutual recognition, under the patronage originating with the Hegelian idea of *Anerkennung*.

We shall not be surprised by the heterogeneous character of the enumeration of forms of social capacities brought together here. Their very diversity, owing to the disparate character of the accepted referent of the different disciplines in question, contributes to a convergence resulting from their ultimate reference to the same anthropological ground, namely, the characterization of the human in general by the power to act, agency. This reference is not always explicit. It remains nonetheless the base from which the different disciplines in question diverge.

Social Practices and Collective Representations

In order to stay with disciplines that are most familiar to me, namely, the historical ones, I shall seek a first argument in favor of the idea of a social capacity in one of the contemporary French schools of historiography. I shall focus here on the attempt led by Bernard Lepetit, one of the successors of Fernand Braudel and the *Annales* school, to ascribe to social practices, as components of action in common, the sphere of those representations which human beings make of themselves and their place in society.

To gauge the change in direction brought about by Lepetit, we must start from the difficulties encountered by historians when they wanted to add to economic, social, and political history a third dimension relative to cultural facts in the broadest sense of the word *culture*, which there is no reason, in this context, to oppose to the idea of civilization. What was at issue was nothing less than how to take up again those problems posed at the end of the nineteenth century and the beginning of the twentieth by historians influenced by the sociology of Émile Durkheim and Lucien Lévi-Bruhl as those of "mentalities." The advantage of this notion was that it overlapped approximately the same field as that indicated by the term *Weltanschauungen* (or "worldviews") used in German schools of social psychology. By contrast, it had the disadvantage, apart from its impreciseness, of reflecting an embarrassing kinship with the idea of "primitive" or "prelogical" thought, with its overtone of superstition and "mystical" survivals.[39] But what was most lacking from this notion of mentality was that it did not really reveal its tie to the field of social practices. Substituting the term *representation* for that of *mentality,* in spite of the ambiguities this new term raises, has opened the way to investigations bearing on the coordination between the sphere of phenomena accessible to description and to historiographical explanation, on the one hand, and the rest of the historical field on the other.

Here is where the conceptual revolution proposed by Lepetit in *Les formes de l'expérience: Une autre histoire sociale* comes in.[40] His reinterpretation of the role assigned to collective representations presupposed a more fundamental reorientation in the task of the historian.

Lepetit's explicit aim, as indicated by his programmatic statement "Histoire des pratiques et pratiques de l'histoire," was twofold. On the one hand, the idea of social practices was to be held up as the referent of historiography; on the other, history itself takes on the status of a pragmatic discipline. In this way, a relation of congruence is established between practices as the object of history and as the historiographical operation.

A new continuation can be given to the history of mentalities under the condition of this double change in direction. It is no longer merely an appendix to economic, social, and political history, but it has to do with the universe of representations that go with the situations in which they are employed.

This connection between representations and social practices is expressed through the role of symbolic mediation these representations exercise when there is something specific at stake with regard to the social practices, namely, instituting the social bond and the modes of identity attached to it. Representations are not therefore abstract ideas floating in some autonomous space, but, as said, symbolic mediations contributing to the instituting of the social bond. What they symbolize is identities that confer a particular configuration on these social bonds as they are formed. Reciprocally, we must grant that "social identities or social ties have uses, not a nature." The meaning of this statement becomes clear only if we clarify the idea of instituting the social bond by adding that of an *agreement*, as what is at stake in the quest for identity. It is a question, says Lepetit, of "reorienting the hierarchy of questions in terms of one of them, that of *agreement*, agreement among subjects, about subjects and things—of knowing how the social bond comes about, fails to come about, or unravels" (15).

Whatever may be said about Lepetit's ambition not only to reorient but also to rearrange the discipline of history overall, under the rubric of pragmatic reason, in the wake of the crisis that struck the Braudelian model, it is the enlarging of the concept of capacities following from these changes that most interests me.

The idea of social capacities finds its justification in the pairing of collective representations and social practices. On the one hand, the sphere of representations takes on the role of symbolic mediator and in this way brings to the fore the question of the identity of the social entities in question. On the other hand, the field of social practices restores the change agent, the social protagonist, to the place of honor, as much on the collective as on the individual level. We can speak here of capacities to generate history—that is, in Lepetit's own terms, that ability to institute the social bond in the guise of the identities that are attached to it. We could speak equivalently of a competence as representing itself, recognizing itself, in the identities it engenders on the social level.

This interesting approach to the relations between collective representations and social practices, to which we owe the extension from the idea of individual capacities to that of societal capacities, finds reinforcement if we take into consideration the notion of an "interplay of scales" and of changes of scale in historiography.[41] This notion is part of the revision in chronological models that occurred earlier in the discipline of history, whether it was a question of the interlacing, so dear to Labrousse, of structures and conjunctures, or of Braudel's superimposing of the long time span belonging to an almost static geohistory, the intermediate time spans characteristic of institutions and social structures, or of the short time span of contingent events. The idea of an interplay of scales along with its corollary of a change of scale brings with it the idea of a variation in point of view that is applicable to our inquiry into the social forms of the idea of capacity. The key idea here is that one does not see the same thing on these different scales. In contrast to the notion of scale in cartography, in urban planning or architecture the divisions established on different scales applied to social changes are incommensurable. For example, what the historian sees on the scale of macrohistory is more readily structures of the long time span, but especially anonymous structures, norms felt as constraints by the protagonists of social practices, when they are not models of behavior progressively internalized, unbeknownst to socialized individuals, as is the case for those models of "civility" whose development was traced by Norbert Elias from "courtly" behavior to the governing of each person's own passions on the most intimate individual level.[42] On the microhistorical scale, chosen by the Italian practitioners of *microstoria*, we see considerations of strategy at the level of villages, families, and individuals confronted with opaque economic realities and indecipherable hierarchical relations viewed from below. For these individuals and their immediate social environment, the question is how to reduce an uncertainty that goes beyond the ordinary unpredictability of the future and that proceeds, as Jacques Revel puts it, "from the permanent awareness of having only limited information at their disposal about the forces at work in the social setting in which they must act."

This, in short, is the fruitfulness, for our investigation, of the idea of an interplay of scales. It provides the occasion for reconstructing the resources of innovation available to social agents whose power to act on the social plane is, so to speak, laid bare in circumstances of uncertainty.

Recognition and Collective Identities

Exploration of the social forms of the power to act within the framework of the cultural history of collective representations does not seem to refer to the idea of recognition in its reflexive form. Nevertheless, just as, following Bernard Williams, we adopted the expression "recognizing responsibility" to designate the way in which the heroes in Greek epic and tragedy argue among themselves about their plan of action, so too must we seek the basis for a comparable recognition of responsibility in the exercise of competence of agents of social change. This key point is located, if we use the vocabulary of Bernard Lepetit, at the juncture between the instituting of the social bond, understood as what is at stake in social practices, and the collective representations that constitute its symbolic mediations. These representations symbolize the identities by which the social ties being instituted are knotted together.

We have known from the opening pages of this work that the idea of recognition has a special connection with that of identity, whether it is a question, as in the previous chapter, of the recognition-identification of something in general or of the recognition-attestation in terms of individual capacities being considered in this chapter. Someone may say that the gap is great between those identities which imply personal capacities and those identities relating to the instituting of the social bond. In the former case, it is a question of recognition-attestation. But the identity of the social actors engaged in some collective action cannot be so directly expressed in terms of recognition-attestation, even if we take into account the complexity of the linkages arising from the diversity of capacities in play. Still, however close to "the practice of history" the "history of practices" wishes to remain (according to the title of Lepetit's programmatic essay), reflection on collective identities cannot elude a higher order of sophistication than the identity-ipseity of the individual subjects of action. The kind of explicit recognition actors on the societal level expect for their individual capacities calls for a second-order reflection reconstructing them.

I found part of an answer to this question of the identity of collective agents of social change in the work that Jean-Marc Ferry offers concerning "the forms of identity" in the modern era.[43] What is interesting for us about this work of reformulating forms of identity is that it is not limited to narration and narrative identity, whose relevance Ferry does not deny, particularly as regards the categories of "event" and "destiny." His suspicion regarding an exclusive use of the narrative form of identity has to do with its being based on tradition and foundational myths. Like me, he sees in interpretation the critical turn to which we owe the rationalizing of mythical and religious images of the world. But the real turning point in his analysis has to do with his taking argumentation as a critical force, in an openly Habermasian manner. As for Habermas, the categories of subject, laws, and justice stem, according to Ferry, from this level of argumentation. In the next chapter we shall see how this argumentation works in situations placed under the heading of the struggle for recognition. But it is not with the form of identity linked to argumentation that Ferry ends his review of forms of identity. Instead, he places the idea of reconstruction above that of argumentation. And he audaciously links this promoting of reconstruction to the idea, coming from the philosophy of language, of the Word in its openly creative aspect, in contrast to the closure of the subject in its claim to some formal, transcendental identity.

I agree with this updating of the forms of identity on the societal level insofar as I am presuming that this reconstruction is implicitly at work on the level of collective representations that render public the instituting of the social bond. Any such instituting is potentially reconstructive in nature as soon as it no longer remains caught up in simple repetition but reveals itself to be in some way innovating. In this sense, there is a continuity between spontaneous reflection on the level of social agents and the rational reflection of the philosopher. The first kind of reflection anticipates the second, which, in return, contributes retroactively to the articulating of the first. This back-and-forth between levels of reflection of different orders is characteristic of that "contemporary identity" Jean-Marc Ferry attempts to theorize.

Capacities and Capabilities

Following this critical pause which has allowed us to make more precise the tie between the collective capacity to make history and the forms of identity that are at stake in the instituting of the social bond, the moment has come to carry a step further our extending of the concept of social capacities, which is at issue in this part of this chapter. I owe the most unexpected, if not the most audacious, of these extensions to the work of Amartya Sen, the 1998 Nobel Prize winner in economics. In his *On Ethics and Economics,* and more precisely in an important work from 1985 titled *Commodities and Capabilities,* Sen places the concept of "capabilities" joined with that of "rights" at the center of his argument in favor of reintroducing ethical considerations into economic theory.[44]

How did a highly skilled economist, one well trained in mathematical techniques, arrive at this conclusion? From the opening pages of *On Ethics and Economics,* he announces his intention to take into account the role of "moral feelings" in "economic behavior." "It is difficult to believe that real people could be left out completely by the reach of the self-examination induced by the Socratic question: 'How should one live?'" (2). Economists are almost unanimous in considering economic actors in terms of their motives where such motivation has been reduced to its rational core, itself interpreted as the maximizing of self-interest, in accordance with the principle of utility. But human beings, Sen argues, do not act in reality in an exclusively self-interested way. "I have tried to argue . . . that there is an essential and irreducible 'duality' in the conception of the person in ethical calculation. We can see the person, in terms of *agency,* recognizing and respecting his or her ability to form goals, commitments, values, etc., and we can also see the person in terms of *well-being,* which too calls for attention. . . . But once [the] straitjacket of self-interested motivation is removed, it becomes possible to give recognition to the indisputable fact that the person's agency can well be geared to considerations not covered—or at least not *fully* covered—by his or her own well-being" (41). In this way, each person's ability to act comes to the fore, his agency, which Sen takes as open to a nonsubjectivist evaluation, inasmuch as the aspects of "action" and "well-being" of a person do not completely overlap. It is the moral feelings and evaluations stemming from the aspect of action that the model of *homo economicus* undercuts, in the distortedly simplified image of this model of what motivates a person to act.

The freedom of the individual comes into play here, and with this freedom, the question of the rights that transform abstract freedoms into real opportunities. We need to understand here that Sen's argument is not Kantian, but utilitarian (even if authors close to Sen, like John Rawls, situate themselves at the crossroads between these two great traditions of moral philosophy). It is not so much that utilitarians such as John Stuart Mill overlooked the juridical dimension, Sen argues, but rather that for them rights were only the means to obtain other goods, in particular, utilities. Thus, it is in the great tradition of English political liberalism that Sen formulates his argument, rubbing shoulders in this way with, besides Rawls, such important thinkers as Robert Nozick, Ronald Dworkin, J. L. Mackie, and others.[45] Sen's contribution as an economist to this discussion is his having associated the idea of freedom on the one hand with a life choice and on the other with collective responsibility. To make sense of this rare conjunction, he refers to Isaiah Berlin's well-known distinction between negative and positive liberty.[46] In the negative sense, liberty consists in the absence of hindrances that some individual—or principally the state—can impose on an individual. Civil rights (freedom of opinion, of assembly, of property, and so on) are connected to liberty in this sense, which when extended leads to the idea of "libertarianism." Considered in its positive sense, liberty represents everything that a person, taking everything into account, is capable or incapable of accomplishing. Even if this sense of liberty presupposes the former sense, it adds to it the capacity of a person to lead the life he or she chooses. According to Sen, therefore, the rights that political economy must incorporate into the motives for economic action are components of the idea of "capabilities," as he argues in his *Commodities and Capabilities*. The most noteworthy expression in this regard is that of "rights to certain capabilities," which transcends the usual dichotomy between the prescriptive and the descriptive. Within the context of the discussion among English-speaking philosophers, it is a question of getting beyond the alternative between consequentialism, stemming from the theory of well-being (such as in utilitarianism), and a deontological approach, founded on constraints external to agency. The mixed concept of "rights to certain capabilities" stems, according to Sen, from an "evaluation of situations."

This concept of an "evaluation of situations" is close to that of the "strong evaluations," which for Charles Taylor conjoin self-assertion and an ethical position expressed in terms of the good rather than of obligation. But, unlike the discussion by Taylor, who preserves the moral philosopher's reflective distance, the "evaluation of situations" is in sync with the behavior of economic agents. What is at stake is a new definition of social justice centered on the idea of "rights to certain capacities."

It is within this "evaluative" framework that the actual exercise of the freedom to choose calls on collective responsibility. It is up to such collective responsibility to ensure individual liberty in both its positive and negative forms, as well as the integrity of reciprocal relations between these two forms of liberty.

Sen has become well known for the application he makes of his conceptual analysis to a concrete case that has to do with the economy, that of famine. Himself a native of Dacca, Bangladesh, he has shown, with the example of a series of famines on the Indian subcontinent, that there exists no mechanical connection between the available reserves of foodstuffs and famines. The first thing that makes a difference is the "rights" allocated to vulnerable groups, that is, the rights of appropriation these groups can make use of.[47] In the light of this diagnosis, it turns out that the policy of enhancing the revenues of people (by offering them public employment or paying the poorest among them a salary, for example) turns out to be one of the most efficient means of preventing famines. In fact, it is in this way that famines have been systematically avoided in India since independence. Thus Sen does not hesitate to draw a connection between the nondemocratic nature of a political system and famines, such as those which occurred in China in 1958 and 1961. In short, it is the different positive liberties existing in a democratic state, including the freedom to hold regular elections, freedom of the press, and freedom of speech, that embody the actual force responsible for eliminating famines.

Armed with this demonstration based on empirical evidence, Sen can return to the theoretical problem, that of the social evaluation of the capacity to act, of agency. Contrary to the utilitarian tradition that bases this evaluation on results already accomplished, themselves reduced to utility, it is in terms of the liberty to accomplish things, as an extension of positive liberty, that Sen bases social evaluation—for example, of competing policies. In this way, individual liberty understood as a life choice becomes a social responsibility.

It is on this ground that Sen takes up John Rawls's great work, *A Theory of Justice*.[48] As regards the political and ethical dimension of individual liberty, Sen acknowledges that Rawls's "principles of justice" safeguard the priority of individual liberty, on the condition that similar liberty be given to everyone. Similarly, for Rawls, the fact of inequality brings to the fore, not the distribution of utilities, but of "primary goods," such as income, wealth, and those public liberties which assist individuals in freely pursuing their respective objectives. I shall not consider here the quarrel between Rawls and Sen over the relation between "primary goods" and positive liberty, which does not affect our reaching the category toward which I am aiming this review of Sen's work, in light of my topic in this chapter. Let it suffice to emphasize a conception of *social* responsibility that makes *individual* liberty the primary objective of a theory of justice. In return, liberty becomes an element in the evaluation of social systems, including their economic dimension. In short, what must be taken into account is "all the realizations that are rooted in the life that a person may lead."

In the final analysis, it is the pair "rights" and "capacities," summed up in the concept of "rights to capabilities," that counts most for our investigation. It converges on the pair "representations" and "social practices" discussed earlier. It stems from the preference given to positive liberty over negative liberty in the English-language tradition of political liberalism. As Sen's works on famine have confirmed, when the capacity to act, in its minimal form as ability to survive, is not assured, the phenomenon of famine is unleashed. One consequence is that protection against the abusive interference of others, which libertarians place at their pinnacle, is vain if specific measures are not taken that guarantee this minimal capacity to act. And this capacity to exist and to act turns out to be inseparable from those liberties ensured by political and juridical structures.

The conceptual revolution introduced with the pair "rights" and "capabilities" will be understood only if we contrast it with the evaluation of action in terms of utility and well-being. It is as a real capacity for choice about life that this capability is promoted to the rank of a criterion for evaluating social justice.

At the end of this brief incursion into the domain of economics, what is important is our having discovered reinforcement for a concept of human action as rooted in a fundamental anthropology. It is at this level that the convergence is warranted between the pair uniting representations and social practices and the pair bringing together the concept of "rights to capabilities."

At the end of this chapter, it will be helpful to cast a glance back over the path we have traveled. Starting from the beginning and moving toward this ending, we can affirm that the theme of recognizing responsibility, deciphered by Bernard Williams from Greek epic and tragic literature, has remained the thread that runs through our whole investigation. We can agree with Williams that an agent's recognition of his power to act, his agency, constitutes a cultural constant that confirms a readability of the classics of Western literature we can call transcultural. Nevertheless, unlike Williams, who is skeptical concerning the philosophical sophistication that has opened a gulf between the ancients and the moderns, I continue, as in my previous chapter, to take seriously the discontinuous thought events to which we owe the properly philosophical problematizing of the leading concepts of the philosophy of action, from Aristotle to contemporary authors. This is how a diverse and multifarious rumination for which action remains the main theme has been able to grow from the anthropological base of the spontaneous recognition of responsibility for their actions by its agents. The remainder of this chapter will try to illustrate this conceptual proliferation, whether it is a question of the epistemic sense of the act of recognition or of the modes of the abilities claimed.

As regards the second point, we can take the passage from the idea of individual capacities to that of social capacities as an insight into the increasing complexifying of the idea of capacities against the stable background of the anthropological theme of the capacity to act, of agency. The effect of dispersal commenced with our remarks devoted to individual capacities. It continued to grow, from the ability to speak to imputability, and from there to the pair memory and promise. However, it was in our remarks devoted to capacities of social rank that the differences really began to open between analyses stemming from the heterogeneous disciplines that make up the broad field of the human sciences, such as history and economics. The effect of convergence that compensates for this divergence is all the more striking in that it strengthens our basic idea of a power to act stemming from a common anthropological base.

As regards the epistemic sense of the recognition at work over the entire course of our investigation, it presents the same equilibrium between stability and diversification as does the thematic treatment of the capacities enumerated. The basic equation remains that of recognition and attestation, in an extension of the lexical sense that our dictionary places under the rubric of avowal. The kind of certitude that characterizes avowal cannot be reduced to *doxa* on the theoretical level. It is a certitude sui generis, arising from the practical dimension of knowledge. The whole of this chapter is set within this dimension of practical certitude. This does not prevent the third section of this chapter from enriching the key idea of attestation in an important way. It is the forms of identity brought to the fore by the disciplines considered that structure the progressive enriching of this practical certitude. The symbolic connection between collective representations and the instituting of the social bond marked a decisive phase in the process of our gaining insight into the complexity of the forms of identity. But it was with the theme of rights to certain capabilities and with Amartya Sen that our investigation made a leap forward, without for all that breaking the tie to earlier forms of the avowal of such capacities. Attestation has become a demand, a right to require, under the rubric of the idea of social justice. This convergence, once again, is assured by the underlying anthropological base from which stems the pivotal idea of power to act. The innovation on the conceptual plane lay in the recourse to the theme of positive liberty, borrowed from the English-language tradition of political liberalism. But nothing prevents us from placing this modern concept of positive liberty face to face with the Aristotelian theme of a human *ergon*. The idea that there is a function for human beings, a task irreducible to techniques, skills, or some particular craft, emerges magnified from the eminently modern discussions about the liberty to act.

A backward reading of this chapter starting from its *terminus ad quem* is no less instructive than a reading starting from its initial stage. The passage from the idea of capacity to that of capability, itself enriched by its being conjoined with that of a right, in the phrase "rights to certain capabilities," does not leave the earlier analyses intact.

The conjunction between the ideas of rights and capabilities projects its light retrospectively over the whole previous course of our itinerary. The question that arises is whether the idea of capacity can be taken as ethically neutral at any stage whatsoever of the analysis. What is called into question, at the very heart of attestation, is the opposition between description and prescription. Capacities are not observed to be true, but attested. And to this idea of attestation remain attached those of appreciation, of evaluation, as the idea of ascription suggests, which, itself coming from the region of right and law, is carried over into that of everyday avowal. "Ascription" as a practical category transcends the opposition between description and prescription, which bears the imprint of theoretical empiricism. This ethical mark placed on the attestation of capacities and on the claim to such capacities is in the end common to the thought of both ancients and moderns. The right to certain capabilities leads back to the Greek idea of *arête*, which we must not forget fundamentally signifies excellence in action. It is at the level of the anthropological base of the idea of a power to act, of agency, that the evaluation of our capacities, subterraneanly linked to the idea of living well, operates. Amartya Sen and Bernard Williams agree in praise for the desire to live one's life freely.

At the end of this discussion, we need yet to say what is lacking from this segment of the course of recognition, which the rights-capabilities pair can convey. Considered from a prospective, and not a merely retrospective, point of view, and taking into account the notions it anticipates, the idea of a right to capabilities is valuable as a criterion of social justice in the comparison between competing political programs and ideas. In this way, the conflictual dimension of actual situations submitted to this criterion of evaluation is revealed. With conflict, a new conceptual chain is uncovered. The ideas of plurality, alterity, reciprocal action, and mutuality that will be at the center of my next and concluding chapter belong to this chain.

CHAPTER 3

MUTUAL RECOGNITION

———

As soon as one man was recognized by another as a sentient, thinking Being similar to himself, the desire or need to communicate feelings and thoughts to him made the first man begin to look for ways to do so.

—Jean-Jacques Rousseau, *Essay on the Origin of Language*

The next step in our journey brings onto the philosophical stage the third occurrence of the term *recognition*. After the Kantian moment of *Rekognition* and the Bergsonian moment of recognizing images, now comes the Hegelian moment of *Anerkennung*.

In our first chapter, identification was the identification of something in general. The relation between the same and the other was then one of exclusion, whether it was a matter of a theoretical judgment of perception or a practical matter of choice. In this first case, to identify is to distinguish. The one is not the other. Something appears, disappears, reappears. After some hesitation—because its appearance has changed or because a long time has elapsed—one recognizes it. It is indeed the same thing and not another. The risk here is that of making a mistake, of taking one thing for another. At this stage, what is true of things is also true of persons. The mistake is just more dramatic in the latter case, identification being confronted with the threat of misrecognition. We recall the episode of the Prince de Guermantes's dinner toward the end of Proust's *Time*

Regained. The familiar people, who have suffered the ravages of time, seem to have "put on a disguise," and the question becomes pressing: Is this still the same person or someone else? Trembling, the spectator of this scene exclaims, "Yes, it's she all right! It's he himself!" This relation of exclusion between the same and the other is no less clear when perceptual judgment yields to preferential judgment. Choice takes the form of an alternative: one or the other. Once hesitation is overcome, it is the one rather than the other.

In our preceding chapter, recognition was still based on procedures of identification. The self took the place of the thing in general. In this case, the bifurcation between sameness and ipseity did not weaken the opposition in principle between the same and the other, except for the fact that by the same we had to understand me and not the other, others, the other person. Locke gave this relation of exclusion its canonical form: the self is the same as itself and not another. In his vocabulary, "identity" is opposed to "diversity."

But the recognition of the self by the self implied more than a substitution of the self for something in general. Thanks to the semantic proximity between the notion of recognition and that of attestation, a vast realm of experiences opened up for description and reflection, that of the capacities each person has the certitude and confidence of being able to exercise. Self-recognition thus found in the unfolding of the figures of the "I can," which together make up the portrait of the capable human being, its own space of meaning. But what is most important for our pursuit of the course of recognition is that identification, which has not ceased to be the hard core of the idea of recognition, not only has changed its referent in passing from something in general to the self but has been elevated to a logical status dominated by the idea of the exclusion between the same and the other, and to an existential status thanks to which the other is likely to affect the same. The preceding chapter touched only lightly on this dialectic with the ideas of help and hindrance in the exercise of one's own capacities. It will be the task of this chapter to target the dialectic of reflexivity and alterity through the figure of mutual recognition. Reciprocity and mutuality (which we will not differentiate at the start) will give what has since Kant been called reciprocal causality or community, in the categorical sense of the term, its space for manifestation.

The Greeks had just a single term to speak of this relationship of mutuality: the genitive form *allelōn*—reciprocally—which can be translated as "one another," or, more succinctly, "each other."

We shall first consider the categorical structure of this "one another," in order to discern in it a paradox that will accompany us tacitly to the conclusion of our whole enterprise—namely, the resistance that opposes to the idea of reciprocity the originary dissymmetry that widens the gap between the idea of the one and that of the other. This categorical preamble will serve as a warning for the remainder of our inquiry, inasmuch as the praise of reciprocity through the more intimate figure of mutuality runs the risk of reliance on forgetting the insurmountable difference that accounts for the fact that the one is not the other at the very heart of the *alleloi,* the "one another."

Once this warning has been stated and held in reserve, we shall apply to the theme of mutual recognition the same genealogical method used in the previous chapters, that is, a consideration of the chain of "thought events" for which the Hegelian moment of *Anerkennung* will constitute the central link. One hypothesis will govern the first part of this inquiry, that the Hegelian *Anerkennung* is to be understood as a rejoinder to a major challenge, the one that Hobbes threw in the face of Western thought on the political plane. Our reconstruction of the theme of *Anerkennung,* as Hegel articulated it during his Jena period, will be guided by this idea of a rejoinder to Hobbes's challenge, in which the desire to be recognized occupies the place held in the Hobbesian conception of the state of nature by the fear of a violent death. This reconstruction, presented as an *explication de texte,* will serve in turn as an introduction to

Mutual Recognition · 153

some attempts to reactualize the Hegelian theme under the heading "The Struggle for Recognition." We shall follow these attempts to the point where doubt arises concerning the very idea of a struggle, which will give me the opportunity to shape another hypothesis: that the struggle for recognition would lose itself in the unhappy consciousness if it were not given to humans to be able to accede to an actual, albeit symbolic, experience of mutual recognition, following the model of the reciprocal ceremonial gift.

From Dissymmetry to Reciprocity

On the categorical plane, the relation of reciprocity is not self-evident. Already in our chapter discussing recognition as identification, the notion of reciprocal action was a problem. In the *Critique of Pure Reason* Kant placed it third in the Analogies of Experience in the Analytic of Principles, after substance, which is a synonym for permanence in time, and after the law of causality, which is a synonym for a law-governed succession. The third analogy then stated: "All substances, in so far as they can be perceived to coexist in space, are in thoroughgoing reciprocity."[1] It is quite remarkable that the principle of reciprocal action should also be called a principle of community or even of commerce. What is important is that on the temporal plane simultaneity wins out over succession, as in the case of the law of cause and effect. It is indeed a kind of existential simultaneity that is at issue in mutual recognition, or in intersubjective commerce, or better still, in appearances, as when we speak of the appearance in court of the plaintiff and the defendant in a trial.

As stated earlier, I want to bring to light the novelty of the existential category of reciprocity through an argument drawn from the difficulty phenomenology encounters in deriving reciprocity from a presumably originary dissymmetry in the relation of the ego to others. Phenomenology gives two clearly opposed versions of this dissymmetry, depending on which pole one starts from, the ego, or the other person. One version, that of Husserl in his *Cartesian Meditations*, remains a phenomenology of perception. In this sense, his approach is theoretical. The other, that of Levinas, in *Totality and Infinity* and *Otherwise than Being or Beyond Essence*, is straightforwardly ethical and, by implication, anti-ontological.[2] Both approaches have their legitimacy, and my argument here does not require us to decide in favor of one or the other of them. What matters is the seriousness with which each of the two parties undertakes to overcome the dissymmetry that, in a way, persists in the background of experiences of reciprocity, leaving reciprocity to appear as an always incomplete surpassing of this dissymmetry.

Husserl's fifth *Cartesian Meditation* represents the most radical and most audacious attempt to account for the status of alterity of the "stranger," starting from the ego pole and, in a second movement, from the derived status of the community of egos on the basis of the constituting of the alter ego. The difficulty is thus doubled by the obligatory passage through the constituting of the alter ego.

The dissymmetry is imposed by the self-sufficiency of the ego within the realm of the reduction of all natural transcendence to a transcendental consciousness for which all reality stems from the self-explication *(Selbstauslegung)* of my ego as the subject of all possible knowledge. This egological understanding of consciousness is reached at the end of the fourth *Meditation*.

Then the objection of solipsism arises, coming from the outside, but this is an objection that phenomenology transforms into a challenge willingly taken up. The constitution of the phenomenon of the "other person" then presents a paradoxical twist. The alterity of the other person, like all other alterity, is constituted *in* me and starting from *(aus)* me. Yet it is precisely as other that the stranger is constituted as an ego for himself—that is, as a subject of experience just as I am, a subject capable of perceiving me as belonging to the world of his experience. Husserl makes the task particularly difficult for himself by pushing the reduction of the ego to the point of the "sphere of ownness" or the "sphere of belonging," centered on my lived body, with no reference to another person external to this sphere. It is precisely from this extreme version of reduction to a sphere of belonging—which, like solipsism, has the value of a philosophical fable, as Hobbes's description of the state of nature will have further on—that will emerge the attempt at a solution of the paradox of the constitution in and by me of the other as other. It is my own flesh that presents itself as the first *analogon* of another flesh, whose immediate, intuitive experience will remain inaccessible to me. In this regard, it is the unsurpassable truth of the dissymmetry on the perceptual and intuitive planes. Nevertheless, the notion of an analogical apprehension makes sense not as a reasoning by analogy, but as a precategorial, preintellectual transposition, referring back to a first creation of meaning that makes the relation from me to the stranger a relation of a model to a copy of it. This presumed analogical apprehension authorizes us to speak of an "appresentation," for want of a presentation, or again of an apperceptive transfer *(Übertragung)*. Whatever we call it, this analogizing apprehension receives a threefold reinforcement. First, that of a relation we can call a pairing *(Paarung)*, for which examples can be found in sexual experience, friendship, ordinary conversation, and the exchange of ideas, all experiences conferring a kind of existential "fulfilling" on the originally logical notion of *Paarung*, of pairing. Second, we have the confirmation of the coherence with itself of the other's existence in the agreement of expressions, gestures, and postures, which announces the unity of the same style. Finally comes an open appeal to imagination. The other is over there, where I could be if I were to move. In this way, imagination makes the other's "here" coincide with my "over there."

We could discuss endlessly the innumerable variations on this idea of an analogizing apprehension. Its merit is that it preserves intact the enigma of alterity and even that it exalts it. The other person does not remain completely unknown to me, of course; otherwise I could not even talk about him. He remains "apperceived" not only as other than me, in the exclusive sense of the term, but as another me, an alter ego, in the analogical sense of the term. Hence, the analogy protects the unknowability in principle of the other's experience as he experiences it. In this sense, the ego and the other don't really "appear" together. I alone appear, am "presented." The other, as presumably analogous, remains "appresented."

A common natural world and historical communities having values in common are constituted step by step, starting from this dissymmetry that is at the same time surmounted and preserved. These two new degrees of constitution are presupposed by the relation of reciprocity. We must give the greatest importance to those operations leading to community (those of *Vergemeinschaftung*), which draws reciprocity out of asymmetry. It really is a matter of a second-degree constitution. The other must be my analogue, so that beyond my experience of myself I come to terms with that of others on a basis of reciprocity, even though this chain of constitutions draws its basic meaning from me as ego. For this kind of phenomenology there is only one ego, multiplied through association. We can be assured that however real these communities may be, they never amount to an absolute, in the sense that only the *ego cogito* is, for reflection. Here too, as in the first degree of constitution, we can follow in this "intentional sociology" the trace of the negotiation between two demands: one that requires respecting the new meanings that the analysis discovers as it progresses, the other that requires deriving the ontic status of these communities from that of the ego. What Husserl attempts here is the equivalent of Leibniz's monadology, which makes multiple perspectives intersect in the common experience of nature, in what Husserl calls the synthesis of identification. Intermonadic communities are built upon such an experience in common of nature. What for the sociologist comes first as given, is last for the phenomenologist as constituted.

Whence the calculated slow pace of the last paragraphs of the fifth *Cartesian Meditation,* which multiply an almost overwhelming number of preliminary steps: equalization of points of view, which makes me an other among others, elevation of historical communities to the rank of "persons" of a higher order, each one having the privilege of directing at its own level the problematic of ownness and the foreign, at the horizon of which stands the "archontic society of scholars and philosophers," where a universal awareness *(universale Selbstbesinnung)* is realized.

Yet to the end of this laborious course, the lived experience of the other always remains inaccessible to me. The analogical relation can only repeat itself again and again. And it is as an unstable equilibrium that the "explication" holds itself at equal distance from description, in the sense of British empiricism, and construction, in the sense of German idealism, something that Husserl really did not know well.

With Emmanuel Levinas, the dissymmetry between the ego and the other proceeds from the pole of the other person toward that of the ego. This reversal is linked to a more basic one that places ethics in the position of first philosophy in relation to ontology. In *Totality and Infinity* the idea of being is assimilated to the process of assimilating all differences, including those instituted between me and the other person in a phenomenology of perception like that of Husserl. In this regard, the two ideas of being and totality overlap, while that of infinity serves as an exception.

It is not that the question of life together, to which we give the name mutuality, is absent from *Totality and Infinity.* Does the book not begin with a meditation on war, which, by suspending morality and breaking the continuity between persons, offers a simulacrum of the "ontology of totality" (22), by means of the terrifying operation of general mobilization? And it is with a single bound, under the prodding of the eschatology of peace, that the gaze reverses itself and opens itself to the "gleam of exteriority or of transcendence in the face of the Other" (24). The rigorously developed concept of such transcendence is "expressed by the term infinity" (25). In a way, everything is said in one page. Yet it will require a thick volume to actually carry out the reversal from ontological totality to infinity according to ethics, through the grace of the mediation of the face.

In this conquest of exteriority, whose importance is indicated by the book's subtitle, the ego is not ignored. It has its own consistency in the self-identification that encapsulates the enjoyment of the world. The self is "at home with itself" in this world that it inhabits. The stranger is what troubles this sense of being at home with oneself. The same and the other enter into a relation whose terms never form a totality.

The question of living together is not absent from *Totality and Infinity*. Once the exordium on war imposes its consideration, language, discourse take the place of the relation, but this is not a totalizing relation. It leads to no history that amounts to a system. Ontology, that is, reduction of the Other to the Same.

Levinas's pages about the face, where it is said that it does not appear in the sense of a representation but expresses itself, are well known. The face teaches: "In its non-violent transitivity the very epiphany of the face is produced" (51)—to the point that in the face-to-face relation, the face of the other summons me. This is not given to vision: its revelation is "speech" (193). It is "present in its refusal to be contained" (194). In an inverse relation to Husserl's "analogizing grasp," the face conjoins transcendence and epiphany. This epiphany is not an analogizing grasp, but rather a revelation sui generis. The summoned ego is uprooted from its state of separation and self-enjoyment and called upon to respond. Responsibility, from that moment on, is no longer an affirmation of ipseity but a response, on the model of Abraham's "Here I am."

It is the possibility of murder—the theme with which Hobbes inaugurates modern political philosophy—a possibility evoked in

Levinas's initial pages on war—that opens up the question of a mutual relation. If it is true that "the Other is the sole being I can wish to kill" (198), on what recourse, what aid, can "ethical resistance" (199) call? *Totality and Infinity* does not take up the institutional aspect of this resistance. The book ends with the obligation to enter into discourse and to allow oneself to be instructed by kindness, the nonviolence of peace. The underlying figure of the other is that of the teacher of justice. Justice, which brings onstage the third person, touches me only through the face of the other: "The third party looks at me in the eyes of the Other—language is justice" (213). In this sense, the ethics of the face excuses *Totality and Infinity* from having to provide a distinct elaboration of the problematic of the third person. "The asymmetry of the interpersonal" (215), which was there at the beginning, as the originary situation, comes back at the end as the truth of the discourse of fraternity and kindness. A relation wherein I and the other would become interchangeable leads back from infinity to totality. The "height" [*hauteur*] of the word of instruction responds to the initial inequality.

Is there in *Totality and Infinity* a "beyond the face"? Yes. This is the title of section 4. But its place is that of a phenomenology of eros that gives rise to the wonderful pages on the caress, feminine beauty, and fecundity. The third party is named again, in the conclusion, with something like the weightlessness of a dream: "Metaphysics, or the relation with the Other, is accomplished as service and as hospitality. In the measure that the face of Other relates us with the third party, the metaphysical relation of the I to the Other moves into the form of the We, aspires to a State, to institutions, laws, which are the source of universality. But politics left to itself bears a tyranny within itself; it deforms the I and the Other who have given rise to it, for it judges them according to universal rules, and thus as in absentia" (300). In the end, the visible for politics is what the face leaves invisible. Unlike "the cruelty of this impersonal justice" (300), fecundity remains the true "beyond the face."

We had to wait for the book by Levinas that I take to be his most accomplished work, *Otherwise than Being or Beyond Essence,* to receive a worked-out answer to the question that motivates my reading—namely, in what way a philosophy of the originary asymmetry between the ego and the other, an asymmetry starting with the ethical primacy of the other, can account for the reciprocity between unequal partners. Levinas's repeated references to justice, to kindness, to war and peace, and finally to institutions in *Totality and Infinity* seems to justify stressing this question.

The theme of this later book is more rigorously centered than the one in *Totality and Infinity.* The greatest gamble undertaken by this book, I have written elsewhere, "is that of linking the fate of the relation to be established between the ethics of responsibility and ontology to the fate of their respective language: *Saying* on the side of ethics, the *said* on that of ontology" (82).[3] If it is true that ethics upsets the kingdom of being—which is the sense of the recurring adverb *otherwise*—what language then ensures that the "saying" does not fall into the "said"—that is, into the thematic articulation of ontology, into what semantics calls propositions? Do we not run the risk of being satisfied with words by invoking "unsaying" [*dédire*] as a synonym for the an-archy of "saying"?[4] Yet surely something is being *said* when proximity, responsibility, and substitution for the persecutor are discussed over the course of the entire book in a tone that can be said to be declarative, not to say kerygmatic? We can even observe a kind of move to the extreme case, a verbal overbidding, when we pass from the theme of proximity to that of substitution—that is, from the theme of suffering by others to suffering for others—and when the vocabulary of wounds inflicted gives way to the more extreme vocabulary of persecution, of being taken hostage.[5] There is more. The "traumatic effect" of persecution is to signify the "irremissibility of the accusation" (112)—in short, an unlimited guilt. Here Dostoevsky takes over from Isaiah, Job, and Quoheleth. There is something like a crescendo here: persecution, outrage, expiation, "an absolute accusation" anterior to freedom (121). Is this not to admit that ethics disconnected from ontology lacks its own language? This hyperbolic language poses the problem of a language to which an ethics radically disconnected from ontology can appeal. It is this question which itself leads to my hypothesis for reading concerning the strategic role played by the theme of the third party in Levinas's discourse. This theme of the third party is imposed by the very position of the philosopher when he writes; the place where he is, is that of the third party. And the occasion for its evocation is the comparison between incomparables. The philosopher of dissymmetry grants that "there must be justice among incomparable ones" (16). Justice is, essentially, this comparison between incomparables.[6]

I shall stop with this enigma rather than really conclude this review of the difficulties that both versions of the originary asymmetry between the ego and the other confront in their own way. Whether one starts from the pole of the ego or the pole of the other, in each case it is a question of comparing incomparables and hence of *equalizing* them.

Hobbes's Challenge

Having ended my categorical introduction, I want to return on the thematic level to my attempt to place in sequence the "thought events" that highlight the central theme of Hegelian *Anerkennung*, either preceding or succeeding it, without forgetting the subversive sting of the originary dissymmetry between the ego and the other. Just as recognition-identification in going from something in general to single persons continues to face the test of the *unrecognizable*, reciprocal recognition runs the risk of never getting beyond *misrecognition* in the sense of a refusal of recognition. With these reservations in mind, we will now attempt to respond directly to the demands of the prepositions *with* and *among* in the expressions "being-with" or "being-among," where the latter preposition re-calls the *Inter-esse* so often referred to by Hannah Arendt.

I shall begin with the hypothesis announced in my introductory remarks to this chapter, that the theme of *Anerkennung* has to be treated as a moral rejoinder to the challenge launched by a natural-istic interpretation of the sources of the political. In so doing, we tacitly admit that the problematic of being among and with is fun-damentally political in nature. I take this primacy of the political in the sense Aristotle gives to it at the beginning of his *Nichomachean Ethics* (1094a24f.), following Plato in this instance. The science of argument in the broadest sense leading to the nature of the sover-eign good is "politics," the "most authoritative art." This is the one that tells us what sciences are necessary in states and cities. Here Aristotle includes strategy, economics, and rhetoric. The argument is not so much about the subordination of ethics to politics as about the hierarchical relation of the different protagonists. "For even if the end is the same for a single man and for a state, that of the state seems at all events something greater and complete both to attain and to preserve; for though it is worthwhile to attain the end merely for one man, it is finer and more godlike to attain it for a nation or for city-states" (1094b7–10).

Hobbes, who knew these texts, as well as that of the *Politics,* which develops them further, overturns the homology between the good of the individual and that of the state, which is in a sense a common feature of every ancient moral and political philosophy, to the point that Leo Strauss, in his *Political Philosophy of Hobbes,* will designate Hobbes as the founder of modern political theory.[7]

My reading of *Leviathan* will not deal with the figure of Levia-than, which resolves the enigma created by the theory of the "state of nature" in chapter thirteen of that work. It is not Hobbes's con-ception of the state that constitutes the primary challenge to which Hegel will reply with his concept of recognition, but the very theory of a "state of nature." What is at stake is knowing whether an originarily moral motive underlies life together, one that Hegel will identify with the desire to be recognized. Thus it is as a theory of misrecognition that the Hobbesian theory of the state of nature will be revisited.

What we need first to recall is how his thesis is a thought experiment. Not that this hypothesis lacks preparation or support in the vision of the world or the doctrine of man that go with it. A desire for demonstration, which has its first model in Euclid's *Elements,* subsequently found its most powerful development in the search for and practice of a method in Bacon, Galileo, and Descartes, for which the "resolutive-compositive" method (Strauss, 153) developed by the School of Padua forms a close second. Strauss is undoubtedly correct when he says that the theory of the "state of nature" finds an a posteriori justification, rather than a necessary foundation, in physical materialism. The human mind is directly apprehended as a bundle of activities governed by desire, while this desire is itself guided by a capacity for calculation, without which it would not be possible to have the chain of arguments leading from the fear of a violent death to the conclusion of the contract from which is born the mortal god whose figure is Leviathan.

That Hobbes's description of the state of nature is a thought experiment is confirmed by the fact that the features I have placed under the heading of misrecognition result not from the observation of some fact, but from the imagining of what human life must be like without the institution of a government. It is true that this imagining finds converging signs in the reality of wars between states and of episodes of subversion within states, as well as in what we can call everyday fear—fear of theft, of assault, of murder— even in the most allegedly civilized societies. Yet the radicalization that leads to the fear of violent death at the outset of Hobbes's enterprise constitutes as such an unforeseeable thought experiment in the history of political and moral ideas.

The names of the three primitive passions that together characterize the state of nature as a "war of all against all" are well known. They are competition, distrust (Hobbes says diffidence), and glory. "The first maketh man to invade for gain; the second, for safety; and the third, for reputation."[8] It is worth noting that none of these passions is conceivable without some reference to others. Everyone knows himself to be, in comparison, equal to everyone else on the plane of passions. This equality by nature of human beings among themselves is affirmed in the opening sentence of the chapter titled "Of the Natural Condition of Mankind, As Concerning Their Felicity, and Misery." Here, what men do is more important than what they think about themselves. But without comparison there would be no enmity to push men to "endeavour to destroy or subdue one another" (75). "One another" in this sense is a structure of denying recognition that finds its clearest experience in distrust, and its deepest motive in vanity.

Leo Strauss can say that in relation to vanity (another name for glory), a source of illusion, the fear of death constitutes the principle of truth from which derive those reasonable measures that will lead to the decisive political contract. In this sense, the state of nature harbors the origin of the antinomy between vanity and the fear of a violent death. Another noteworthy feature as regards our re-reading in terms of the refusal of recognition in this description of the human condition in the state of nature is that it is not possible to pronounce the word *war* (borrowed from historical experience) without pairing it with the word *peace*. At this point, Hobbes introduces an odd reference to time. He says, "The notion of time is to be considered in the nature of war" (76). The word "time" is still taken in the double sense in the English of the seventeenth century of a lapse of time and of inclement weather. The "nature of foul weather" only makes sense by contrast with another, more favorable time: "all other time is peace" (76). I interpret this as saying that misrecognition knows itself to be a refusal of this recognition called peace.

Having written that "the life of man is solitary, poor, nasty, brutish, and short," Hobbes returns to his main path. "It may seem strange, to some man that has not well weighed these things, that nature thus dissociate, and render man apt to invade and destroy one another. And he may, therefore, not trusting to this inference from the passions, desire perhaps to have the same confirmed by experience" (76–77). There follow examples of fear drawn from everyday life. But is it not from the point of view of peace that one feels surprise here?

Hobbes's challenge would not be understood in its full scope if we were not to complete what he says about the state of nature in chapter 13 with those placed under the heading of "natural laws" in chapter 14 and "other laws of nature" in chapter 15. In fact, without the establishing of these laws, which already obligate everyone by appealing to the state of nature, the emergence of the state would remain incomprehensible; for it is necessary that this state should stem from a contract to which, it is true, the sovereign is not a party, but which at least engages all those human beings in the state of nature who are unaware of any evaluation in terms of what might be morally preferable. All that remains is the fear of death to govern the evaluations listed as permitted at the end of chapter 13. What is permitted is measured by what is required for the preservation of each person, namely, the augmentation in power over people. This being necessary to self-preservation, "it must be permitted." The permitted then is nothing other than the last link in the chain: vanity, distrust, preventive attack. At the end of chapter 13 the demand for what will satisfy the idea "law of nature" in chapters 14 and 15 appears: "Reason suggesteth convenient articles of peace, upon which men will be drawn to a agreement. These articles are they which otherwise are called laws of nature" (78). The reason invoked here is nothing other than the calculation provoked by the fear of a violent death.

To speak of laws of nature on the basis of a state of nature is for

Hobbes to enter the territory of his great rivals, the theorists of a *jus naturale*. What we must understand at this critical point of his argument is that before becoming a challenge to Hegel, Hobbes's theory—combining state of nature and law of nature—was a challenge to the theorists of natural law who succeeded him, but who first preceded him in the person of Grotius. Grotius had published *De Jure belli ac pacis* in 1625, while *Leviathan* dates from 1651.[9] There we find this definition of right: "A moral quality attached to a person [*qualitas moralis personae*] in virtue of which one can legitimately have or do certain things [*competens ad aliquid juste habendum vel agendum*]" (cited by Zarka, 9).[10] It is just such a moral quality of the person, conceived of as a "faculty" opening out onto the "capacities" we have spoken of, that Hobbes openly rejects in the definition he gives at the head of chapter 14: "The Right of Nature, which writers commonly call *jus naturale*, is the liberty each man hath to use his own power, as he will himself, for the preservation of his own nature, that is to say, of his own life, and consequently of doing anything which, in his own judgment and reason, he shall conceive to be the aptest means thereunto" (79).

Having said this, how are we to understand that this positive liberty turns into prohibitions and first of all the prohibition "by which man is forbidden to do that which is destructive of his life or taketh away the means of preserving the same, and to omit that by which he thinketh it may be best preserved" (ibid.)? Here is where the subtle turn lies that allows us to make the distinction between *law,* which forbids, and *right,* which authorizes and permits. This difference between law and right nevertheless runs the risk of being misunderstood once we give the underlying prohibition visible expression in a sequence of "precepts"—Hobbes enumerates no fewer than nineteen of these!—the first of which enjoins that "every man ought to endeavour peace," without for all that renouncing "by all means we can, to defend ourselves." And the second precept says that we ought "to lay down this right to all things" (80). At this point law is clearly dissociated from right. The contract from which the state is born would be incomprehensible without this "precept." To "lay down a man's right to anything is to divest himself of the liberty of hindering another of the benefit of his own right to the same" (81) is what is preliminary to every act of making a contract. In turn, this relinquishment of a right divides into a simple *renouncing* and a *transfer* to the benefit of another, whence proceeds the first obligation: not to prevent this other from drawing some benefit from this transfer. For the first time, the epithets *reciprocal* and *mutual* are pronounced, under the sign no longer of the state of war, but of the search for peace. Through surreptitious and subtle shifts we have entered the domain of the contract. But although it is a matter of relinquishing something, of a transfer, a contract, it in no way amounts to a moral constraint, but rather is a question of an entirely voluntary and sovereign precaution that calculation recommends under the pressure of fear. That one relinquishes one's right can go so far as to become a gratuitous gift, that is, one without reciprocity, thereby exceeding any possible contract: "This is not contract, but Gift, Free-Gift, Grace, words that signify one and the same thing" (82), Hobbes notes. This nonethical motivation can hardly go any further in its mimicking of the ethical motivation that underlies the definition of right by the natural law theorists as "the moral quality of the person." It does not go as far as the promise, which is set in motion by the precepts of the law of reason, once the gratuitous gift refers to the future: "I will that this be thine tomorrow and I will to give it to thee tomorrow" (83).

No doubt Hobbes has need of this idea of a unilateral relinquishment of right by each person, just as he does of those of transferring a right, a contract, and a promise, to make plausible the idea of a waiver of the totality of individual rights to the benefit of one ruler on the condition that this waiver be reciprocal. Mutuality was inscribed in the definition of the contract, as just said. As for the promise, if it is not mutual, it is made to another to whom one promises to give something tomorrow—hence as ceding in exchange for a benefit previously received. A *covenant* is implied at the end of this sequence of contractual acts. The transfer of right, and hence of liberty and power, constitutes the linchpin for the whole chain of notions considered. The reciprocity of the covenant is henceforth joined to the unilateral nature of the transfer. "Covenants entered into by fear, in the condition of mere nature, are obligatory" (86). This simple assertion reinforces the paradox of the concept of "right of nature." How can calculation, motivated by fear, give rise to such a gap attaching to the liberty to do everything that the conservation of life recommends and the laws and precepts that attach obligations to everything that follows from the voluntary relinquishment of this right: transfer, contract, promise, *covenant?* The only null and void convention is the one by which I renounce making use of force to defend myself against force. The inalienable right *to resist,* under the governance of the state, is the result.

From Hobbes's long enumeration of "other laws of nature" in chapter 15, I shall retain only the ninth, which expressly introduces *acknowledgment* as a technical term. "That every man acknowledge the other as his equal by nature. The breach of this precept is *pride*" (97). This pretext makes the law of nature coincide, curiously enough, with the state of nature. The original equality is reaffirmed, but as consented to, recognized. Acknowledgement, following the law of nature, overcomes distrust, following from the *state* of nature, through the grace of a unilateral relinquishment of right and the reciprocal contract that this makes possible.

One indispensable condition for the definition of the state through each person's relinquishment of the right to govern himself is still lacking, if the sovereign must be a single person who represents a multitude. What is lacking is the new definition of the person that is a rejoinder to that of Suarez and Grotius. To the natural person, "possessing" his words and acts, is added—and this is the critical point—the fictive or artificial person who "represents" the words and acts of another. This, Hobbes claims in chapter 16 ("Of Persons, Authors, and Things Personated"), is a return to etymology: the person as a mask, as a role, as a vicarious representative, in short as an *actor,* unlike the proprietary *author* of his words and actions. Authority derives from this, a mandate that authorizes. We are not far from the definition of the state: "A multitude of men are made *one* person, when they are by one man, or one person represented so that it be done with the consent of every one of this multitude in particular." Indeed, it is the *unity* of the representative, not the *unity* of the represented, that makes this one person. The representative is this person and it is just one person. "Unity cannot otherwise be understood in a multitude" (104). We have surreptitiously passed from the natural to the artificial with this idea of a fictive or artificial person and what follows from it: essentially the turning of the many into the one through the intermediary of the idea of representation, as a part of the fictive or artificial person. On the transfer resulting from each natural person's relinquishment of his right is superimposed the transfer—through representation and mandate from author to actor—from the natural to the artificial person.

The definition of the state at the beginning of chapter 17, "Of the Causes, Generation, and Definition of a Commonwealth," with which we come to the end of our discussion of Hobbes, turns out to have been prepared well in advance: "I authorize and give up my right of governing myself to this man, or assembly of men, on the condition that thou give up thy right to him, and authorize all his actions in like manner. This done, the multitude so united in one person is called a Commonwealth, in Latin *Civitas*. This is the generation of that great Leviathan, or rather (to speak with more reverence) of that Mortal God to which we owe, under Immortal God, our peace and defense" (109). The leading terms—*authorization, relinquishment, condition of reciprocity*—take on, to the benefit of one individual, all the components of the mutual promise that makes the state rest on a commitment by all to all through language.

If we retrace the path of Hobbes's argument in the opposite direction, the idea that we had at the beginning of this section on Hobbes's challenge has to be nuanced considerably, or to put it a better way, corrected. Starting from naturalist premises—"nature hath made men so equal in faculties of body and mind"—and from the apparently transparent definition of the state of nature as a "war of all against all," the dissociation between right as liberty without limits and the law as bearer of prohibition made room for precepts that we can call para-ethical, in that they imitate the rules of a morality of obligation. What has become, along the way, of the motive of the fear of a violent death? Does it suffice, through the intervention of calculation, to carry the whole edifice of contracts and promises that appears to reconstitute the conditions of a commonwealth? This doubt means that Hobbes's challenge is double: that of the naturalistic, and in this sense, anti-ethical premise, and that of a contractual, para-ethical order.

In my opinion, the fault line lies in the absence of a dimension of alterity in the sequence of concepts culminating in the idea of a covenant. In the first place, the notions of relinquishment of right, of letting go of power, bear the mark of a virtually arbitrary voluntarism. It is the calculation arising from the fear of violent death that suggests those measures that have an appearance of reciprocity, but whose end remains the preservation of one's own power. No expectation coming from others justifies the letting go of such power. The same deficiency is to be seen in the passage from the natural person, that person who is still the author, "he that owneth his words and actions" (101), to the artificial person, that actor who plays the role of another that he is representing. It is not so much the self-identification of this person that is lacking (Locke will supply this), but the part of an alterity that cooperates in his ipseity, as seems to be required by the notions of transfer, contract, and covenant.

It will be left to Leibniz to place others at the heart of this legal relation, with the idea that the object of right "is everything that we do that is important to others and that is in our power" (cited by Zarka, 983). Whether it is a question of "not injuring others, of attributing to each what is his due," or even more "of taking pleasure in the happiness of another," all these Leibnizian formulas attest that it is not only the invention of the subject of rights that is important for our conceptual history of the idea of mutual recognition, but the conjunction between ipseity and alterity in the very idea of right.

Hegel at Jena: *Anerkennung*

I have placed the political philosophy of Hobbes under the rubric of a challenge. The question it poses is whether a political order can be founded on a moral exigency that is as originary as the fear of violent death and the rational calculation that this opposes to vanity, following the summary proposed by Leo Strauss. As Axel Honneth observes at the beginning of his book consecrated to the struggle for recognition, it is Hegel's concept of *Anerkennung*, considered in its whole development, that satisfies this threefold demand.[11]

First, it ensures the link between self-reflection and orientation toward the other. This reciprocal determination of the relation to oneself and intersubjectivity, inherited from Fichte, as we shall discuss, constitutes the principle of Hegel's rejoinder to Hobbes. The ground of political philosophy that found its first articulation in the philosophical fragments Hegel produced at Jena between 1802 and 1807 lies in this duplication of subjectivity.

Second, the dynamism of the whole process proceeds from the negative toward the positive pole, from disregard toward consideration, from injustice toward respect. This second component of the notion of mutual recognition is typically Hegelian, in that we find in it the chief expression of the role assigned generally to negativity in his philosophy, as stated in the well-known preface to *The Phenomenology of Spirit,* the work that closes the period at Jena with a bang. Its irruption onto the practical plane will be indicated by the regenerative power assigned to crime on the juridical plane. Ethical and practical negativity extends throughout the figures of transactions among human beings. In this way, the Hobbesian theme of a struggle to the death will find itself reinserted into a course that is eminently spiritual, in the Hegelian sense of the word.

Third, the theory of recognition draws its systematic aspect from its articulation into hierarchical levels corresponding to specific institutions. From Jena to Berlin, Hegel will continue to diversify this process of the institutionalization of recognition, up to its definitive stabilization in the *Principles of the Philosophy of Right* from 1820 to 1824. Insofar as this hierarchization is immanent in the very process of recognition, it constitutes the rejoinder par excellence to what is artificial in *Leviathan,* which finds its first expression in the distinction between a natural and an artificial person and culminates in the fabrication of the great artifice that is the Leviathan itself. In this regard, the Hegelian concept of *Sittlichkeit,* of the "ethical life," can be taken as the substitute for Hobbes's concept of artifice.

In turn, the specific spheres of recognition distinguished by Hegel do not constitute immutable configurations. They are historical compromises between speculative exigencies and empirical experience, just as in Aristotle's *Politics* the basic conception of justice as equality comes to terms with the limits of a property-based society that excludes slaves, women, children, and even merchants. The same may be said of Hegel's successive elaborations of *Anerkennung.* They open a history of a struggle for recognition that continues to make sense in our own day so long as the institutional structure of recognition remains inseparable from the negative dy-

namism of the whole process, each institutional conquest responding to a specific negative threat. This correlation between the level
of injustice and the level of recognition illustrates the familiar adage
that we are clearer about what is unjust than about what is just. On
this point, indignation, for a political philosophy founded on the
demand for recognition, holds the same role as does the fear of violent death for Hobbes. In this, the inchoative forms of his theory of
recognition in his writings from the Jena period retain their polemical, even provocative, power in contemporary interpretations aiming at actualizing them in favor of a new combination of speculative
exigency and empirical inquiry. But what more than anything else is
preserved in this history of a struggle for recognition is the correlation between a relation to oneself and a relation to the other that
gives the Hegelian *Anerkennung* its recognizable conceptual profile.

We have given the name that fits—the desire to be recognized—to
the motive that from here on will confront the fear of violent death.
In this lapidary expression, the passive form of the verb *recognize* is
essential, inasmuch as each individual's self-recognition, which in
the preceding chapter was placed in the position of a principle, is
henceforth a result of the great dialectic that articulates negativity
and institutionalization in terms of each other.

Having said this, why must we, like other scholars with whom I
associate myself, go back to the fragments from the Jena period
rather than build on the work of Alexandre Kojève, the author of
the well-known *Introduction to the Reading of Hegel* (based on lectures he gave between 1922 and 1930)?[12] These are works that take
the *Phenomenology of Spirit* as their primary reference and thus
give the struggle between master and slave the position we all recognize. My wager was that by confronting the theme of recognition
at its inchoative stage, the reader might hope to see resources of
meaning disclosed that were not exhausted in Hegel's later, more
accomplished books, up to and including *Principles of the Philosophy of Right,* where the theme of recognition and of being recog-

nized has lost not only its density of presence but its subversive virulence. In return, the price to pay is a laborious reading, one that makes nonspecialists dependent on the reconstruction carried out by Hegel experts. For my part, I shall draw on the work of Jacques Taminiaux in his two translations of and commentaries on Hegel's Jena writings: *Système de la Vie éthique* and *Naissance de la philosophie hégélienne de l'État,* as well as on the historical summary that constitutes the first part of Axel Honneth's *Struggle for Recognition,* devoted essentially to the "systematic reactualization" of themes relating to the two fragments dealt with in Taminiaux's books.[13]

The intellectual situation in which Hegel found himself following his youthful writings and those of his Frankfurt period can be characterized by the major heritages that he honors and that are still in many ways ours today.

From Kant comes the idea of individual autonomy as the first moral exigency, without regard for its eventual insertion into historical formations capable of giving it a social and political dimension.

Next, from the confrontation between Machiavelli and Hobbes came the plan to reorient the idea of a struggle, which Hobbes interpreted as a struggle for survival, in the direction of a struggle for reciprocal recognition. In this sense, the struggle for recognition occupies the place held by distrust that the Galileo of politics placed at the center of his trilogy of passions that nourish the war of all against all.

From his precocious admiration for the Greek world Hegel retains, beyond the primacy of the *polis* over the isolated individual, the idea of a living unity between individual and universal freedom. His conviction was that existing customs prefigure the structures of excellence by means of which modern forms of morality and right echo the virtues of Greek ethics. In this regard, the passage from one fragment to another in the Jena period will also be that of the transition from a residual Aristotelianism, by virtue of which the first figures of recognition remain placed under the aegis of nature, to a frankly idealist conception assigning to consciousness the capacity to generate the successive stages of self-differentiation that punctuate the struggle for recognition.

However, it is to Fichte's rereading of the great tradition of natural law that Hegel is most immediately indebted. Without Fichte he would not have been able not only to conceive of substituting the struggle for recognition for that of survival, but also to include the struggle for survival in the dialectic between self-assertion and intersubjectivity. In this sense, we can say that Hegel's writings from the Jena period sanction the unexpected collusion between Hobbes and Fichte.

Is recognition the guiding theme of the *System of Ethical Life?* Posed in these terms, the question at first glance calls for a negative response. The whole speculative apparatus is structured starting from the figure of the absolute identified in ethical terms, which Fichte names Identity; that is, from "customs," to Totality. We are at the heart of a speculative approach far removed from empiricism, a kind of ontotheology in which Fichte and Schelling compete, the latter thinker still finding favor with Hegel in the years 1802–1803, in the name of the preeminence of intuition over conceptuality and in virtue of the absorption of the latter into the former. The key words are *indifference* (in the sense of nondifferentiation), *universality,* and *particularity,* and finally the return to totality. If the theme of the struggle for recognition can claim the patronage of this fragmentary text, it is because of the role assigned to scission in the speculative process. What is more, it is precisely the dynamism of the hierarchized "powers" whereby identity-totality uproots itself from initial indifference to move back to identity-totality which announces the theme that will be ours as we proceed, that of an ordered plurality of models of recognition.

In the fragment considered here, under the rubric A, it is on the plane of "natural" potentialities that the great dramaturgy of ethical life is first enacted. This dramaturgy prefigures absolute ethical life, on the condition of a distance from the unifying instance that justifies the title "Absolute Ethical Life on the Basis of Relation."[14] Unlike the subsequent work that we shall consider later, where the language will definitely be that of Spirit, here the talk is of Nature. We are confronted with a multiplicity of individuals invested with a *Trieb,* a drive, who are driven by the work of returning to the Absolute. The degrees of satisfaction of this or that impulsive relation lead to a hierarchy of "potentiality," in which we encounter successively: natural need, work, the difference between desire and enjoyment, the articulation of work beyond taking possession, and the annihilation of the state of enjoyment in affective possession. Contemporary readers took pleasure in noting the place of honor assigned to love, through the multiple figures of the family tie and in proximity with the idea of a natural potentiality. We find under rubric A the core of a first model of mutual recognition in this course with its multiple articulations. "Potentiality" is still described in positive terms, but the shadow of negative natural forces is projected by the figures of the necessity of death, of the violence of the elements, and the confrontations among human beings and of human beings with nature.

The same figures having to do with ethical life "on the basis of relation" reappear under rubric B from the point of view of the dominant note of universality and the rule of law, which in turn generates a specific negativity to which a subsequent section will be devoted under the heading "Transgression." With exchange, the contract, we can speak of recognition of the person. Indeed, this is the first occurrence of the word *recognition* in this fragment. Taminiaux comments: "This is why the recognition of the individual as alive—what the recognition of the *person* is—is the recognition of the other as an 'absolute concept,' a 'free being,' a 'possibility of being the contrary of himself in relation to some determination,' but this is still a formal recognition which lacks the moment of difference. It is this moment that introduces the relation of *domination and servitude,* a potentiality higher than recognition because real, whereas the preceding was only ideal and formal."[15]

The expression returns with the third potentiality. The first one was that of the power of nature, the second that of "infinity and ideality in form or in relation" (*System of Ethical Life,* 116). We read: "The third level is the indifference of the preceding ones; that relation of exchange and the recognition of possession, which therefore is of property—and hitherto had a bearing on the single individual, here become a totality, but always within individuality itself; or the second relation is taken up into universality, the concept of the first" (123–124). The uneasy stability of this recognition, contemporary on the speculative plane with the relation of domination and servitude (whose fortune we know in the *Phenomenology*), is underscored by the expression "unequal life," which the text describes as "the relation in which the indifferent and free has power over the different" (125).

Hegel does not end his inquiry into the potentialities of nature, however, without giving a second chance to the positive figures of natural being already mentioned, taken up again under the heading of universality at work. In this way in the family "the totality of nature and all the foregoing are united" (127). This truth comes about through the child, of whom it is said that he "is the absolute, the rationality of the relationship; he is what is enduring and everlasting, the totality which produces itself once again as such" (128). And a little farther on: "Might and the understanding, the differentiating characters of the parents, stand in an inverse relation with the youth and force of the child, and these two aspects of life fly from and follow one another and are external to one another" (129).

Something like a thunderclap breaks out in the text segment titled "The Negative or Freedom or Transgression [*Verbrechen*]" inserted between "the ethical life on the basis of relation," which we have been discussing, and "the ethical life." By indicating the opposition to the ascending movement, this moment reveals what was at work in the work of difference, namely, annihilation *(Vernichtung)*, the negative of the natural ethical life. The effect of transgression or crime is that it "negates reality in its specific determinacy, but it fixes this negation" (131). It suppresses, without surpassing itself within the totality. The countermovement to which it gives rise—vengeance, internalized as remorse—participates in this fixation, which recalls that of slavery, but in a register already marked by right—whence the successive figures of barbarism, plundering, and subjection, the figure that most calls for our attention in the political perspective that finally prevails, as being the wound to honor that touches the person as a whole. But it is evoked under the heading of crime. The contemporary reader, avid to learn what finally merits being called the absolute ethical life, that is, one freed of the scaffolding of natural potentialities, beginning with the *Trieb,* and culminating in the family, finds himself confronted with the unique bearer of this absolute ethical life: the people. The idea of an ethical absolute appears in the people *(Volk)* and finds its intuition there. The people and religion bear witness to the absorption of conceptuality into intuition. The discourse then speeds onward, shifting from the static point of view of the constitution of the people to the dynamic point of view of its governance. It is not a question of recognition in the speculation on "the system at rest" (146). Hegel's discourse covers a sequence of virtues assigned to distinct instances *(Stände).* These are bravery, uprightness, and finally mutual trust, where the relation to servitude is abolished. Recognition can be named only at the point of the passage from the state of rest to the dynamic one that incarnates the act of governing *(Regierung).* The privileged moment is situated between the first system of government under the heading of need and what "exceeds it" in terms of procured satisfaction, and the third system, that of discipline, which is hardly detailed. This interval is that of the "system of justice," "the public authority as thinking and conscious, is the government's administration of justice" (174). Property relations become mutual relations only within this framework: "I recognize the other man's competence to possess property; but force and theft deny this recognition. They are compulsive, affecting the whole; they cancel freedom and the reality of being universal and recognized. If crime did not give the lie to this recognition, it could equally well surrender to another, to the universal, what it accomplishes" (175).

Returning to our initial question whether the *System of Ethical Life* can be taken as an actual antecedent of the theory of the struggle for recognition, we can nuance in the following way what we have said. On the one hand, we can detect the presence of the word *recognition* at two precise moments, the first linked to the formality of right, principally in terms of exchange, the second linked to the governing of a people under the aegis of justice. These are both intermediary moments in a hierarchy of potentialities. On the other hand, it is plausible to assign the patronage of the theme of recognition to the whole dynamics of the essay, inasmuch as the person is contemporary with right, but also because public liberty remains faced with the negative challenge to which Hegel devotes a distinct sequence wherein liberty is associated with transgression or crime. In this sense, recognition is never referred to apart from its negative shadow: crime as the refusal of recognition. This sequence is itself in an intermediary position in this long fragment.

This being said, what keeps Hegel's problematic distant from our own is the speculative reference, with no empirical counterpart, to identity, totality—along with its corollaries: intuition versus conceptuality, indifference versus difference, universality versus particularity. It is this form of ontotheology that prevents human plurality from appearing as the unsurpassable reference for the relations of mutuality, punctuated by violence, that Hegel considers, from the levels of the drive and of love up to that of mutual trust within the heart of the totality of a people. This is a course similar to the one proposed by Axel Honneth, but in a configuration he will call postmetaphysical, following Habermas. In this configuration human plurality will occupy the place of Identity and Totality.

Accompanied by my two mentors, Jacques Taminiaux and Axel Honneth, I want now to turn to the second important text from 1805 to 1806 of Hegel's Jena period. Its editors title it the *Realphilosophie,* because it constitutes the part of the total system of philosophy in which the Spirit is grasped in its real as opposed to its ideal phase.[16] Let us begin by emphasizing this reference to Spirit at the expense of what in the earlier text remained dependent on a quasi-Aristotelian concept of nature, which becomes the distinct theme of a philosophy of nature as the first "real" stage of the philosophy of Spirit. It will therefore be a matter of the coming—or rather return—of Spirit to itself, under the heading of the major distinction between Ideality and Reality. How does Spirit render itself "equal to itself" in making itself other than itself? We are not surprised to rediscover interlocking sequences of levels similar to those of the system of ethical life. But now nature figures in each instance as what is "suppressed." This setting the theme of nature at a distance is particularly interesting for my project, which has from the beginning of this chapter been seeking a rejoinder to Hobbes through the promotion of an originary moral philosophy. Hegel, in this sense, chooses to combat Hobbes in assuming with him that "it is necessary to go beyond nature." His rejoinder to Hobbes consists entirely in the course of moments of the realization of Spirit and the description of the return of Spirit to itself in its ipseity. The state will appear at the end of this long detour and return. As for the theme of recognition, it will not be, as it will become in post-Hegelian philosophies of human finitude and plurality, the dynamic energy behind the conquest of mutuality, but it does indicate certain noteworthy phases of Spirit's return to itself. In any case, it is not only named but also articulated with a precision that was still lacking in the system of ethical life. This is sufficient to make its treatment in the *Realphilosophie* a genuine precedent and, if I may put it this way, a speculative source for contemporary reflections dedicated to this theme.

In a broad sense of the word *politics,* we can say that Hegel definitively inscribed the theme of recognition at the heart of political philosophy. His break with Hobbes will be, as we have said, in line with a kind of ontotheology, indicated here by the Spirit in its Idea, which says that the way in which the Spirit finds itself in its other remains fundamentally a relation of a self to itself. In other words, Spirit makes itself other starting from its relation to itself. The steps in its "realization" nonetheless continue to be an unsurpassable speculative resource for Hegel.

Three parts can be distinguished in this work.

The Spirit according to Its Concept

What is at issue is a speculative psychology centered on the mind, then upon the will. It is in the discussion of the will that the theme of recognition appears in the first part, a discussion marked by the ego's mastery over its images, by the positing of the self in the internalization that takes place through the skill that makes it master names, and through the prevailing rule of conceptualization. This course of the will has to do with its conclusion *(Beschluss)* and its argumentation *(Schluss),* or "syllogism." In this context, we rediscover drive, the *Trieb,* its lacking something, and its satisfaction. We also find the tool, in its singularity and its universal capacity to transform things; love; male and female; the family as the elective setting for education, in conjunction with work; and above all, the child, that third person in whom the parents "see their love—their self-conscious unity as self-conscious" (Rauch, 109). It is in this moment of love, the family, and the child that Honneth will discern the first of his three models of recognition, thanks to an extrapolation that will allow for abandoning the absolute speculative point of view. For Hegel at Jena, however, recognition comes up with relations having to do with right. Right is reciprocal recognition. His relation to Hobbes is quite complicated here. Hegel sees the determination of right in Hobbes as coming from outside the individual. But how can it be seen as proceeding from the not-right, after the break with the idea of "ethical life on the basis of relation," still marked by its reference to nature? It is within a philosophy of the same that recognition occurs. For Hegel, notes Taminiaux, it is a question of following in the content itself a movement toward the right of recognition. A state of nature, the juridical state, and recognition are neither mixed together nor dissociated from one another. Hegel makes the moment of recognition coincide with the passage from taking possession to legitimation. This latter signifies the reversal of the relation of excluding the other. And this is what recognition means: "Such recognition must come about" from the interweaving of love and right. "The individuals are *love,* this *being-recognized* without the opposition of the will—(i.e., wherein each would be the entire 'conclusion,' [and] wherein they enter into only as characters, not as free wills). Such a recognition is to come about. There must become for them what they [already] are in themselves. Their being for one another is the beginning of it" (114). Some wonderful passages about the interweaving of love and right are worth citing here. Speaking of the object, in general, as "itself this creation of right, i.e., the relation of *recognition,*" the text goes on to say: "In recognition, the Self ceases to be this individual; it exists by right in recognition, i.e., it is no longer [immersed in] its immediate existence. The one who is recognized is recognized as *immediately* counting as such [*geltend*], through his *being*—but *this being is itself generated from the concept;* it is recognized being [*anerkanntes Seyn*]. Man is necessarily recognized and necessarily gives recognition. This necessity is not his own, not that of our thinking in contrast to the content. As recognizing, man is himself the movement [of recognition], and this movement is what negates [*hebt auf*] his natural state: he is recognition; the natural merely *is*, it is not the *spiritual* aspect" (111).

Everything turns on the moment of possession sublated into right. Recognition equalizes what offense had made unequal. It proceeds from the overcoming of the exclusion (116), at the price of the assumed danger of the ruse. We find the same sequence again in "the life-and-death struggle" as in the earlier text. At this price, "this knowing will is now *universal*. It is the state of *being recognized*." Opposed to itself in the form of universality, it is Being, actuality in general, and the individual, the subject, is the *person*. The will of individuals is the universal will, and the universal will is individual. "It is the totality of ethical life [*Sittlichkeit*] in general, immediate, yet [as] Right" (118).

Actual Spirit

The second part of Hegel's text is titled "Actual Spirit" in opposition to the abstraction of the intelligence and the will. With recognition, we pass from the faculty to the actualization. This is why mention is made straightaway of being-recognized, or more precisely of "the element of universal recognition" (119). The effective reality of the universal succeeds the uprooting from nature. The dynamism of this speculative mode compels once again the traversal of these levels, as if we were passing through the same sites, but at a different altitude: desire, and no longer drive; machine, and no longer tool; property, and no longer possession. "In the possession being has the unspiritual significance of *my* having, as this individual having. Here, however, the *being recognized* [enters]—the *being* of the possession, such that the thing is and I am, and the thing is grasped as in the Self. Here being is the universal Self, and the having is the mediation through another, i.e., it is universal. Value is what is universal [here]; the movement, as perceptible, is the exchange. This same universality is mediation as conscious movement. Property is thus an immediate *having,* mediated *through being recognized. That is, its existence* is [shaping, recollection, value]—is the spiritual essence" (122–123).

Here is the place for the contract, which makes being-recognized coincide with the will, both the individual and the common will. Next comes crime, in the breaking of the contract. It is the person, not the property, that is injured—"my honor," not the thing. This is why the sanction raises itself above vengeance to justice, once it undertakes to restore not "my generally injured self, but rather my injured self [as] recognized" (129). The person is the name for this injured being, recognized and restored (ibid.).

In these terms, the opening of Hegel's second part links up with the conclusion of the first part. An immediate being-recognized corresponds to actuality in the advent of recognition in the abstraction of speculative philosophy. I shall not continue my reading of this text beyond this point: this immediate being-recognized follows from the rule of law, which binds together autonomous beings, whether in terms of marriage, the industrious management of wealth and poverty, or the legal system and the trial as execution of the law. Room is also left for the constituting act of "the universal will" (153) by which a state is established.

Constitution

Does recognition really still have a place in this theory of the constituting act of the State? With the dominant problematic of power *(Macht)* another semantics is set in place, one that is centered on the term *alienation (Entäusserung),* in the sense of a transfer and giving up of possession. In one sense, in section 3, titled "Constitution," there is a prolongation of the being-recognized from section 2, as the persistence of the vocabulary of being-recognized testifies.[17] Nevertheless, the semantics of recognition fitted better with the transition phase of mutual-exchange operations. With the political problematic, the emphasis is no longer on reciprocal action, but on the hierarchical relation between the allegedly universal will and the individual will. This is why Hegel has to take a detour through the foundation of tyranny, the Machiavellian moment. Machiavelli's *Prince* is written from the perspective that in "the constituting [*in der Constituierung*] of the state, in general, what is called assassination, fraud, cruelty, etc., carries no sense of evil but rather a sense of that which is reconciled with itself." The problematic of recognition seems entirely left behind: "Through tyranny we have the immediate alienation [*Entäusserung*] of the individual's actual will . . . this is education toward obedience" (155–156). The only thing equivalent to recognition in this context would be "trust": "the individual likewise knows his Self, therein, as his essence." In this sense, the individual "finds himself sustained in it . . . through [some] connections and arrangements" (157). Hegel does not seem to regret the loss of Greek freedom which was and still is envied (155), at a time when the beautiful public life was "the common morality." The harsh law of the modern age must be taken as a "higher principle," that is, as an education through "externalization" (160). The vocabulary of being-recognized will reappear a last time only in the final course, that of the "absolutely free spirit," through art, religion, and science. The absolutely free spirit, which has taken back into itself its determinations, will henceforth produce a new world, a world that has the figure of itself, where its work lies within itself, and where it accedes to intuition of the self as itself (173). Hence it can be said that "being-recognized [*Anerkanntseyn*] is the spiritual element," with all the reticence and reservations that go with the dissemination of the arts, the finitude of figures, such as the statues of god (175). In absolute religion only God is the depth of spirit certain of itself: in that very way God is "actual selfhood. He is a *Person,* having a common spatial and temporal existence—and this individual is what all individuals are"

(176). The vocabulary is no longer either that of recognition or that of alienation, but that of reconciliation. With this barely sketched-out philosophy, the activity of spirit as world history is announced. As the final sentences of this work state, "in it, this [antithesis] is overcome—namely, that only in themselves are nature and spirit one being [*Wesen*]. Spirit becomes the knowing of them [and thereby unites them]" (183).

Systematic Renewals of Hegel's Argument

The part that follows is devoted to the systematic renewal of the Hegelian theme of *Anerkennung*. Let me begin by acknowledging my debt to Axel Honneth. I have borrowed more from him than just from the title of part 2 of his book.[18] I want to think of this section as a dialogue with him, where my contribution will run from some complementary to a few critical considerations, which will in turn open the way to an argument directed against the exclusive emphasis on the idea of a struggle, in favor of a search for more peaceful experiences of recognition. The final section of this chapter is devoted to this argument and this search.

The renewal undertaken by Honneth draws its strength of conviction from the equilibrium it maintains between fidelity to the Hegelian theme and rejection of Hegel's metaphysics of the absolute during the Jena period, influenced by Schelling and also by Fichte. I agree with his accusation regarding a monological approach, directed against a philosophy of consciousness where it is the self that fundamentally is set over against itself in differentiating itself. Like Honneth, I too start from the unsurpassable character of human plurality in all intersubjective transactions, whether it is a question of struggle or of something other than a struggle. What Honneth retains from Hegel is the project of founding a social theory with a normative sense. This theory is meant to serve as a rejoinder to Hobbes, inasmuch as the struggle proceeds from moral motives capable of occupying the place held by the triad of rivalry, distrust, and glory in the description of the alleged state of nature in *Leviathan*. I accept the essence of this project. In my own vocabulary, it is a question of seeking in the development of conflictual interactions the source for a parallel enlarging of the individual capacities discussed in my second chapter under the heading of the capable human being out to conquer his ipseity. The course of self-recognition ends in mutual recognition.

Honneth's strategy rests on a combination of procedures. First, there is the pairing of a speculative argument with an empirically based theorizing about interactions among individuals. Honneth borrows from George Herbert Mead the model of a social genesis of the identifying of the "I." I see this pairing of Hegel and Mead as the model for an interweaving of speculative conceptualization and the test of experience. And I shall propose several variations on it. What is most important is that the speculative structure should keep the theme of recognition from slipping into banality, as today is more and more the case. But there is also a second aspect to Honneth's strategy. From his reconstruction of Hegel's Jena writings in the first part of his book, he borrows the idea of an interconnected sequence of "three models of intersubjective recognition," placed successively under the aegis of love, law, and social respect. I shall adopt this tripartite scheme, which has the principal advantage of framing the juridical with structures that both anticipate and go beyond it. In the third place, Honneth has these three half-speculative, half-empirical models correspond to three figures of refusal of recognition which are capable of providing a moral motive in a negative sense for the social struggles that the latter part of his work takes into consideration. This moral motivation for struggle has to be reconciled with individual or group interests in order to give the practice of such social struggles a complete explanation. This last component of Honneth's strategy is only sketched, but here is where a comparison with other such enterprises I shall briefly discuss may turn out to helpful. For the most part, however, I shall concentrate on the correlation between the three models of recognition inherited from Hegel and the negative forms of disregard. This comparison strikes me as the most important contribution of Honneth's book to the theory of recognition in its post-Hegelian phase. The three models of recognition provide the speculative structure, while the negative sentiments give flesh and blood to the struggle for recognition. In return, a structural analysis of the figures of refusal of recognition would not be possible if the normative demands arising from the successive models of recognition did not give rise to expectations whose disappointment corresponds in scope to those demands.

My additional comments will fit within this framework, while opening some new avenues of exploration along the way. The critical considerations I have mentioned will have to do with the third model of recognition Hegel places under the heading "The People" and, more precisely, the state and its "constituting act." I shall not, however, undertake a discussion of Hegel's political philosophy having to do with the structure of the state, just as I stopped short in my discussion of Hobbes at the threshold of the question of sovereignty linked to the emergence of a "mortal God." Hence the following section will be a discussion centered on the very idea of struggle, coming from Hegel, and seek to round out the problem of struggle with an evocation of peaceful experiences of recognition. If this discussion does not reach its goal, it will at least afford us a glimpse of the defeat of the refusal of recognition.

Love and the Struggle for Recognition

The first model of recognition, placed under the heading of love, covers a range that encompasses erotic relations, friendship, and family ties "constituted by strong emotional attachments among a small number of people" (95). What is at issue here is a prejuridical degree of reciprocal recognition, where "subjects mutually confirm each other with regard to their concrete needs and thereby recognize each other as needy creatures" (95). The Hegelian formula of "knowing oneself likewise in its other" finds its first application here.

In undertaking his renewal, Honneth seeks in the psychoanalytic theory of object relations an empirical complement to Hegelian speculation as it applies to this first model of recognition. Honneth is particularly interested in those successors of Freud who situated the initial structures of conflict at the level of the emotional forms of attachment of the mother-infant type that precede intrapsychic conflicts of the "ego-id" type. He points especially to the importance of "interpersonal disturbances in the process of the child's detachment" (97). Not only does adult experience preserve traces of these first conflicts—it enriches the schema. It is a question, at different ages, in particular at the stage of maturation where love reaches an adult level, of going beyond the state of absolute dependence that gives rise to a fusional libidinal tie. Just as the young child must face the test of the absence of the mother, thanks to which she regains her own capacity for independence, if for his part the child is to attain the autonomy suitable at his age, in the same way love relationships in adulthood face the test of separation, whose emotionally costly benefit is the capacity to be alone. And this grows in proportion to the partners' confidence in the permanence of the invisible bond that develops in the alternation between presence and absence. Between the two poles of emotional fusion and self-affirmation in solitude, relations of relative dependence are established, over the course of lovers' shared history, that suffice to destroy fantasies of omnipotence carried over from earliest childhood. In this regard, the detachment acquired at the price of many disillusions can be taken as the counterpart of the confidence that keeps a couple together. This maintained order, in the strongest sense of the word, is supported by mediations, principally from language and culture, that recall the "transitional objects" of childhood discussed by D. W. Winnicott. Honneth cites one text from this author that evokes the continuity between those transitional objects so strongly imbued with the spirit of play and the cultural models that people the space of separation that distance and absence open up between adult lovers.[19] We can say that lovers recognize each other by recognizing themselves in models of identification that can be held in common.

Simone Weil extends to forms of friendship the potentially conflictual configuration that erotic love implants in the depths of the unconscious and its drives. (Did Hegel not already at the beginning of the nineteenth century give the name *Trieb* to this power more primitive than desire, in that it is the desire of the desire of the other?) She writes: "There are two forms of friendship: meeting and separation. They are indissoluble. Both of them contain the same good, the unique good, which is friendship. . . . As both forms contain the same good, they are both equally good. . . . Lovers or friends desire two things. The one is to love each other so much that they enter into each other and only make one being. The other is to love each other so much that, having half the globe between them, their union will not be diminished in the slightest degree."[20]

These magnificent lines where, as in Aristotle, friendship is raised to the level of the good—the "unique good," Weil writes—describe the phase of maturity where the empirical forms of love resonate with the speculative structure received from Hegel. We may even speak in this regard of a dialectic between binding and unbinding that is common to both the speculative and the empirical features of love. The unbinding speaks of the suffering of absence and distance, the test of disillusionment; the binding speaks of the strength of spirit that is embodied in the capacity to be alone. But it is confidence in the permanence of a reciprocal solicitude that makes such unbinding a salutary tribulation.

What, then, would be the form of disregard corresponding to this first model of recognition? If the correlation proposed by Honneth between three models of recognition and three of disregard has any heuristic value, it does not seem as though threats to physical integrity, all kinds of physical abuse—torture or rape—"that destroy a person's basic self-confidence" (133), will suffice to delimit this first type of disregard. Honneth proposes here more complex kinds of threats than those relating to mere physical integrity. The normative idea in the model of recognition under the rubric of love, which conveys the extent of the disappointment characteristic of this first type of humiliation, seems to be more completely identified by the idea of approbation. Friends, lovers—to reflect Simone Weil's calculated indecision—mutually approve each other's existence. It is this approbation that makes friendship the "unique good" Weil speaks of, as precious in the state of separation as in togetherness. Humiliation, experienced as the withdrawal or refusal of such approbation, touches everyone at the prejuridical level of his or her "being-with" others. The individual feels looked down on from above, even taken as insignificant. Deprived of approbation, the person is as if nonexistent.

It is impossible to cross the threshold from this first to the second model of recognition unless we take into account the constraints and regulations that, without as such being formally juridical in nature, have to be regarded as institutions, in the true sense of the word, even though they are rich in possible juridical developments. Does Hegel not devote a long discussion to the institutions appropriate to the broad affective realm that he places under the heading of love? This is the case for the parent-child and husband-wife relations, and even of the family itself seen as the educator for our first point of initiation into culture. Unlike the city or the state, the family constitutes a form of living together, whose figure is the household, that brings together only a limited number of people.

In the family the vertical ties of filiation intersect with the horizontal ties of conjugality. As Françoise Héritier reminds us at the beginning of her *Masculin/Féminin*, three unvarying factors structure our being-in-the-world through the family: each of us is born from the union of a man and a woman (whatever fertilization techniques, with the exception of cloning, may apply); each of us is born as part of a set of possible siblings; finally, the birth order of those siblings is fixed.[21]

The conjugal bond, whatever juridical status it may claim, is the obligatory place of interchange between these vertical and horizontal relations. It is itself subject to a constraint imposed on all the socially accepted variants of conjugality: the incest prohibition. This prohibition inscribes sexuality in the cultural dimension, by setting up the difference between the social bond and that of consanguinity. It is no exaggeration to say that the constraint linked to this prohibition is the tacit presupposition of the Hegelian theme of desire for the other, inasmuch as the demand that distinguishes desire from a simple drive can be held to be the affective benefit of this constraint.

I want to concentrate on the phenomenon of filiation within the institutional framework roughly laid out here, and to place the following remarks under the heading "Recognizing Oneself in One's Lineage."

What is striking at first glance about the genealogical system is the position of the ego at the base of a family tree that divides into two lines: paternal and maternal, which divide again in turn as we retrace the succession of generations, in each instance splitting lines that are themselves already double, as patri- and matrilineal (with, along each line, sibling relations, which are themselves implied in such vertical lineage relations).[22] Different names are assigned to these different places: father, mother, grandfather, grandmother, uncle, aunt, nephew, and so on, according to the countable degrees. It is in this system of places that one can read the degrees of kinship for which marriage is excluded by virtue of the incest prohibition—sexual relations between father and daughter, mother and son, and brother and sister being forbidden first and foremost.

If we shift from this external perspective to the meaning experienced by the ego in this system of places, what first draws our attention is that one is, by the very fact of being born, assigned a fixed place in one's lineage. This, before any egological self-awareness, is what confers an identity on me in the eyes of civil institutions, the identity of being the son or daughter of . . . In thinking about the meaning of this civil identity for myself, I discover with astonishment that before being able to think about myself or wanting to be a subject of perception, action, imputation, or rights, I was and still remain this "object," this *res* that Pierre Legendre, in the title of his book, terms "that inestimable object of transmission." I am struck by the epithet *inestimable*. My birth made me a priceless object, something outside ordinary commerce. The parental project from which I issued—whatever it may have been—transformed the static aspect of the genealogical table into an instituting dynamic, one indicated by the word *transmission*—a transmission of life, itself instituted as human by the genealogical principle; transmission of the family legend; transmission of an inheritance of commercial and noncommercial goods; a transmission finally summed up by the assigning of a name: I am called . . . , my name is . . . It is this contraction of a transmitted treasure into the naming process that authorizes our speaking for the first time of recognition in terms of a lineage. I was recognized as a son or daughter—whatever family, civil, or religious ritual may have marked the recognition of which I was the object for the first time. The Romans had an appropriate institution for this event, adoption, which authorized, in the true sense of the word, this admirable performative sentence: "Titus shall be my heir." In one sense, every birth welcomed is an adoption, not only by the father, but also by the mother, as soon as she has accepted or chosen to "keep" this fetus become "her" baby and to give birth to it. Both these adoptions were authorized by the system transmitting a family name and choosing a given name for me. In return for this authorization to name me, I am authorized to continue the transmission in my turn, in the name of those who made me their heir, and to occupy when the time comes the place of the father or the mother. In short, because I was recognized as the son or daughter of . . . , I recognize myself as such; and I *am*, as such, *this* inestimable object of transmission. Thanks to this progressive internalizing of the genealogical perspective, the ego, zero function on the table of places, becomes actual when such transmission is experienced as mutual recognition, as both paternal and filial.

Thanks to this act of recognizing oneself in one's lineage, it is possible to go in two opposite directions: backward, from birth, and forward toward the permissions and constraints that the genealogical principle exercises over the whole course of a life of desire.

Reflecting on birth is difficult. Anyone who recognizes him- or herself in his or her lineage has already been born. What we have been speaking of is a reflection on this being already born. What birth proposes, on this side of the growing blurriness of early childhood memories, is the enigma of an origin, which cannot be reduced to an explanation in terms of a beginning. The beginning of life was preceded by biological antecedents, desires, perhaps by a project we might call paternal—all things that go beyond the simple awareness of having been born. The beginning refers back to something before it. An origin is something else again—it only refers to itself. The appearance of a new being is in this sense unprecedented: this being, I. We speak of children as the flesh of their parents existing in another being. Confronted with birth as an origin, speculative thought does not know how to choose: between the contingency of the event (I might not have been born or might have been someone else) and the necessity of existing (it is because I am here, in an undeniable way, that I can ask questions). Near the end of *The Human Condition*, Hannah Arendt writes: "The miracle that saves the world, the realm of human affairs, from its normal, 'natural' ruin is ultimately the fact of natality [*Gebürtigkeit*] in which the faculty of action is ontologically rooted."[23] Arendt can thus speak of birth as a "miracle" (perhaps as a retort to Heidegger's being-toward-death). In this way, we find ourselves at the unfathomable origin of "that inestimable object of transmission" that each of us is at birth. We escape this speculative vertigo only by replacing ourselves and our parents in the sequence of generations, under the heading "Recognizing Oneself in One's Lineage."[24]

If we now proceed forward from our awareness of having been born, we have to acknowledge the genetic principle in terms of its polar opposition to the incest drive, insofar as this latter creates an absence of difference. Legendre, whose analysis interweaves juridical and psychoanalytical considerations, says that the genealogical principle "objects to the incest drive." This objection is foundational, in that its prohibition orders kinship relations and sets up distinct, identified places and as a consequence recognized relationships of filiation. In ordering conjugality, the genealogical principle organizes filiation. But to reach its target, the objection to incest has to strike down the fantasy of omnipotence, itself closely akin to the "narcissistic capture." In trying to kiss his own image, Narcissus reveals "man caught up in his desire" (541). If the incest drive were not so deeply grounded in the operation of desire, and if this drive did not threaten the entire genealogical system with destruction, we would not understand why incest could have been elevated in myth and tragedy to the rank of the most horrible crime, alongside its corollary, parricide. Nor would we understand why it required the lucidity of a Tiresias, the blind seer, to uncover, denounce, and charge Oedipus. To be sure, in the delayed aftermath of the tragedy of Oedipus at Colonus, common sense supplies the old man with excuses, but it thereby strips his ancient crime of its mythic and tragic dimension, and at the same time conceals the antagonistic relation between the genealogical principle and incest. It is only within the aura of horror aroused by Oedipus's crime that conjugality, itself instituted in one form or another as a kind of long-suffering and faithfulness, can reveal its deep meaning as mediating between the genealogical principle and the incest drive, between the distinction that comes with order and confusion based in fantasy. This does not prevent conjugality, in turn, from unfolding its own conflictual aspects, principally at the point where erotic love intersects with conjugal affection. In any culture, erotic love may remain rebellious toward the institution and toward the discipline of desire that this institution tries to establish. Yet it remains the case that conjugal affection makes possible the parental project that enables those involved to think of themselves not as mere progenitors, but as the parents of their children. The filial recognition that gives its meaning to *self-recognition through filiation* corresponds to this mutual recognition between the parents.[25]

The Struggle for Recognition on the Juridical Plane

At this second level, between that of love and that of social esteem, is where any "systematic renewal" of Hegel's speculative suggestions from the Jena writings most markedly distances itself from its source of inspiration. It is easy to understand why. For Hegel, the question posed by the juridical relation was largely dominated by his rejoinder to Hobbes, insofar as in *Leviathan* it is from the state, conceived of as an entity external to conflict within the state of nature, that every process of institutionalization receives its legitimacy. In seeking in this state of nature a properly moral reason for moving beyond the war of all against all, Hegel discerns the first features of being-recognized on the juridical plane in the access to legal possession of material goods—in short, in the contractual form of exchange. The dynamics of conflict relating to this type of recognition proceeds from the breaking of a contract and the response to it, consisting in legal restraint, in coercion. Thus it was crime that revealed the nonrecognition characteristic of this type of subversion of the individual. It also provoked a new evaluation of the offense as harm done to a person in his or her universal dimension. It was in this sense that Hegel could speak of a struggle for recognition pertaining to the juridical relation in general in the process of formation of the "universal will." For me, crime as a catalyst must not be lost from view in the confrontation between the individual will and the universal will in the modern era. This analysis, in effect, places the emphasis on the material conditions for what we call equality of chances in gains made through the rule of law. A kind of nonrecognition cannot fail to attach to the institution of the law. In this regard, in some of the contemporary forms of discourse brought together by Axel Honneth some new figures of disregard will take over the role played by crime in Hegel's Jena writings.

But first we need to speak of the ambitions that attach to the juridical relation in conjunction with those modes of recognition pertaining to the sphere of love; so we made the connection between emancipation when it comes to fusional affective ties and confidence in the permanence of a reciprocal relationship between partners. A new logic is now at work. On the one hand, the predicate *free* takes the place of the "capacity to be alone" on the affective level—"free" in the sense of the rationality presumed to be equal in every person considered in his or her juridical dimension. On the other hand, "respect" takes the place of trust. It is stamped with a claim to universality that goes beyond the proximity of ties of affection. Juridical recognition can also be characterized in the following terms: "We can only come to understand ourselves as the bearers of rights when we know, in turn, what various normative obligations we must keep vis-à-vis others" (*Structure of Recognition,* 108). In this sense, recognition intends two things: the other person and the norm. As regards the norm, it signifies, in the lexical sense of the word, to take as valid, to assert validity; as regards the person, recognition means identifying each person as free and equal to every other person. Thus juridical recognition adds to self-recognition in terms of capacities (in the sense considered in my earlier chapter) new capacities stemming from the conjunction between the universal validity of the norm and the singularity of persons. These two dimensions of juridical recognition thus consist in the connection between the enlarging of the sphere of rights recognized as belonging to persons and the enriching of the capacities that these subjects recognize in themselves. This enlarging and enriching are the product of struggles that mark the inscription in history of these two associated processes.[26]

As much as we may have set aside the cultural history of conflicts having to do with the affections, just so much is the historical evolution important on the juridical plane, insofar as it is an enlarging of the sphere of rights and an enriching of individual capacities that are at issue on this level of the struggle for recognition. It is also on this plane that the notion of a passage to modernity is not just inevitable, but inseparable from the gains we shall consider.[27]

In this context, the concept of respect *(Achtung),* which comes from Kant, offers an indispensable guidepost. For Kant, respect is the one motive that practical reason imprints directly on affective sensibility. In this sense, it stands outside history. But it has been thinkers open to the historical character of the passage to modernity who have been able to reinsert this notion of respect into a history of rights as well as of the rule of law. No one can dismiss this history of moral knowledge relative to the juridical obligations we have toward autonomous persons, any more than the interpretation of situations where persons are allowed to claim these rights. In this respect, the return to the Aristotelian notion of *phronesis* is indicative of the contemporary recourse to the category of an "applied hermeneutics," whenever it is a question of interpreting situations where the correlations can be borne out between a recognition of validity on the plane of norms and the recognition of capacities on the human plane. The struggles for juridical recognition stem from this mixed understanding of normative constraints and situations in which persons exercise their competencies.

The enlarging of the normative sphere of rights, to which in a moment the extension of capacities of the juridical person will apply, can be observed in two directions: on the one hand, on the plane of an enumeration of personal rights defined by their content; on the other, on the plane of the attribution of these rights to new categories of individuals or groups.

As regards the enumeration of such personal rights, I shall adopt the division into civil, political, and social rights, following Robert Alexy, Talcott Parsons, and Honneth himself.[28] As Honneth puts it, "The first category refers to negative rights that protect a person's life, liberty, and property from unauthorized state interference; the second category refers to the positive rights guaranteeing a person the opportunity to participate in the processes of public will-formation; and the third category, finally, refers to the similarly positive rights that ensure a person's fair share in the distribution of basic goods" (*Structure of Recognition*, 115). I would add that this three-fold division offers an excellent conceptual grid for analyses and discussions about human rights. The struggle is older when it comes to civil rights. It dates from the eighteenth century and is far from over. As for the establishment of political rights, it dates from the nineteenth century but continued into the twentieth in the framework of debates over the representative character of democratic governments, once the battle had been won concerning the sovereignty of the people and the expression of this sovereignty through elections. But the larger problem in the twentieth century was the opening of the question of social rights relating to a fair share in the distribution of marketable and nonmarketable goods on a planetary scale. In this respect, what the citizens of every country suffer most from is the painful contrast between the equal attribution of rights and the unequal distribution of such goods. A theory of justice like that of John Rawls finds one of its raisons d'être in the formulating of the rules for a fair distribution in nonegalitarian societies, the only ones we know. If these social rights principally concern education, healthcare, and the guarantee of a decent standard of living, then economic security appears to be the material means for the exercise of every other right.

As a result of this distribution of personal rights, the corresponding acquisition of competencies on the personal plane makes specific forms of disrespect appear relative to the claims that a person may expect to see satisfied by society. In this regard, the humiliation that relates to a denial of civil rights is different from the frustration that relates to not being able to participate in the shaping of the public will, which is again different from the feeling of exclusion that results from the refusal of any access to the most basic goods. As a refusal of recognition, the loss of respect that a person feels in each case takes a different affective form in each case. This is the place to recall that negative feelings are important impulses in the struggle for recognition. In this regard, indignation constitutes a structure of transition between the experience of disregard, felt as anger, and the choice to become a participant in the struggle for recognition. The most telling thing about indignation has to do with the unbearable contrast, just referred to, between the equal attribution of rights and an unequal distribution of goods in societies like our own, which seem condemned to pay for progress in productivity in every domain through a noticeable increase in inequalities. But indignation can disarm as well as mobilize people. In this regard, the idea of responsibility draws one of its meanings from this passage from humiliation, felt as a blow to self-respect, passing through indignation as moral riposte to this hurt, to choosing to participate in the process of enlarging the sphere of personal rights. Responsibility can be taken in this regard as the capacity recognized by both society and oneself that "a subject is capable of acting autonomously on the basis of rational insight" (114). Responsibility as a capacity to take responsibility for oneself is inseparable from responsibility as the capacity to participate in a rational discussion concerning the enlarging of the sphere of rights, whether they are civil, political, or social. The term *responsibility* therefore covers self-assertion and the recognition of the equal right of others to contribute to advances in the rule of law and of rights.

However, enlarging the sphere of personal rights has a second aspect that does not have to do with the enumerating and apportioning of these rights into different classes, but rather with the expansion of that sphere to include an ever larger number of individuals. This is the second dimension of the concept of universality, which no longer applies just to the meaning of such rights, but to extending its sphere of application. The forms of equality gained by some are meant to be extended to all. But a separate analysis has to be made regarding the three categories of rights as regards their extension. It is principally through a comparison of the types and standards of living attained elsewhere that demands relative to the different categories of personal rights gain their strength. The negative experience of disregard then takes on the specific forms of feelings of exclusion, alienation, oppression, and indignation that have given social struggles the form of a war, whether one of revolution, liberation, or decolonialization. In turn, the self-respect arising from the victories won in this struggle for a geopolitical extension of personal rights deserves the name of pride. The correlation between normativity when it comes to rules and capacity when it comes to persons, which is at the heart of this sense of pride, finds apt expression in a formulation of Joel Feinberg's in his *Rights, Justice, and the Bounds of Liberty,* cited by Honneth: "What is called 'human dignity' may simply be the recognizable capacity to assert claims."[29] The feeling of pride corresponds to this higher capacity.

The Third Model of Mutual Recognition: Social Esteem

Within the framework of the threefold schema of mutual recognition inspired by Hegel's Jena writings, it is not so much the constitution of the state as the social dimension of politics in the broadest sense that Honneth chooses to emphasize in the third step in his "systematic renewal." Rather, it is the Hegelian concept of *Sittlichkeit* in its broadest sense that is taken as the focal term. On this plane "ethical life" reveals itself as irreducible to juridical ties.

The concept of social esteem is distinct from that of self-respect, just as the latter was distinct from that of self-confidence on the affective plane. As such, it functions to sum up all the modes of mutual recognition that exceed the mere recognition of the equality of rights among free subjects. This raises several questions: What new normative demand is this social esteem supposed to satisfy? What kinds of conflict attach to mediations on the postjuridical level? What personal capacities correlate with these forms of mutual recognition? Honneth devotes only a few pages to this architecture of questions that I propose to examine more closely. According to him, it is the existence of a horizon of values common to the subjects concerned that constitutes the major presupposition of this third cycle of considerations. At the same time, it is the axiological dimension of esteem that is emphasized. It is by the same values and ends that individuals measure the importance of their individual qualities for the life of others. By stating that these relations of esteem vary over time, Honneth opens the way to a multidimensional exploration of social mediations considered from the point of view of their symbolic constitution; the cultural conception that a society has of itself makes up the sum of values and ethical ends in question in each case. The idea of a community of values thus appears as the presumed horizon of an inevitable axiological diversity that stands in contrast to the presumed universality of personal rights in the juridical order. The examination of the concept of social esteem thus finds itself dependent on a typology of the mediations contributing to the formation of a horizon of shared values, the very notion of esteem varying depending on the kind of mediation that makes a person "estimable." The notions that go with the idea of social esteem, such as prestige or consideration, do not escape the axiological pluralism that results from the variety of such mediations. As a result, social esteem does not escape the interpretative conditions corresponding to the symbolic character of such social mediations. Struggles different from those tied to the enlarging of the juridical rights have to be taken into consideration as regards both their content and the range of persons to whom they apply.

Before returning to the idea of solidarity with which Honneth ends his discussion, I would like to describe briefly a few of the paths I have encountered in my own reading in which the term *social recognition* is deliberately used in connection with specific forms of conflict on the axiological plane.

Orders of recognition: I will begin with the detailed analysis that Jean-Marc Ferry proposes for what he calls orders of recognition in the second volume of his work devoted to the *puissances de l'expérience*. At issue is the development of a concept of identity at the juncture of the lived experience of intersubjectivity and sociability organized into a system. In his first volume, he considered the general conditions of communicability governing "acts of discernment." There he takes up narration, as the organ of narrative identity, interpretation on the level of the great symbolic systems of religions and philosophies, argumentation relative to orders of validity (principally of the juridical order), and above all, the reconstruction—his major concept—that presides over the hermeneutic comprehension of the world.[30] Taken together, these mediations of communications contribute to the "acts of discernment" constitutive of personal identity. Under the title "orders of recognition," Ferry's second volume proposes an examination of those organized mediations that mean that "the neighbor is always already recognized [*reconnu*] without having already been known [*connu*]" (9).[31] It is not just a matter of describing social systems from the point of view of their organization, but of seeking a "handhold from which to understand the demands of an expanded responsibility in time and space" (10). In this regard, relations among human beings also have to include those between human beings and nature, as well as those relating to the dead, those guardians of how the past is seen. Given such considerations, the "organization of social systems" can be articulated as regards the reconstructive type of discernment discussed in volume 1 and can contribute to the formation of the identity of individuals on the moral and political plane.

Let me confine myself to simply enumerating the "systems" taken as the leading paradigms for the social world, integrated into communicative activity: the socioeconomic complex (which includes technology, as well as monetary and fiscal systems); the sociopolitical complex (which to the legal system adds the bureaucratic and the electoral systems, along with the parallel organization of public opinion); the sociocultural complex (which brings together the media system and its impact on the cultural reproduction of societies, and on the scientific system considered from the point of view of its institutional organization). What is interesting about this vast undertaking for our concerns is that it gives moral and political identity a differentiated significance that cannot be reduced to the argumentative practice emphasized by an ethics of discussion. The work of Arnold Gehlen finds its legitimate place here, as do his fears that with the decay of nature our humanity may be lost.[32] Similarly, Hans Jonas's reworking of the "principle of responsibility" ought to be taken into account here. Ferry is not deaf to these fears or to this appeal to new forms of responsibility on a different temporal and cosmic scale from Kant's idea of responsibility.[33] Therefore we ought not to dwell upon vulnerability unless we also rework the idea of normativity. The critical resources of an argumentative and reconstructive identity, elaborated in Ferry's first volume under the title of "powers of experience," find use on the social level when identity is confronted with systems of organizations considered as "orders of recognition."[34]

Economies of standing: In my reading I also came across the work of Luc Boltanski and Laurent Thévenot.[35] I have elsewhere discussed their work from the point of view of the plurality of sources of justice, in tandem with the work of Michael Walzer.[36] Here I would like to take up the problems connected with the plurality of structural mediations in relation to public esteem. Where I speak of recognition, Boltanski and Thévenot speak of justification. Justification is the strategy by which competitors give credence to their respective places in what Boltanski and Thévenot call economies of standing. Hence we need first to speak of this concept of an economy of standing before taking up the enterprise of justification as a qualifying operation of individuals in relation to the situation they occupy on the different scales of such kinds of standing. The first idea that imposes itself is that of an evaluation of the social standing of individuals making some claim on the idea of justice, but one that makes use of diverse criteria that mean that a person can be "great" or "small" as a function of the different measures of standing our authors call economies, because of their coherence in relation to a certain type of social success. A situation of dispute is engendered by the qualifying tests in a given order of such standing. This competition agrees well with our concept of a struggle for recognition. Straightaway, our authors grant that the forms of justification present "a great variety of kinds of justification, those we may call civic, domestic, industrial, commercial, or types of opinion" (De la justification, 25), referred to earlier in the initial description of their project. For example, there is the question of "inspired greatness" as applied to artists and other creative individuals. In each case, the evaluation of performances is based on a battery of tests that the protagonists must pass in competitive situations, if they are to be said to be "justified." The disputes in question are not violent, but argumentative, something that political philosophies which place the principal emphasis on power, domination, or force tend to underestimate. This is why the aim of constructing a common humanity, too quickly characterized by solidarity, is in no way incompatible with this pluralization of different criteria of standing. Forms of justice have to be specified, not as for Walzer on the basis of "shared values," but on that of strategies of justification, stemming in each instance from what Boltanski and Thévenot call cities or worlds, to emphasize the internal coherence of the systems of transactions or the mechanisms and objects involved in these transactions. Therefore, their enterprise comes from a sociology of action, even if Habermasian concepts of discussion and argumentation are used. There is rarely agreement without some dispute, and the legitimate common good is aimed at through many "goods"—as the word *standing* is meant to convey. In short, it is the evaluation of individuals in relation to such criteria and their corresponding tests that is at work in the attribution of standing by means of tests of justification.

The negative finds its place here in the form of feelings of injustice arising, for example, from the corruption of such tests and in proportion to the differences of opinion to which that corruption gives rise. This is why Boltanski and Thévenot favor figures of compromise over those of consensus in dealing with the idea of agreement. In the end, it is the relation between agreement and disagreement that can be taken as what is really at issue in their analysis, beyond the opposition between a sociology of consensus and a sociology of conflict, or between holism and methodological individualism. Forms of agreement are to be described in connection with the justifications that support them. In each case, to what is the attributed standing to be assigned? At the end of what test of justification is it taken to be legitimate? So it is agreement that is in question, but under the condition of a plurality of principles of agreement.

Boltanski and Thévenot thus attempt to outline on the scale of a plurality of orders of standing what English-speaking authors have successfully discussed only at the level of the commercial marketplace.[37] But the commercial city for our authors is just one of the cities that has to be taken into account. To identify these cities as a function of their respective kinds of argumentation, they had the interesting idea of pairing canonical texts appropriate to one order or another with manifestos, instruction manuals, public relations guides, and handbooks used by unions, professional associations, pressure groups, and the like, where the ultimate arguments are "acceptable" without being fundamentally "justified." The authors come up with a division of the orders of standing based on six common higher principles to which individuals make recourse in order to support a litigation or establish an agreement worthy of being taken as one form of the common good.

To cite one example, Saint Augustine, in *The City of God,* gives the reasons for the construction of the standing of the "city of inspiration." The principle of grace is what allows us to detach inspired standing from other forms, which are denounced as sullied by worldly interests corrupted by "vainglory," and to arrange hierarchically the kinds of good through which love binds human beings to one another. (We shall rediscover an echo of this in remarks I shall make later about states of peace.) In this city, no credit is accorded to recognition by others, at least in terms of renown.

But renown is precisely what the *city of opinion* refers to, in which standing depends only on the opinion of others. Ties of personal dependence are what decide one's importance in the eyes of others. Here honor depends on the credit conferred by other people, as Pascal's discourse on established forms of greatness confirms.

If we move to the domestic city, our authors turn to Bossuet's writings meant for the education of princes to find the most fully elaborated argument in favor of this city, with its values of allegiance, goodness, justice, and mutual assistance, which correct for the aspects of subjection linked to paternity.[38]

As we might expect, Rousseau's *Social Contract* is taken as the ultimate reference for the "civic city," with its subordination to the general will as the legitimating principle of civil standing. There relations between citizens are mediated by the relation to a totality on a second level and are founded on reason in *The Social Contract,* which holds that everything happens as though each citizen freely made a contract with him- or herself and voted only as he or she thought best, unlike the contract of submission to be found in Hobbes's *Leviathan*. Adversity here comes down to private intrigues and deceit. The real break is between this city and the triad of standing based on inspiration, the domestic city, or renown.

The commercial city, which is the first one named, finds its paradigm in the works of Adam Smith. The intermediary term here is rare goods being submitted to everyone's appetite. "The commercial bond unites individuals through the intermediary of rare goods submitted to the appetites of everyone, and the competition among desires subordinates the price attached to the possession of some good to the desires of others."[39] In this sense, Smith's *Theory of Moral Sentiments* constitutes a necessary preface to his *Inquiry into the Nature and Cause of the Wealth of Nations*. There the social bond appears as founded on an interest in exchange, but in the absence of all feelings of envy.[40]

The confrontation between the commercial and industrial worlds constitutes one of the central parts of Boltanski and Thévenot's "presentation of worlds" in their sixth chapter (241–262). The industrial city finds its paradigm in Saint-Simon's *Du système industriel* (1869), far removed from Rousseau's *Social Contract*. It is up to industrialists to manage "utilities" expertly.

I shall not say anything more here about the examination of the kinds of justification that make up the greater part of *De la justification*. But things, objects external to individuals, contribute to the characterization of cities or worlds as large-scale sociocultural entities. There is no justice without justification, no justification without some adjustment between the status of persons and that of things. Disputes and differences of opinion do not consist solely in disagreements over the standing of individuals; they have to do also with the reliability of physical mechanisms that give consistency to some "situation that works." Sheltered by these limited forms of consensus, different individual ways of living come from a "phronesis" applicable to the variety of situations of "deliberation" (to use an Aristotelian vocabulary).

In seeking to be attentive to negative motives, following Hegel who gave "crime" an institutional fruitfulness, and Honneth, who bases the dynamics of struggle for recognition on forms of disrespect, we need next, following Boltanski and Thévenot, to refer to situations of disagreement inherent in the relations among the different worlds. Beyond the rivalries created by the tests of justification in each world having to do with questions of standing, acquaintance with other worlds tends to extend such disagreement to the tests themselves, even to the point of challenging their contribution to the common good. This accusation may even go so far as to invalidate them as a result of such a confrontation between two worlds. The challenge then takes on the form of a difference of opinion, in the absence of a basis for argumentation stemming from a single system of justification—a difference of opinion affecting not only the criteria of standing in a given world, but the very notion of standing. What is the standing of a great industrialist in the eyes of a great orchestra director? The capacity to become great in another world may even be eclipsed by success in some order of standing. On this basis, we can develop a typology of the types of criticism directed by one world to another in the form of denunciation.[41] But the most interesting issue, in my opinion, lies elsewhere. It lies in the capacity to awaken the actors of one world to the values of another world through such criticism, short of their changing worlds. A new dimension of personhood is thereby revealed, that of understanding a world other than one's own, a capacity we can compare to that of learning a foreign language to the point of being able to appreciate one's own language as one among many. If translation can itself be interpreted as a way of making what is incomparable comparable, to echo the title of a book by Marcel Détienne, it is then the capacity for compromise that opens a privileged access to the common good.[42] "In a compromise," write Boltanski and Thévenot, "one agrees in order to work things out—that is, in order to suspend the difference of opinion—without its having been governed by recourse to a test in just one world" (337). The fragility of any compromise applies as well to the common good, itself in quest of its own justification. A compromise is always threatened with being denounced by pamphleteers from all sides as a surrender of principle. Compromises too thus lend themselves to a typology.[43] This typology invites us to reread the procedures leading to an expansion of personal rights described in the preceding section. We can take compromise, then, to be the form that clothes mutual recognition in situations of conflict and dispute resulting from the plurality of economies of standing.

The question that arises in the end is whether the common good is a presupposition or a result of processes of compromise. The paradox is perhaps that the status of being a presupposition, which seems to impose itself as the goal of processes of compromise, is verified—justified—only by the aptitude of the common good to relativize our belonging to a given city. On the side of individuals, what corresponds to this is the capacity to recognize oneself as one figure in the passage from one city to another without allowing oneself to get caught up in the oscillation "between disillusioned relativism and the accusation of the pamphleteer" (421), through the lack of some position overarching all these arbitrations. In this regard, nothing allows social actors to dispense with turning to practical wisdom, which does not separate justice from the correctness of the search, in every situation, for a fitting action.

Be that as it may, I do not want to leave behind an analysis that takes the idea of standing as its guiding concept without having examined what the problematic of justification does not take into account—namely, the vertical dimension implied in the opposition between great and small, which seems to stand in contrast to the horizontal dimension of recognition on the plane of self-esteem. Here we run up against the difficult concept of authority, which Boltanski and Thévenot do not discuss as such. Nor can we avoid this difficulty, given that Hegel, it will be recalled, devoted the final section of his *Realphilosophie* to a reflection on the "formation of a constitution" and the obedience that this imposes. There it was a question of the "renunciation" in the face of the strength, or even the praise, of a founding tyranny. In this regard, our lexicons point in the same direction, in that they underscore the asymmetry of a relation such as authority that brings together those who command and those who obey. Max Weber's analysis of the forms of domination and the beliefs that correspond to them on the part of the subject are well known. The right to command, to be sure, is not violence, insofar as such power is held to be legitimate and, in this sense, authorized, or to put it a better way: accredited. The problem posed by authority first ran into that of standing in Pascal, who opposed greatness and wretchedness. In his *Pensées,* he writes, "All these examples of wretchedness prove his greatness. It is the wretchedness of a great lord, the wretchedness of a dispossessed king."[44] He was certainly not fooled by the prestige of greatness, which he pragmatically justifies as a remedy for the inevitable rifts in the social bond, like those we see in the *Conseils au jeune prince* and in the *Traité de la grandeur* in the ethical writings of Pierre Nicole.

This is not the place to take up this problem in its full scope.[45] I shall limit myself to the cultural aspect of authority, leaving aside the blind spot of institutional and, more precisely, of political authority, which our emphasis on the social bond leaves aside. In this respect, a vertical element already slipped into our lexical analyses that opened the first chapter. The recognition-adhesion characteristic of "taking as true" contained a "having greater worth," confirmation of which already includes a dimension of height. The whole enigma of the idea of authority in this way finds itself at the heart of the lexical analysis of the term *recognition* by means of this "having greater worth."

One aspect of authority, more easily compatible with the horizontal aspect of living together, stands out clearly from the power to command that calls for obedience. With Gadamer, we can call it the recognition of superiority.[46] Boltanski and Thévenot's notion of standing seems close to this Gadamerian idea of recognition of superiority, insofar as each of the argument forms considered refers to shared beliefs concerning the superiority of the values that distinguish each kind of lifestyle belonging to a city. It must be admitted that the relation is circular between the superiority of the values evoked within this limited framework and the act of recognition that is expressed through participation in the qualifying tests throughout the process of justification.

The most complete model of a recognition of superiority has to be sought in the relationship between a teacher and a disciple. In *De Magistro,* beginning with the exordium, Saint Augustine confronts two acts, that of teaching and that of learning, linked together by that of questioning, of inquiring. It must be said that the kind of superiority claimed for the argument forms in each of the worlds discussed by Boltanski and Thévenot is far from this model of recognition of superiority proposed by the relation between the teacher—whose words have authority—and his or her disciple. To be fair to Boltanski and Thévenot, we have to grant them the right to carve out of the immense field of procedures that institutionalize the social bond the relatively autonomous set of forms of allegiance justified by the procedures of justification discussed in their book. Yet it remains the case that the vertical relation of authority, even when considered within the limits of discursive or written claimed authority, constitutes a thorn in the flesh of an enterprise like my own, deliberately limited to *reciprocal* forms of mutual recognition.[47]

Multiculturalism and the "politics of recognition": I have kept for last the form of struggle for recognition that has most contributed to popularizing the theme of recognition, at the risk of turning it into something banal. This theme is linked to the problem posed by multiculturalism, as well as to battles on other fronts, whether those of feminist movements or of racial or cultural minorities. (I shall reserve the term *multiculturalism* for claims for equal respect coming from different cultures that in fact have developed within one and the same institutional setting.) The stake common to these disparate but often convergent struggles is the recognition of a distinct identity for culturally underprivileged minorities. Hence, it is a question of identity, but on a collective level and in a temporal dimension that embraces discrimination against these groups in a past that may date back a few centuries, as in the case of the history of slavery, or even many centuries, as in the case of the status of women. The demand for equality on the social plane involves self-esteem, as made widely known by the public institutions of civil society—for example, the university—and ultimately the political structure itself.

One reason for keeping this form of struggle for recognition for the end, despite its public visibility, in particular in English-speaking countries, lies in the highly polemical character of a notion such as multiculturalism, which makes it difficult to hold to the descriptive stance we have adopted up to this point. It is difficult not to become what Raymond Aron called a committed observer—an observer, in that one's primary duty is to understand the warring arguments and to give the advantage to the side with the better argument.

I found in one of Charles Taylor's essays, entitled "The Politics of Recognition," a model that considers the intersecting of such arguments within the limits of a polemical situation in which the author finds himself personally engaged, the question of the future of francophone Quebec.[48] In the spectacle of struggles for recognition carried out by minority or subaltern groups, Taylor sees a confirmation of "the thesis that our identity is partially shaped by recognition or its absence, often by the *mis*recognition of others" (25). The corollary also holds true: the harm in question affects the image that members of the affected groups form of themselves, an image that they perceive to be scornful, disdainful, even debasing. The seriousness of the lack of recognition of which members of these

groups feel themselves to be the victims comes from the internalizing of this image in the form of self-depreciation. Taylor begins his
effort to make sense of the situation by noting that this eminently
modern preoccupation, which joins together identity and recognition, was made possible, as Habermas and Honneth also recognize,
on the one hand only by the collapse of social hierarchies that
placed honor at the apex of values of esteem and on the other hand
by the promotion of the modern notion of dignity, along with its
corollary, the egalitarian form of recognition. Yet to this universal-
izing version of dignity was added the affirmation of an individual
identity that can be traced back to Rousseau and Herder, and that
finds its distinctive *pathos* in the contemporary vocabulary of au-
thenticity at the same time that it preserves, not to say reinforces,
the fundamentally "dialogical" character of a demand that assumes
a frankly collective dimension. It is collectively, one could say, that
we demand an individualizing recognition.

Given his concern for careful formulation of his argument, Taylor focuses his discussion on the claims of a "politics of recognition" that comes from the profound changes that have occurred in
the idea of social esteem, a politics that he opposes to that founded
on the principle of universal equality. Taylor tries hard to see in the
passage from one kind of politics to the other a gradual shift rather
than a head-on confrontation, a shift brought about by a change in
the definition of the meaning of equality implied by the very idea of
dignity. It is equality itself that calls for a differential treatment,
right up to the institutional level of rules and procedures for "af-
firmative action." Abstract universalism is reproached for having
remained "blind to differences" in the name of liberal neutrality. In
this way, two policies, equally founded on the notion of equal respect, enter into conflict starting from the same central concept,
that of dignity, with its egalitarian implications.

This benevolent approach that tries to take both sides into account finds its limit, however, when it comes to its institutional ap-

plication in the reverse discrimination demanded in the name of the wrongs done in the past at the expense of the populations in question. These institutionalized procedures would be acceptable if they were to restore that social space which is allegedly blind to differences and not to turn into something permanent. This situation of extreme conflict then brings to the foreground underlying oppositions concerning the very notion of dignity. The classic version of liberalism is grounded on the status of being a rational agent, which everyone shares, as a universal human potential. It is this potential which we saw at work in the preceding section as regards the enlarging of the sphere of individuals who have access to personal rights. In the case of the politics of recognition, the demand for universal recognition proceeds from the differentiated cultural background, the affirmation of an allegedly universal human potential itself being seen as the expression of some hegemonic culture, that of whites, or of males, which reached its apogee during the Enlightenment. For this argument, it is universal identity that appears as discriminatory, a form of particularism disguising itself as a universal principle.[49] Hence, it is the general will, which operates in Rousseau's argument, that finds itself accused of a homogenizing tyranny by the politics of recognition. The question then is whether "any politics of equal dignity, based on the recognition of universal capacities, is bound to being equally homogenizing" (51).

The sticking point will therefore lie in the refusal to accord the idea of different collective destinies and of a right to survival (as in the case of Quebec) a kind of legitimacy distinct from that invested in the constitution and the associated notion of constitutional rights. Today in the English-speaking world, and particularly in Canada (where Taylor teaches), it is in educational institutions and the rules governing commerce that the politics of recognition and that of universal liberalism clash.

A less committed observer than Charles Taylor might be tempted to transpose onto these conflicts over legitimacy the model of compromise considered earlier in which allegiances do not take the form of a collective destiny, and still less of a right to survival. The committed observer must ask his opponents to bring their best arguments into the discussion, as he himself seeks to do. This is a great necessity for liberal societies, in the political rather than economic sense of this term, inasmuch as today they find themselves confronted with the problem of minorities, as the configuration of the nation-state does not completely overlap with the map of ethnic and cultural differences. In the future, it will be said that a liberal society "singles itself out as such by the way in which it treats minorities, including those who do not share public definitions of the good, and above all by the rights it accords to all of its members" (59).

This last maxim defines a "politics of recognition" whose benefit is an increase in self-esteem.

At the end of our consideration of the figures of the struggle of recognition, I would like to question the importance of the idea of struggle at each stage along the way. Let me recall the reason for this angle of attack on the experiences we have been considering. At first, it was a question of finding a rejoinder to the naturalist version of the state of nature in Hobbes, itself already opposed to the theses of the founders of the school of "natural law." *Leviathan* excludes every originally moral motive, not only to get out of the state of the war of all against all, but in order to recognize the other as a partner in the primitive passions of competition, distrust, and glory. In this regard, Hegel provides a powerful speculative instrument, one that puts the resources of the negative at the service of a process of the actual realization of consciousness or of Spirit. We have not forgotten his pages on "crime" as generating accepted norms. In this way, being-recognized becomes what is at issue in the whole process, which is named a struggle for recognition in the "systematic renewal" of Hegel's argument, with a strong emphasis being given to the negative forms of disrespect, of refusal of recognition. As for this being-recognized itself, toward which the whole process leads, up to the end it has retained an aspect of mystery. With regard to these normative demands, and wounds commensurate with them, we have taken into consideration the tally of new personal capacities evoked by the struggle for recognition. As correlated with the successive models of recognition, here we could mention self-confidence, respect, and self-esteem, whose details we have also discussed. Nevertheless, this promotion of new subjective capacities, when added to those considered in the previous chapter, has not precluded a certain sense of unease from developing with regard to the claims attaching to the very idea of a struggle.

When, we may ask, does a subject deem him- or herself to be truly recognized?

It might be possible to remove some of the virulence from this question by arguing that our investigation has stopped at the threshold of politics in the precise sense of a theory of the state. In this regard, we have stopped well short of the certitudes associated with a completed political philosophy. Here we might refer to the peremptory declarations of Hegel's *Philosophy of Right:* "The state is the actuality of the ethical Idea. It is ethical mind *qua* the substantial will manifest and revealed to itself, knowing and thinking itself, accomplishing what it knows and in so far as it knows it."[50] And recognition is named once again: "The state is the actuality of concrete freedom. But concrete freedom consists in this, that personal individuality and its particular interests not only achieve their complete development and gain explicit recognition for their right . . . but, for one thing, they also pass over of their own accord into the interest of the universal, and, for another thing, they know and will the universal; they even recognize it as their own substantive mind; they take it as their end and aim and are active in its pursuit" (160). Yet we need to recall also that, lacking a comparable development

218 · THE COURSE OF RECOGNITION

of the law of nations, the *Philosophy of Right* ends with a sketch of the "world history," whose pretensions, we have said in another work, have become unbelievable.[51] Nor should we overlook the fact that the *Philosophy of Right,* however imposing its development may be, covers only the meaning space of objective Spirit and then surrenders the field to absolute Spirit, which makes way for another problematic than that of recognition, one which coincides only with the ethical sphere where I am a We.

Our doubt has to do, therefore, only with this region of Objective Spirit and the models of recognition that arise within it. Within these limits, our doubt takes the form of a question: Does not the claim for affective, juridical, and social recognition, through its militant, conflictual style, end up as an indefinite demand, a kind of "bad infinity"? This question has to do not only with the negative feelings that go with a lack of recognition, but also with the acquired abilities, thereby handed over to an insatiable quest. The temptation here is a new form of the "unhappy consciousness," as either an incurable sense of victimization or the indefatigable postulation of unattainable ideals.

To ward off this worry about a new "unhappy consciousness" and the consequences that follow from it, I propose to take into consideration our actual experience of what I shall call states of peace, and to pair them with the negative and positive motives for an "interminable" struggle, something like what analysis can be in the psychoanalytical sense of the word. But allow me to say right away what I expect or do not expect from this pairing. Experiences of peaceful recognition cannot take the place of a resolution for the perplexities raised by the very concept of a struggle, still less of a resolution of the conflicts in question. The certitude that accompanies states of peace offers instead a confirmation that the moral motivation for struggles for recognition is not illusory. This is why we have to turn to days of truce, clear days, what we might call clearings, where the meaning of action emerges from the fog of doubt bearing the mark of "fitting action."

The Struggle for Recognition and States of Peace

The thesis I want to argue for can be summed up as follows: The alternative to the idea of struggle in the process of mutual recognition is to be sought in peaceful experiences of mutual recognition, based on symbolic mediations as exempt from the juridical as from the commercial order of exchange. The exceptional character of these experiences, far from disqualifying them, underscores their importance, and precisely in this way ensures their power to reach and affect the very heart of transactions stamped with the seal of struggle. Before developing this thesis, related to that of Marcel Hénaff in *Le prix de la vérité* (whose title I shall explain in a moment), I think it necessary first to take on arguments that may serve as an obstacle to an overly hasty adoption of an interpretation too favorable to my attempt to pair up the idea of a struggle for recognition with what, with other authors, I am calling states of peace.[52]

The obstacles are two in number. The first is linked to the existence in our culture of models of states of peace known by their Greek names as *philia* (in the Aristotelian sense), *eros* (in the Platonic sense), and agape (in the biblical and postbiblical sense), where the third term, *agape,* seems to refute in advance the idea of mutual recognition, inasmuch as the generous practice of gift giving, at least in its "pure" form, neither requires nor expects a gift in return. The question will be whether the unilateral character of the generosity belonging to agape must not be held in reserve to counter the opposite peril, one imposed on the idea of mutual recognition by a logic of reciprocity that tends to wipe out the interpersonal features that distinguish what, at the beginning of this chapter, I have preferred to term mutuality, to distinguish it from the kind of autonomous circularity attaching to the logical forms of reciprocity. The paradox of the gift and the gift in return will constitute in this regard the polemical site par excellence where the unilateralness of agape will be able to exercise its critical function with regard to a logic of reciprocity that transcends the discrete acts of individuals in the situation of an exchange of gifts. In this way, the ground will be cleared for an interpretation of the mutuality of the gift founded on the idea of symbolic recognition.

A STATE OF PEACE: AGAPE

Luc Boltanski takes up love and justice as competencies within the framework of a sociology of action. The problematic of this discipline is summed up in the phrase "What people are capable of" (the title of the first part of his book).[53]

It is remarkable that "states of peace," with agape at their head, are globally opposed to states of struggle that are not summed up by the violence of vengeance, which our next model sets in reciprocity together with the gift and the market, but also and principally as including those struggles having to do with justice, as indicated by the law court and the trial process. Boltanski even constructs his text around the opposition between struggles under the heading of justice and the trilogy of states of peace of which agape is the privileged type.

Therefore, it is first in contrast to justice that agape presents its credentials. Justice, in effect, does not exhaust the question of putting an end to the dispute begun by violence and reopened by vengeance. The reference in justice to the idea of equivalence contains the seed of new conflicts ignited by the plurality of principles of justification relative to the conflictual structure of "economies of standing" introduced earlier by Boltanski and Thévenot. There is nothing surprising about this observation. We have emphasized the reference to justice in our models of the struggle for recognition. If ending the dispute is the first criterion for a state of peace, justice fails the test. Agape, by contrast, renders unnecessary the reference to equivalents because it knows nothing of comparison and calculation.

The boundary is less clear between agape and the state of peace apparently closest to it, *philia*. It has to do exactly with reciprocity.

Aristotle's analysis of friendship in his *Nichomachean Ethics* has to do with the conditions most propitious for mutual recognition, that form of recognition which brings friendship close to justice. Without being a type of justice, Aristotle says, friendship is akin to it.

Still more subtly, agape is distinct from Platonic *eros* through the absence of the feeling of privation that nourishes its desire for spiritual ascent. The overflowing heart, in the case of agape, excludes this sense of privation. The most important feature for our investigation lies in the lack of concern about any gift in return in the effusion of the gift in the realm of agape. This is a corollary to the absence of any reference to the idea of equivalence for agape. It is not that agape remains unaware of the relation to the other, as what it says about the neighbor and the enemy attests. Rather, it inscribes this relation of an apparent search for equivalence by exempting it from judgment. At best, it is a matter of an equivalence that neither measures nor calculates. The only reciprocity evoked in this context stems precisely from the order of judgment and takes the form of a curse, something like the *nemesis* of a judgment of condemnation: "Judge and you will not be judged." Calculation falls away along with judgment; and with calculation, all worry. The insouciance of agape is what allows it to suspend a dispute, even in cases of justice. The forgetting of offenses that it inspires does not consist in setting them aside, still less in repressing them, but in "letting go," to use one of Hannah Arendt's phrases in speaking of pardon. Agape is not, for all that, inactive. Kierkegaard could write at great length about "works of love." In moving beyond comparison, agape cares for "the person one sees." The "incommensurable" character of people makes "reciprocity infinite through and through."[54] Love remains without a rejoinder to questions because justification is entirely foreign to it, as is attention to self. More enigmatically still, agape lives in permanence, in that which endures, its present knowing neither regret nor expectation. And if it does not argue in general terms, it speaks through examples and parables, whose extravagant tale disorients hearers without any assurance of reorienting them.

The question that agape poses for Boltanski's sociology of action is my own as well: "The theory of *agape* poses one central problem, which is that of its status: Is it a construct allowing description of actions carried out by persons in reality, or a partially realizable ideal, a utopia, or a deception?" (*L'amour et la justice,* 199). The seriousness and weightiness of this question comes from the credit accorded discourse about agape once we do not take it to be something illusory or hypocritical. This credibility has to do with its impact on the very practice of reciprocity, which its concept of the neighbor reopens: the neighbor is not just someone nearby, but someone to whom one draws near. Hence the test of credibility for any talk about agape lies within the dialectic of love and justice, opened up by this act of drawing near to someone.

Agape lends itself to this test first of all thanks to its entering into language, which makes it in some ways commensurable with talk about justice. For agape speaks. However strange we may find its expressions to be, they are offered up to common understanding. The discourse of agape is above all else one of praise—in praise, human beings rejoice in the sight of its object reigning over every other object of their concern. In the words of Charles Taylor, praise is a "strong evaluation," uttered in the mode of song. Paul's hymn to love in I Corinthians 13 is its paradigm. The height of agape is also celebrated in the optative mode of the beatitudes: "Blessed are they who . . ." Agape takes another step in the direction of justice by assuming the verbal form of the imperative: "You shall love," which Rosenzweig in *The Star of Redemption* contrasts with the law and its moral constraints.[55] The commandment that precedes all law is the word that the lover addresses to the beloved: Love me! Love commends itself through the tenderness of its supplication. We could even dare to speak here of a poetic usage of the imperative, close to that of the hymn and the benediction. And let us add to these two discursive features the power of metaphorization that attaches to expressions of agape, which make it link up with the analogical resources of erotic love, as the Song of Songs bears witness.[56]

That agape enters into language, of course, does not abolish the disproportion between love and justice, which Pascal took to an extreme in his famous fragment on the orders of greatness.[57] The dialectic of love and justice takes place precisely through this disproportion, which continues up to the paradox of the gift returned. And it is again on the level of language that this discordant dialectic can be apprehended: agape declares itself, proclaims itself; justice makes arguments. In the law court, this argumentation remains in service of dispute, to which states of peace are opposed. The distance between a juridical dispute and such states of peace is in one sense brought to its peak when the handing down of a judgment puts an end to the trial process and its clash of arguments. The judgment operates as a word that separates, setting the victim on one hand and the guilty party on the other. The judge thus appears as bearing not only the scales of justice but a sword. The dispute is settled, but it is merely spared from vengeance, without yet being a state of peace.

However, it is not only on the plane of penal justice that the connection between justice and argumentation is flagrant. It is also so in many different ways in situations where individuals are submitted to the tests of justification arising out of the conquest or defense of a position in one or another of the cities having to do with economies of standing in Thévenot and Boltanski's sense of this term. These situations of justification belong to societies such as our own that can be defined in terms of the distribution of commercial or noncommercial goods (roles, tasks, rights and duties, advantages and disadvantages, prerogatives and burdens). Individuals would lack social existence without such rules of distribution which confer upon them a place within the whole. Here is where justice, as distributive justice, intervenes as the virtue of institutions presiding over every form of exchange. "To give to each his or her due" is, in some situation having to do with distribution, the most general formula for justice. Ever since Aristotle, moral philosophers have emphasized the connection between the just, so defined, and the equitable: "Treat similar cases in similar ways."

Can we build a bridge between the poetics of agape and the prose of justice, between the hymn and the formal rule? It is a bridge that must be built, for these two realms of life, that based on agape and that based on justice, both refer to one and the same world of action, in which they seek to manifest themselves as "competencies." The privileged occasion for this confrontation is precisely that of the gift. For agape, we have said elsewhere, is a stranger to desire. Not being marked by privation, it has only one desire—to give—which is the expression of its generosity. Therefore, it appears as a surprise in the everyday world, where a gift takes on the social form of an exchange, and where the spirit of justice is expressed, as it is throughout its realm, by the rule of equivalence. Whatever may have been the archaic origins of the economy of the gift, which will be the object of our next discussion, gifts are still given in our societies, even when these are dominated by the market economy where everything has a price, albeit as dominated by social codes governing the relations between gifts and gifts in return. People who act out of agape, to whom the sociology of action assigns a type and certain kinds of behavior, find themselves lost in this world of calculations and equivalences, where they are incapable of providing some kind of justification. Being, as they are, unaware of the obligation to give in return, they do not go beyond their initial gesture, because they expect nothing in return.

Dostoevsky gave an unforgettable figure to this innocence: the idiot.[58] It is not that Prince Myshkin is what we ordinarily call an idiot. He has a stupefying awareness of situations that causes him to appear wherever there is a dispute or argument. But he does not arbitrate them according to the rules of justice. In each case, his action is what is "fitting," without having to take the detour through the general rule. We might even characterize his actions in terms of their justness rather than in terms of justice. Because of this, the dominant tonality of the actions of the person who makes the first gesture, the person who acts out of agape, and those of the person who makes the second gesture, that of justice, can be characterized only by misunderstanding. Agape loses the "purity" that excludes it from the world, and justice loses the security conferred upon it by its submission to the rule of equivalence. If, with Boltanski, we add that in the concrete situations of life it is permissible for each partner to "topple" from one realm into the other, the misunderstanding will be complete.[59]

THE PARADOXES OF THE GIFT AND THE GIFT IN RETURN AND THE LOGIC OF RECIPROCITY

The interpretation of the concept of reciprocity that I take to be an alternative to the thesis that makes the idea of mutual recognition the key to the paradoxes of the gift and the gift in return comes from the discussion of Marcel Mauss's *The Gift*.[60]

To put it quickly, Mauss places the gift within the general category of exchanges, on the same level as commercial exchange, of which he takes it to be the archaic form. It is these archaic features that hold the attention of the sociologist-ethnologist. What is enigmatic about the practices of exchanging gifts among some peoples, such as the Maori of New Zealand, is not the obligation to give something, nor even that to receive, but that of giving something back in return. How are we to explain "the prestations which are in theory voluntary, disinterested and spontaneous, but are in fact obligatory and interested"? What accounts for the connection linking these three obligations: to give, to receive, to give in return? Mauss formulates the question as follows: "What force is there in the thing given which compels the recipient to make a return?" (1) With this formulation, he adopts the language of the populations being considered, not only in making his question bear on the energy of the bond that underlies the obligation to give a gift in return, but in placing this force in the thing given, which is taken to be not inert: "In the things exchanged at a potlatch there is a certain power which forces them to circulate, to be given away and repaid" (41). Sticking close to the Maori tradition, Mauss adopts in this way the latent conceptuality that this tradition attaches to the word *hau* to designate this force in the gift that obligates a gift in return. It is the ethnologist's crediting of the interpretation given by the indigenous people themselves to their practice that launched the discussion.

In his *Introduction to the Work of Marcel Mauss,* Claude Lévi-Strauss criticizes him for accepting the interpretation in terms of the *hau.*[61] He asks whether Mauss has not thereby allowed himself to be mystified by the natives. The rational explanation for the enigma of the gift in return lies elsewhere. "*Hau* is not the ultimate explanation for exchange; it is the conscious form whereby men of a given society . . . apprehended an unconscious necessity whose explanation lies elsewhere" (48). By turning to the notion of the unconscious, Lévi-Strauss shifts the explanation to another level than that of conscious life, the level of the rules of symbolic thought. It is the truth about exchanges, in that they obey rules that the notion of the *hau* conceals from the eyes of the Maori. Where magical thought invoked a hidden force, something like the "dormative virtue" of medieval thought, the scientist brings to light a simple rule governing any exchange.

As Luc Boltanski reminds us, Claude Lefort was one of the first to criticize Lévi-Strauss for overlooking "the immanent intention of behavior" in his ambition to reduce the social to a universe that could be explained by rules.[62] What is thereby eliminated is the very meaning of the gift. This meaning remains hidden so long as we refuse to relate the obligation to give a gift in return to "the obligation to give as it manifests itself in the first gift, the act of gift giving." Lefort anticipates the interpretation that will be proposed later when he writes: "The idea that the gift must be returned pre-supposes that the other person is another self who must act as I do; and this return gesture has to confirm for me the truth of my own gesture, that is, my subjectivity. . . . Human beings [thereby] con-firm to one another that they are not things." A sociology of action, in contrast to a sociology of the social fact, like that of Durkheim, is able to take up for its own purposes Lefort's critique, which is in-spired by Merleau-Ponty's phenomenology. It will refuse to sacrifice the actors' own justifications to the constructs of an external ob-server.

It is this sacrificing of the social agents' own justifications that I see consummated in a logic of reciprocity such as that proposed by Mark Rogin Anspach in *À charge de revanche: Figures élémentaires de la réciprocité*.[63] In his preface, he declares: "A relation of reci-procity cannot be reduced to an exchange between two individuals. A transcendent third term emerges in each instance, even if this third term is nothing other than the relation itself, imposing itself as a separate actor entirely" (5).

But if we leave the plane of the sociology of action, we leave not only that of the justifications given by the actors, but also one where we can oppose two "competencies": justice and love. Lost from sight, agape has then to be held in reserve for that moment when the phenomenology of mutuality will claim its rights in the face of a logic of reciprocity.

But first we need to discuss the merits of this logic of reciprocity, in order to gauge exactly the novelty of the interpretation through a form of recognition that announces itself to be immanent in inter-personal transactions.

The evident merit of this theory of reciprocity is that from the beginning it covers a vast territory that includes vengeance, the gift, and the market, where these three categories constitute the "elementary forms of reciprocity," to use the subtitle of Anspach's book.

Its second merit is to assimilate reciprocity to a circle that can be either vicious or virtuous. This poses the problem of the passage from the vicious circle of vengeance (blow for blow) to the virtuous one of the gift (gift for gift), where sacrifice opens the way to a positive reciprocity.

The vicious character of the circle of vengeance is felt by the actors, without their necessarily being able to formulate the rule "Kill the one who has killed." It is this rule which turns the avenger into a murderer, by transforming him into the anonymous agent of a system that surpasses him and one that perpetuates itself as a system only through these oscillations. Considerations like those of Hegel on the power of the negative in crime—or those of François Tricaud on ethical aggression or those of Verdier on the role of social regulation exercised by vengeance in the experience of some societies—find themselves neutralized from the outset.[64] What happens "between" the actors is subordinated to the self-reference—in the sense of "upholding a system of behavior"—of an autonomous system, to use the terminology of Jean-Pierre Dupuy.[65] Some noteworthy phenomenological features, such as those of someone who, for example, offers himself up to the executioner for beheading, are there to recall the offering-like character of the sacrifice, supposed to underlie the transition from the vicious circle of vengeance to the virtuous circle of the gift. But in such a systematic conception we must not lose sight of such concrete gestures as renouncing responding to violence with further violence, or freeing oneself from the grip of the principle "Kill the one who has killed," to transfer all these transactions to a third party, one that is taken as divine in religious systems. The emergence of "someone killed who has not killed," at the source of the violence of a sacrifice, is always an event. And if the formula for making a sacrificial offering is "Give to one who is going to give," there is still the gesture of making the sacrifice, the "offering" that inaugurates the entry into the realm of the gift.

Yet what nevertheless pleads for a systematic vision of the sequence of gift and gift in return is the raising of enigma to the rank of paradox, in the strong sense of an inconsistent thought. This paradox says: How is the recipient of the gift obliged to give back? If he is obliged to give a gift in return if he is generous, how then can the original gift have been generous? In other words, in recognizing a present by giving one in return, does one not destroy the original gift as a gift? If the first gesture in giving is one of generosity, the second, given under the obligation to make some return, annuls the gratuitous nature of the original gift. The systematic theoretician sees this circle, which is once again a vicious circle, as a double bind. And the proposed solution, based on something like Bertrand Russell's theory of types, is to place on two different planes the rule of reciprocity and transactions between individuals. Then the circle results from confusing these two different levels, that of exchange considered in itself and that of the actual individual acts.

Anspach grants that there is an important difference between the functioning of the circle of vengeance and that of the gift. The circle of vengeance is actually experienced; that of the gift exists only in theory for a modern observer of archaic societies. Indigenous peoples, in this sense, perceived something of this functioning when placing the spirit of the gift in a third term, the *hau*.[66] Yet it remains the case that it is the theorist—unlike the avenger, whom the paradox paralyses—and not the actual actors in a situation of vengeance who constructs the argument that results in the double bind. And it is the theorist who distinguishes between two levels, that of reciprocity and that of the actual exchange. Thanks to these distinctions, the theorist can point to "a circular, but not vicious, hierarchy between the exchange as a transcendent unity and the individual operations that constitute it" (44). The transcendence of the exchange does not prevent its existence from depending on the successful unfolding of these same operations.

What is the status of this transcendence in an age in which the world has become disenchanted? According to the model elaborated by Jean-Pierre Dupuy, it is something like a process of self-transcendence that can be expressed only in terms of a "circular causality," both on the level of the system of reciprocity and between the two levels themselves: "a first level where the separate operations take place between the actors and the metalevel where the third term resides that incarnates the exchange as something transcendent" (45). In this regard, the greatest merit of this interpretation is that it sees both Mauss and Lévi-Strauss as being correct, Mauss as regards the transcendence of the *hau*, Lévi-Strauss as regards the logical explanation of the reciprocity of the exchange.

For my part, I shall not take a position on the logical consistency of the concept of the self-transcendence of an autonomous system. What interests me is the way in which the overall circulation "emerges from their interaction through a process of self-transcendence." Therefore we need to be attentive to the features of the "separate operations that take place between the actors," since it is from them that the system emerges. Hence we should concentrate less on "the enigma of the third person" and on the modern reinterpretation of the mystical transcendence of the *hau* than on what the actors do when they recognize the gift as a gift. Thus we make the transition from a sense of recognition that is still that of recognition *for*—a kind of identification—to that of mutual recognition, which is our own preoccupation.[67]

In fact, Anspach helps us to preserve this "immanent" dimension of mutuality (in order to oppose it to the self-transcendence of reciprocity) by a number of comments concerning individual behavior: to stop fighting, to offer in the moment of giving, to expect to receive something back in one way or another, without counting the act of taking the initiative—"without taking the initiative, there is no gift possible" (225). Such behavior places the first gift at the center, the first gift becoming a model for the second gift. There are many variations of "so that" in the expression "to give so that the other gives." It is from these very variations that the neutralized formula of reciprocity that operates above our heads is supposed to emerge, unlike the mutuality that circulates between us. But if reciprocity does circulate fluidly, it is important that the actors not interrupt this flow, but help maintain it. It is trust that makes this possible. Mauss speaks here of the "security" provided by the *hau*. And Lévi-Strauss noted the necessity of "being confident that the circle will close." In other words, giving, on the plane of actual action, is not without risk. When the theory says, "It is always owing to a global circuit that a return can be expected," the giver and the receiver, on the plane of action, bear the risky, contingent burden of undertaking and carrying through the exchange between themselves. Hence, we can take what Anspach says in two ways when he proposes that "we must try to get beyond the problematic of a return" (48). The theorist does this by changing levels. The agents in an exchange may do so by returning from the question, Why give something in return? to the question, Why give at all? The gift in return comes in the wake of the generosity of the first gift. As I shall say later, something of the "giving without return" of agape can be retained in the practice of a gift in return.

Yet it is within the difference between the gift and the commercial exchange that the phenomenology of the gift comes back in force. And the theorist readily concedes it: "The system of exchanges where the group as a whole plays the role of mediator of reciprocity in the strongest sense is undoubtedly the one where there is no longer a gift in any sense of the word in the transactions between individuals, I mean the modern marketplace" (57). Here is where "the law of impersonality," along with the alleged self-transcendence of the social, rules. We can go even further: in the marketplace, there is no obligation to give in return, because there is no requirement of reciprocity. Payment ends the mutual obligations between those involved in a commercial exchange. The marketplace, we could say, is reciprocity without mutuality. In this sense, it stands in contrast to the original mutual bonds characteristic of the exchange of gifts within the wider realm of reciprocity. Thanks to this contrast with the marketplace, the emphasis falls on the generosity of the first giver rather than on the requirement to give something in return. Anspach agrees with this: "To give a gift in return, to recognize the generosity of the first giver through a corresponding gesture of reciprocity, is to recognize the *relation* for which the initial gift is only a vehicle" (59). The verb *to recognize* in this passage functions on two levels at the same time. In the first part of the sentence, *recognition* denotes the redoubled generosity of the very gesture of giving; in the second part, it refers to the relation involved, in identifying it, but is this second kind of recognition still something that operates at the level of those involved in the exchange or only something constructed by the theorist?[68]

GIFT EXCHANGES AND MUTUAL RECOGNITION
The two preceding discussions have brought to the fore the question of reciprocity as it operates between parties in the exchange of gifts. Our first discussion, based on an examination of the model of a state of peace constituted by agape, led us to place on hold for later discussion the idea of a generosity present in the first gift without any regard for the obligation thereby engendered to give something in return. This is a generosity freed from the rules of equivalence governing justice. Our second discussion, starting from the enigma of the obligation to give in return, considered the possibility of establishing the circularity of figures of reciprocity on another, more systematic level than that of actual lived experience burdened by the paradoxes that go with this idea of a return gift. However, the recourse made to a concept of mutual recognition amounts, at this stage of our discussion, to a plea in favor of the mutuality of relations *between* those who exchange gifts, in contrast with the concept of reciprocity that the theory places *above* social agents and their transactions. In accord with linguistic convention, I shall reserve the term *mutuality* for such exchanges between individuals,

and use *reciprocity* for those systematic relations for which such ties of mutuality constitute only one of the "elementary forms" of such reciprocity. I shall take this contrast between reciprocity and mutuality from here on as a fundamental presupposition of my central thesis concerning the idea of symbolic mutual recognition. And from here on I shall compare the exchange of gifts to commercial exchange, without further regard either for the rule of equivalence of the judicial order or for other forms of reciprocity—for example, those of vengeance.

In doing this, we can say that we have an intuitive conviction that the commercial sphere has its limits. This conviction is supported by the argument in Michael Walzer's *Spheres of Justice*.[69] Basing his case on a still-vibrant cultural heritage, he asserts that there are goods, which he calls "shared values," whose nature makes them nonvenal. What is the source, though, from which our resistance to the encroachment of the commercial sphere draws its energy, particularly in societies like our own which have resolved the problem of an equal attribution of rights, but not that of an equal distribution of goods, as we said earlier in discussing our third model of the struggle for recognition? To find an answer, we must take such "shared values" as a telling example.

I owe to the work of Marcel Hénaff entitled *Le prix de la vérité* the idea of resolving what he calls "the enigma of ceremonial reciprocal gift giving" by resorting to the idea of symbolic mutual recognition.[70]

The second part of Hénaff's book builds on the discussion opened by Mauss's *The Gift*. But the originality of the strategy employed in Hénaff's book lies in his delaying the discussion of this literature and in subordinating it to a prior examination of the category of what is "without price." The benefit of this long detour will be to unlink the practices of gift giving and those of the economic sphere when the time comes, so that the gift ceases to appear as an archaic form of commercial exchange. The archaism that would

234 · THE COURSE OF RECOGNITION

have continued to be a problem is transferred to the ceremonial character of such exchanges, whose link with the symbolic character of recognition has still to be demonstrated.

Everything turns on the intersection of two problems of different origin. That of what is "without price" is posed in our culture by the relation between truth—or at least the search for truth—and money. We are eternally indebted to Socrates for having opened this discussion. Socrates, Plato tells us, taught without requiring any salary in return. It was the sophists who expected to be paid. But Socrates would only accept gifts that honored him at the same time that they honored the gods. Thus begins the history of a long enmity between the intellectual and the commercial spheres. This enmity finds an echo even in the definition of the Athenian citizen: merchants were excluded from the society of free men.[71] The merchant bought and sold for others. He belonged to the useful, not to discourse or to the sumptuary. Yet despite Socrates, the boundary between the inspired thinker and the useful expert continued to be blurred in the field of intellectual transactions. For its part, commerce was recognized for better or worse to be a technique, a dangerous one, it is true, but a necessary one. It was willingly left in the hands of foreigners, often of freed slaves. The Aristotelian theory of money, whose function of being an exchange between equals places it in the field of justice in book 5 of the *Nichomachean Ethics,* does not redound to the benefit of the merchant's reputation. The medieval historian Jacques Le Goff has spoken of the competition during the Middle Ages between the negative judgments of clerics about the man devoted to gain and the esteem of the people for shopkeepers and artisans. As for the moneylender, he will remain indistinguishable from the usurer, who sells time that ought to belong to God. It is true that this battle was lost during the Renaissance and the Reformation, but the suspicion would remain about money that is used to purchase money and is transformed into merchandise. Flaubert and Baudelaire were no less indignant about such things than was Marx.[72] Nevertheless, the victory of the merchants, which is also that of the market, has not succeeded in blotting out Socrates' words and his behavior at the hour of his death, nor the question whether there still exist noncommercial goods. "It is a question of conceiving of an exchange relation of a noncommercial type," notes Hénaff at the end of the first part of his book (134). This is the point where the question of what is "without price" intersects once again with that of the gift, coming from a different horizon, that of the ethnology of archaic societies. And it is with the theme of symbolic recognition that our two problematics converge.

Hénaff takes up the interpretation of the enigma of the exchange of gifts at the point reached in the discussion of the conclusion of Mauss's *Gift,* principally in the aftermath of Lévi-Strauss's critique. By designating the exchange as Mauss describes it as "ceremonial," Hénaff's own thesis starts from a double break, first with the moralizing interpretation of the gift, which loses its festive and sumptuary force, to which we shall return, and second with the economic interpretation that makes it an archaic form of commercial exchange. The ceremonial reciprocal gift is neither an ancestor nor a competitor of—nor a substitute for—such commercial exchanges. It is situated on another plane, that precisely of what is without price. This said, however, the enigma remains—to wit, the obligation to give in return.

Let us recall that for Mauss the key to this enigma was to be sought in the thing exchanged, in the gift as a present. He adopted for his own purposes the interpretation of the indigenous people, whereby the force that obligated giving in return lay in this thing, like some magical energy capable of making the exchanged good return to its birthplace. We have already referred to Lévi-Strauss's and others' criticisms, which present themselves as a reinterpretation in logical terms of this magical force. By assigning the force constraining the recipient to give something in return solely to the relation between those involved in the exchange, the structuralist thesis does indeed dematerialize this energy which magical thought localizes in the object as something exchanged, but this thesis remains close to magical thinking in that the relation between the givers functions as a third term, one analogous to the *hau* to which the Maori natives refer. However, substituting a force of entailment belonging to the relation of exchange for the magical power contained in the thing exchanged still keeps the emphasis on the third, exchanged term. What is revolutionary about Hénaff's proposal is that he shifts the emphasis from the relation between giver and recipient to seek the key to our enigma in the very mutuality of the exchange "between" the protagonists, calling this shared operation mutual recognition. The initial enigma of a force supposed to reside in the object itself is dissipated if we take the thing given and returned as the pledge of and substitute for this process of recognition. It is the pledge of the giver's commitment through the gift and a substitute for the trust that this gesture will be reciprocated. Hence it will be the quality of the relation of recognition, he says, that confers its importance on everything we call presents. I would add that we can take this relationship of mutuality as a kind of recognition that does not recognize itself, to the extent that it is more invested in the gesture than in the words that accompany it. It can only do so by symbolizing itself in the gift.

Our analysis here can be said to be one applying ideal types in the Weberian sense, in that it gives equal weight to conceptual precision and empirical exemplification. My purpose in the following comments will merely be to demonstrate the possible value of developing such an analysis.

My first remark is meant to underscore the dichotomy of the conceptual analysis, a dichotomy that will have to be corrected later on the basis of data taken from our historical experience. Contrary to what a reading of Mauss's *Gift* might suggest, the exchange of gifts is neither the ancestor nor competitor of—nor a substitute for—commercial exchanges. Presents, whose purchase may cost one dear, do not count at all as commercial goods in the sense of things that one can buy and sell. For they have no value "outside their function of being a pledge of and substitute for the relationship of mutual recognition." Here is where the two problematics of the gift and of what is without price intersect.

Not only do they intersect—they mutually buttress each other. History showcases the ever-increasing defeat of what is without price, driven back by the advances of commercial society. There is no longer a teacher, however Socratic, who does not demand remuneration. At the end of his book, Hénaff considers the "legitimate forms of commercial exchange": the "rehabilitated sophist," the "legitimated merchant," the "remunerated author," and the "paid therapist." The question then arises: Do any noncommercial goods still exist? To which we can reply that it is the spirit of the gift that provokes a rupture within the category of goods, consistent with an overall interpretation of sociability as one vast system of distribution. We can then speak of noncommercial goods, such as security, responsibilities, duties, and honors, where their not having a price is a sign of our recognition of noncommercial goods. Conversely, perhaps we can find the gift in every form of what is priceless, whether it is moral dignity, which has a value but not a price, or the integrity of the human body, and the noncommercialization of its organs, to say nothing of its beauty, or that of gardens and flowers or the splendor of natural landscapes. Here there is a possible bridge to the judgment of taste in Kant's *Critique of Judgment*. Perhaps there is a gift and mutual recognition in this judgment which Kant says lacks an objective referent and depends on its ability to be communicated?

Here is my second set of remarks: to correct the dichotomous character to whose conceptual dimension an analysis in terms of ideal types pays special attention, it is helpful to proceed to a closer examination of concrete experiences of the difference in meaning and intention that remains between an exchange of gifts and an exchange of merchandise, even when they are not opposed to each other, as in the case of ceremonial forms of exchange, but are bound up in everyday practices. In this regard, the point of view of a historian can be welcome, as is the case with Natalie Zemon Davis's work *The Gift in Sixteenth-Century France*.[73] To be sure, the picture she paints of such practices is confined to a single age, that of sixteenth-century France, which is her specialty. But it turns out that this is the century in which Western culture hesitated among several cultural heritages and created new models for life to which we are still indebted. But the greatest benefit of this historical inquiry is that it contributes to our distinguishing between the two orders of commercial and noncommercial exchange at a time when they were not only contemporary with each other but complementary and subtly antagonistic at the same time. In this way the dichotomous aspect inherent in an approach based on ideal types finds its corrective in the attention paid to complex features that historical investigation can make apparent.

Three such complex features resulting from the intermingling of different forms of exchange in the period considered stand out.

The first has to do with the plurality of basic beliefs that are the source of the "spirit of gift giving." The second has to do with the confusion between the benefits of the gift and those of the market. The third one draws our attention to the forms of failure in the actual practice of gift giving.

On the plane of the convictions and prescriptions that preside over the circulation of gifts, the author sees the "spirit of gift giving" as proceeding from a bundle of quite disparate central beliefs. On the one hand, the biblical theme of the precedence of the divine gift in relation to gifts exchanged among human beings excludes any equivalent restitution yet recommends gratuitous giving in human practice: "You have received without payment; give without payment" (Matthew 10:8b). On the other hand, the ethic of liberality, received from the Greeks and Romans and dear to humanists, makes giver and receiver equal again in a circle illustrated by the group of Three Graces holding hands. To these two beliefs are added the favors of friendship and neighborly generosity. As for occasions of gift giving, the relation to time is essential. Festivals are arranged according to the calendar, which marks the return of the seasons, the new year, liturgical and national holidays, the cycle of individual and family life (birth, marriage, death, and other rites of passage)—to which we can add legacies and inheritances. Each one of these powerful prescriptions inscribed in human time "offered ideals for giving and receiving in different social milieus" (15). As Davis notes, "sixteenth-century people were also attentive to the borders of that realm, to the signs that might distinguish a gift from a sale and a gift obligation from a coerced payment" (22). It is just such actual practices that reveal the difficulty in making volition and obligation coincide in the act of giving. We shall return to this later, in the third point.

The second lesson I draw has to do with the complex relations between selling and giving. As much as Davis refuses to accept the thesis of a substitution of the market economy for that of the gift, and argues for the persistence of their coexistence, she also nonetheless warns against a dichotomous vision that would overlook their overlaps and their mutual borrowings, at the risk of the kinds of corruption we shall underscore at the end. Occasions for giving are also occasions for one regime to encroach on another: "What is interesting in the sixteenth century is this sensitivity to the relation between gift and sale, this concern about the border between them. . . . Especially important in the sixteenth century was the possibility of moving back and forth between the gift mode and the sale mode, while always remembering the distinction between them" (44). Numerous examples can be given: sales transactions, especially among neighbors, require the addition of presents, indicating that the partners have not lost their subsequent relationship; loans, even when they include payment of interest, are ensured by something given in security as a sign of trust; contracts for services or apprenticeships, the carrying out of services rendered, are marked by small presents and other courtesies which preserve the sense of gratitude that goes with true gifts. The most interesting cases of preserving yet crossing the boundary line between gift and sale concern transactions having to do with knowledge. Here we rediscover the problem raised by Socrates. The case of the book is exemplary in this respect. With printing, the publisher becomes distinct from the author, who continues to offer his book with a dedication and acknowledgments, whereas the publisher, whether licensed or not, sells books. Davis discusses this case of books making the trajectory that runs from sales, presents, and legacies up to their inclusion in private or semiprivate libraries, with noble or royal libraries offering such books their final resting place. Teachers, physicians, and midwives are remunerated by payments that oscillate between gifts and salaries. Even "honoraria" do not exclude polite or courteous gifts. Examining these mixed cases reinforces the emphasis already mentioned on gratitude as the sentiment in such acts that both separates and connects giving and giving in return. It is the quality of feeling that ensures the soundness of the dividing line that runs through such mixed cases of giving and selling.

But gratitude is also a weak boundary that exposes the gift to those different forms of corruption that bring our analysis in terms of ideal types back to its starting point, the paradox of the relation between the generosity of the gift and the obligation of giving a gift in return. At any moment this paradox can slip into an aporia, even into an accusation of hypocrisy. It is the third lesson of Davis's book that constrains us to take this step backward. "Gifts," she says, "can go wrong, and sixteenth-century people were often fretting about it" (67). The one who receives a gift can turn into a person who feels overwhelmed by the obligation to give something in return. At the same time, a refusal to give in return, or an excessive delay in so doing, or the mediocrity of the gift given in return can give rise to anger or an accusation of ingratitude. And if the practice of gift giving comes close to the theoretical paradoxes of the double bind at the origin of the logic of reciprocity, the examples of "gifts gone wrong" are many: in the family, the revocation of promised legacies; in social relations, maneuvers tied to advancement and reputation, petitions for advantages that call forth fawning behavior; finally, it is perhaps characteristic of this period that everyone gets caught up in obligations without end. It was this kind of constraint that led Montaigne to prefer strict contracts to the perverse game of good turns and favors.[74] As for politics, it was first the administration of justice, but also the granting of royal privileges that sowed corruption, which, truth to tell, moved beyond the cycle of missed gifts to enter that of "bad" ones. Davis ends her chapter on corruption with a question: "But what did a society so committed to the rhythms of gift and obligation do about gifts gone so badly wrong? Stop all gifts? Unthinkable! Sort out good reciprocity from bad? But how?" (99).

This is also a question for our own time, for it has to do with the essence of the problem posed by the exchange of gifts. Yet if this question is to remain a real question for social practice and not simply one for the theory of reciprocity, we have first to take up the exclamation "Unthinkable!" which follows the discouraged hypothesis of giving up all gift giving. Just as true as that "the gift made always brings with it the possibility for conflict" (130) is the conviction upon which Hénaff's thesis is based—namely, that an actual experience of mutual recognition in a symbolic mode is offered by the ceremonial reciprocal gift. To protect the good side of this actual experience of mutual recognition, we must take up the critical task of "sorting out good reciprocity from bad."

We have to undertake this critical task by drawing on the normative resources of an analysis in terms of ideal types (which I take to be less *wertfrei,* less neutral from an axiological point of view, than did Max Weber, even if he himself was not always faithful to this

principle of asceticism). By drawing near to one degree of the ceremonial aspect of the gift with which I would like to conclude, I shall
place the principal emphasis, as Claude Lefort suggested, on the
very gesture of giving, caught in its first rush forward, I would even
say in its forward impulse. Much has been said about the obligation
to give in return, but not enough attention has been paid to the
question, Why give? Undertaking to give a gift is the gesture that
initiates the whole process. The generosity of the gift does not call
for restitution, which would, properly speaking, mean annulling
the first gift, but for something like a response to the offer. At the
outside, we have to take the first gift for the model of the second
one, and think, we could say, of the second gift as a kind of second
first gift. The obligation to give in return, reinterpreted by the logic
of reciprocity in terms of a double bind, remains largely a weak
construction when considered phenomenologically, one that serves
as a pretext for the distinction between two levels, that of actual
practices and that of an autonomous circle endowed with self-
transcendence. The fascination exercised by the enigma of giving in
return leads to neglecting some remarkable features of the practice
of gift giving, considered as actually occurring, such as offering,
risking, accepting, and finally giving something of oneself in giving
some simple thing. Mauss glimpsed the importance of these movements that we may call those of the heart when he wrote: "One
gives oneself in giving, and if one gives oneself, it is that one owes
oneself to others, oneself and one's property."[75]

Here is where I would suggest placing this phenomenology of the
intentions involved in gift giving in relation to our earlier analysis
of agape, where the emphasis fell on the gift with no expectation of
something in return. Does not the risk of the first gift, its being offered, preserve something of the disinterested character of the expectation that first goes with the reception of the gift before turning into an expectation of a gift in return? This expectation itself,
which can be indefinitely postponed, even lost sight of and frankly

forgotten, can also become the expectation of a surprise, placing the second gift in the same affective category as the first gift, something that makes the second gift something other than a restitution. Instead of the obligation to give in return, it would be better, under the sign of agape, to speak of a response to a call coming from the generosity of the first gift. Pursuing this, ought we not to place a special emphasis on the second term in the triad "give, receive, give in return"? Receiving then becomes the pivotal category, in that the way in which the gift is accepted determines the way in which the person who receives the gift will feel obliged to give something in return. A word comes to mind here that we mentioned earlier in passing: *gratitude*. In French, one says *reconnaissance* in speaking of such gratitude.[76] Gratitude lightens the weight of obligation to give in return and reorients this toward a generosity equal to the one that led to the first gift. This would be the answer to the question posed by Davis concerning the possibility of sorting out good reciprocity from bad. In the end, I believe, everything depends on the middle term of the threefold structure of giving, receiving, and giving in return. A *good receiving* depends on gratitude, which is the soul of the division between good and bad reciprocity. Gratitude fills out the relation between gift and return gift, in decomposing before recomposing it. It puts the pair *give/receive* on one side, and that of *receive/return* on the other. The gap that it opens between these two pairs is *inexact* when compared with the relation of equivalence for justice, as also when compared with that of buying and selling. And it is inexact in two ways, both as regards the value and as regards any temporal delay. For the regime of gratitude, the values of exchanged presents are incommensurable in terms of market costs. This is the mark of what is "without price" in such an exchange of gifts. As for the fitting time to return the gift, we can say that it too is without exact measure. This is the mark of agape, which is indifferent about getting something in return, on the exchange of gifts. This gap between giving/receiving and receiving/returning is thus both opened up and bridged by gratitude. It is finally to the forms of failure of the gift that we owe this deepening of our analysis of the exchange of gifts in terms of an ethics of gratitude, based on an analysis of ideal types.

My last set of remarks will bring us back to my initial proposal, which was to confront the lived experience of the gift with the struggle for recognition and the uncertainty of its being accomplished in an actual experience of being-recognized. I want to place the final emphasis on the ceremonial character of the gift. It is not enough to say that this ceremonial character is meant to distinguish the exchange of gifts from commercial exchanges by setting it apart from transactions having to do with buying and selling. Nor does it suffice to say that it underscores the prevalence of the generosity of the first gift over the obligation that governs a gift in return. This ceremonial character stands in a complex relation with the symbolic character of a recognition that I will risk saying is unaware of itself, insofar as it clothes itself and conveys itself in the exchange. There is more: the ceremonial character, as emphasized by the ritual attitudes of the partners, which are meant to distinguish the exchange of gifts from the exchanges of everyday life, are intended to underscore and protect the *festive* character of such exchanges. I want to dwell on this festive character, in order to set it apart from the moralizing reduction we see already sprouting from the Stoic praise of "good deeds" turned into duties, a reduction that takes on the breadth we recognize in organized charities and caretaking institutions which legitimately aim to fill the gaps left by distributive and redistributive justice. This is not to condemn those nonprofit enterprises and institutions, whose social necessity is evident, and which clearly need to be attached to a broader conception of justice. The problem has to do with what there is about the festive that escapes such moralization. Its exceptional character seems to plead against it. It is the same with the festive in the practice of gift giving as it is with solemnity in the gesture of forgiveness, or rather the request for pardon of which I spoke in the epilogue to *Memory, History, Forgetting*, referring to German chancellor Willi Brandt's falling to his knees in Warsaw before the monument to the memory of the victims of the Shoah.[77] Such gestures, I said, cannot become an institution, yet by bringing to light the limits of the justice of equivalence, and opening space for hope at the horizon of politics and of law on the postnational and international level, they unleash an irradiating and irrigating wave that, secretly and indirectly, contributes to the advance of history toward states of peace. The festive, which can inhabit the rituals of love, in its erotic, amicable, or societal forms, belongs to the same spiritual family as do the requests for pardon just referred to. Moreover, the festive aspect of the gift, as a gesture, is like the hymn on the verbal plane, or, more generally, all those uses of language I like to place under the grammatical patronage of the optative, which is neither a descriptive nor a normative mode of speech.

It is now possible to return to the question posed at the end of the preceding chapter concerning the relation between the theme of the struggle for recognition and that of states of peace. When, we asked, can an individual take for granted having been recognized? Does not the request for recognition run the risk of being endless? In regard to this existential question we proposed the hypothesis that in the exchange of gifts social partners experience actual recognition. But I added one reservation to this expectation. We must not expect from this investigation of recognition through the gift more than a suspension of the dispute. So I spoke of a "clearing" in the forest of perplexities. Now we can say why this is so. The experience of the gift, apart from its symbolic, indirect, rare, even exceptional character, is inseparable from its burden of potential conflicts, tied to the creative tension between generosity and obligation. These are the paradoxes and aporias arising from the analysis of the gift as an ideal type, which the experience of the gift carries in its pairing with the struggle for recognition.

The struggle for recognition perhaps remains endless. At the very least, the experiences of actual recognition in the exchange of gifts, principally in their festive aspect, confer on this struggle for recognition the assurance that the motivation which distinguishes it from the lust for power and shelters it from the fascination of violence is neither illusory nor vain.

CONCLUSION: A REVIEW

The question I want to confront in these concluding pages is what justifies the "course" chosen for this book. What kind of connection among arguments does it assume? If I do not claim that overall it amounts to a theory, I am not resigned to seeing in it just a rhapsody of ideas. What place, then, remains between these two extremes for the course of my survey?

In preface to my answer I want to recall the assertion that lies at the origin of this work: that there is a contradiction between the absence of a theory of recognition comparable to that of knowledge in the history of philosophical doctrines on the one hand, and on the other the coherence that on the lexicographical plane allows us to place within a single dictionary entry the variety of accepted uses of the term *recognition* in ordinary language. In fact, this is the first time in my philosophical work that I have taken as my guide, as my principal informant, an alphabetical and analogical dictionary like the *Grand Robert*. My debt to the preliminary work done by lexicographers is great. First of all, I owe to them the discovery of the breadth of the lexical field in question. This first acknowledgment put me on guard against any reduction to one particular sense, so frequent among contemporary thinkers—for example, the recognition of differences among individuals in some particular situation, a theme that did not appear until the end of our journey. Next, I owe to the dictionary the series of uses attested to by their being used in conversation and in literature. I have responded to this with my search for a guideline presiding over my own series. Finally, my last debt has to do with the enigma of the unsaid underlying the process spanning the gaps in meaning between two successive accepted senses encompassed within one and the same word, to which this conclusion is essentially devoted. As a result, my philosophical survey under the aegis of recognition could not simply repeat the rule-governed polysemy constructed by lexicographers under the single constraint of usage in everyday language. This impossibility is a consequence of the connection that the philosophical lexicon sets up between what I take as the "thought events" that lie at the origin of occurrence of previously unknown questions in the space of what can be thought.

I found an initial parry to this semantic disorder on the philosophical level with a grammatical consideration having to do with the difference in the use of the verb *to recognize*, depending whether it is taken in the active voice—"I recognize"—or the passive voice—"I am recognized." It seemed to me that this difference betrayed a clear reversal on the plane of the interconnections among philosophical uses of the term *recognition*, inasmuch as it was possible to make certain uses of the verb *recognize* correspond to the active voice, where the mastery of meaning by thought is expressed, and others to the passive voice; I mean the sense of *recognize* as a request in which "being recognized" is what is at stake. This, in broad strokes, is how the dynamic I could begin to call a "course" of recognition becomes apparent—I mean the passage from recognition-identification, where the thinking subject claims to master meaning, to mutual recognition, where the subject places him- or herself under the tutelage of a relationship of reciprocity, in passing through self-recognition in the variety of capacities that modulate one's ability to act, one's "agency." In this way, a philosophical equivalent can be given to the rule-governed polysemy

produced by the lexicographer's work based on the dispersed accepted senses of the everyday uses of a word taken from natural
language, my own French language.

Yet this ordering based on a merely grammatical argument
would remain a simple expedient if the derivation from one accepted sense to the next on the philosophical plane were not guided
by some underlying problematical issues whose organizing power
really appears only on rereading. While the bridging of gaps on the
lexical plane could be attributed to the unsaid concealed in the
definitions of preceding acceptations, this book can be considered
as focusing on the gaps at work over the whole course of its text. I
have divided it into three distinct lines of inquiry, whose interweaving will contribute in turn to a kind of interconnectedness worthy
of my title *The Course of Recognition*.

I put in first place the progression of the theme of identity, then,
passing beyond it, that of otherness, and finally, in a more hidden
background, that of the dialectic between recognition and misrecognition.

In dealing with identity, I never say that personal identity, even
when taken in terms of narrative identity, eliminates the logical
identity of something in general, as discussed in my first chapter.
Nor do I say that the recognized identity of members of a community through those transactions placed under the heading of mutual
recognition renders superfluous the features of the capable human
being. I would rather speak of a course of identity, beginning with
the identification of "something" in general, recognized to be other
than any other, then passing through the identification of "someone," on the occasion of the break with the conception of the world
as a representation, as *Vorstellung*, or, to speak like Levinas, upon
the "ruins of representation." It is from this transition between
"something" and "someone," dramatized by experience of the unrecognizable, that the transition can be constructed from "someone" to "oneself"—oneself recognizing him- or herself in his or her

capacities. This transition is reinforced by the epistemic synonymy between attestation and recognition. I am confident that "I can," I attest to it, I recognize it. Narrative identity is thus placed at the strategic point in our discussion of kinds of capacities, at that point where, in Hannah Arendt's words, narrative talks about the "who" of action. Unlike one of my earlier works—*Oneself as Another*—here I have not limited this discussion to a short list of capacities. I have opened the list, not only as I had previously begun to do with the idea of imputability, but also now with the addition of the pair memory and promise, where the temporality of the self unfolds in the directions of past and future, at the same time that the lived present reveals its double valence of presence and initiative. What is acquired with recognition-attestation is not lost, much less abolished with the passage to the stage of mutual recognition. First of all, I will say that here it is still a question of identification. Being-recognized, should it occur, would for everyone be to receive the full assurance of his or her identity, thanks to the recognition by others of each person's range of capacities. As for the complement that I believe I had to add to the idea of a struggle for recognition, in the sense of mutual recognition through an exchange of gifts, it now gives me a chance to underscore the persistence even here of the idea of recognition-identification. It is the same dialectic that carries through from the "something" in general, in passing through the "someone" and the "oneself," up to this figure of identity in mutuality for which the Greeks reserved the magnificent pronoun *alleloi* and adverb *allelon*—"one another," "each other."

This is my first justification of the term *course* for this series of inquiries: the course of identity with its gaps and divergent meanings, its reprise of the logical sense of identification in its existential sense, and its recapitulation in being-recognized, thanks to the experiences of the struggle for recognition and that of states of peace. These reprises to me have the value of making sense of the gaps between them that gives its raison d'être to the present work.

The course of alterity unfolds in tandem with that of identity. To take this fully into account, we need to undertake a backward reading of this work. Alterity is at its peak in mutuality. The Kantian schema of "reciprocal action," anticipated in the framework of recognition-identification, finds fulfillment here, on the plane of the human sciences, which Kant did not have in mind in his theory of the schematism or in the complementary analyses of the Analytic of Principles, in the forms of reciprocity we have considered, among them that of the noncommercial reciprocity marked by what is without price. The struggle for recognition, which for me precedes the recognition at work in the ceremonial exchange of gifts, places alterity/confrontation at the center of the picture. My dialogue with Axel Honneth was the occasion for placing the emphasis on the forms of conflict that correspond to the three models of recognition singled out by Hegel in his Jena period. For my part, I referred to other forms of conflict, having to do with social competition. This was the case for what Boltanski and Thévenot call economies of standing, where the justification of each person's position on comparative scales of greatness corresponds to the plurality of cities or worlds among which these economies of standing are distributed. The forms of compromise that these authors refer to at the end of their work recall the kinds of truce that states of agape and their horizon of reconciliation represent. No doubt we should mention as well my analyses, made within another framework, of the dialectic of love characterized by superabundance—and justice governed by the rule of equivalence.[1] In a word, the figures of alterity are innumerable on the plane of mutual recognition. The last ones we considered in this text interweave conflict and shared generosity.

Moving further back in our investigation, I would emphasize, and if need be note, the anticipations of mutuality in the part of this work devoted to self-recognition. I deliberately placed the principal emphasis on self-assertion *(Selbstbehauptung)* in the investigation of human capacities. It was necessary to do this, in order subsequently to give mutual recognition its full meaning. What transactions based on reciprocity are meant to bring to full flower are the presumed capacities of the agents of such transactions, who bring themselves to them through their agency. Social relations do not replace this capacity of individuals to act. In this regard, the equation between attestation and recognition can only reinforce the self-assertive character of self-recognition. That being said, a rereading of the pages devoted to the exploration of human capacities should join to each modality of the "I can" an often tacit correlation between self-assertion and some reference to others. Self-assertion does not signify solipsism. The reference to the responsibility for one's actions beginning with the age of the Homeric heroes would be the first place to undertake such a reconstruction of the relations of alterity implied in each deliberate decision to act. The whole Greek army gathered before its ships bears witness to the exploits of its leaders. Achilles' anger is public; his withdrawing into his tent takes place before everyone. And the final reconciliation around the funeral pyre is not far from being equivalent to some of the states of peace spoken of with reference to mutual recognition. Nor should we forget that the final recognition between Ulysses and Penelope, which ends the labors of the one whom the poet calls "the man of a thousand wiles," comes at the price of a dreadful slaughter of the rivals for her hand. "Vengeance" is the title ordinarily given to this part by editors, and undoubtedly also by the public, and even the bard himself in the closing books of the *Iliad*. Can we think of a worse kind of alterity, joined to the recognition of responsibility for one's action, than the massacre of all the hero's rivals?

In the same spirit, we ought to undertake a further review of those capacities that, taken together, paint the portrait of the capable human being. In relation to the Greeks, I have placed the accent on the reflexivity that justifies the expression of self-assertion. But this reflexivity must not overshadow the alterity implied in the exercise of each modality of the "I can." If it is possible to abstract from every bond of intersubjectivity in analyzing capacities on the level of potential actions, the passage from a capacity to its exercise does not allow for such an elision. To speak—in effect, to say something—presupposes an expectation of being heard. The well-known relation between question and answer is exemplary in this regard. When self-designation takes the form "As for me, my name is . . . ," self-assertion presupposes an act of adoption by others in the form of assigning a name to me, and thanks to my birth certificate, everyone recognizes me as a subject even before I have learned to make use of this capacity to designate myself. Nevertheless, no mutuality is as yet put to the test in this interweaving of self-designation and being named by others.

The case of being able to act, dealt with as the second form of our capacity to act, calls for the same kind of complement as does self-designation in the dimension of being able to speak. Exercising this capacity to make events happen in the physical and social world takes place in a setting of interaction, where the other can take on over time the role of obstacle, helper, or fellow actor, as in meetings where it is sometimes impossible to isolate each person's contribution. Yet it remains the case that if intersubjectivity is here one manifest condition of such an exercise, it is not, like the power to act, its ground.

As for the power to narrate to which I have more than once, following Hannah Arendt, attributed the virtue of designating the "who" of action, it is submitted in its exercise to the same conditions as action itself, whose emplotment constitutes mimesis. There is no narrative that does not mix together different life stories, as is well documented by literature dealing with self-awareness. The plot is the configuration that weaves together events and characters. Finally, narrating, like saying, calls for an ear, a power to hear, a reception (which stems, moreover, from an aesthetic of reception that is not at issue here). Yet here again the superimposed layers of interaction in saying, acting, and recounting must not obliterate the primary reference to the power to act for which self-recognition constitutes the attestation.

Hence the idea of imputability centers on this power to act, over against some other person, who can be by turns an interrogator (who did this?), an inquisitor (admit it—you are the author responsible for this act), an accuser (get ready to bear the consequences of your act, to repair the harm you have done, and to suffer the penalty). It is before the judge, who assigns guilt more often than he offers praise, that the subject admits to being the actual author of his act. In this way, the other in a way encompasses the same.

Memory and promises, which I sought to place under the rubric of assumed capacities, have the virtue of revealing the temporal dimension of each of the powers considered. I refer to them here in order to proceed to another conjunction, that of recognition in time and before others, a pairing that was implicit in the power to speak, and in the moment of self-designation when a story of a life comes together under a proper name that was pronounced by someone else before being said by the one who now names him- or herself.

This pairing of recognition in time and before others takes on different forms, it is true, depending on whether it is a question of memory or of promises. The relation of a memory that is essentially my own to the memories of others which takes place only through the signs they give, principally on the plane of narrative, can of course take on the form of a sharing of memories on the interpersonal level of friendship, or on the public one of reference to the episodes of a common history. But the relating of memories can also turn into a conflict through the competition among memories about the same events that do not agree. In such cases, alterity can lead to people reciprocally cutting themselves off from one another. The relation between recognition in time and recognition before others turns out to be different in the case of promises. The relation of standing before the other person comes to the fore. It is not only before the other person, but for the other's good that one makes a promise. Yet, like testimony, a promise may not be heard, accepted; it can even be refused, rejected, subjected to suspicion. But the relation to time is not absent. Not only does the promise engage the future; the present credibility of the one making the promise sums up a whole personal history that gives signs of a habitual trustworthiness. In this, the promise links up with both recognition in time and recognition before others.

In these different ways self-recognition refers to others without this reference's assuming the position of a ground, like that of the power to act, nor does the "before others" imply reciprocity and mutuality. The mutuality of recognition is anticipated in this "before others," but is not accomplished in it.

Should we then take one more step backward from self-recognition and seek the marks of intersubjectivity in the recognition-identification of something in general? Undoubtedly we should. Taken as an act of language, the assertion invested in the act of judgment requires the commitment of the speaker just as much as do specific performative locutions, for which the promise remains a key example. And this commitment includes an expectation of the approbation of others. The case of Descartes is especially noteworthy in this regard. The *Meditations* were published in the same volume along with the Objections and Replies. The example of Descartes including his own thoughts in a process of philosophizing together with others continues in his abundant correspondence. And Kant, too, in responding in the text of the *Critique of Pure Reason* to the negation of the ideality of time, seeks not just a reader, but a willing accomplice in his Copernican revolution. Here once again, it is before others that the solitary thinker presumes to undertake the discourse of the transcendental ego beneath the signature of the Königsberg professor.

I want now to add to this course of identity and alterity another, less obvious one having to do with the relations between recognition and misrecognition over the course of these reflections. In fact, the shadow of misrecognition continues to darken the light that may come from the work of clarification, of "existential elucidation" (to use the title of the second volume of Karl Jasper's *Philosophy*) that is at issue throughout this book.[2]

In the phase of recognition-identification, the mind's claim to master the sense of something in general found an appropriate expression in the verb *to recognize* used in the active voice. But this claim to "grasp things" was shadowed by the fear of "mistaking" them, which consists in taking a thing or a person for what it or he or she is not. The time-honored Cartesian equating of identifying and distinguishing, expressed as "distinguishing the true from the false," gives us the opportunity to indicate the possible place of mistaking, extended onto the interpersonal plane by misunderstanding [*malentendu*]. We cannot fail to recall here the fear of failure that runs through Descartes from the *Discourse on Method* to its apogee in the fourth *Meditation*. The power to fail, in effect, is the torment that the analysis of judgment is meant to ward off. We think here too of Pascal's painful words from the *Entretien avec M. de Saci sur Épictète et Montaigne* (cited by the *Grand Robert*): "The essence of misunderstanding consists in not knowing." The not knowing is magnified by the fact that it does not recognize itself. No critical vigilance will ever completely remove this threat of failure. In referring to a "return to the things themselves" at the end of my first chapter, I indicated the fallibility of the credit given to the appearance of what is perceived, which Merleau-Ponty called a kind of faith or primordial opinion, in the wake of Husserl's *Urdoxa* or *Urglaube*. The play of appearing, disappearing, and reappearing is the occasion for cruel disappointments that also can include "self-deception." The test of misunderstanding, which ended this chapter, shakes our confidence in the capacity of things and persons to make themselves recognized. An acceptance of a kind of companionship with misunderstanding, which goes with the ambiguities of an incomplete, open-ended life world, has to re-place the fear of error.

In the second chapter, the shadow of misunderstanding continues to deepen. Admitting that every capacity has as its counterpart a specific incapacity is easy to accept in its generality. The details of these incapacities, on the basis of the distinct registers of the power to act, reveals ever more concealed forms of incapacity whereby misunderstanding leads to "self-deception." The mistake then is to mis-take oneself, to take oneself for what one is not.

The power to speak, which we deliberately placed at the head of the modalities of the "I can," is burdened by a difficulty in putting things into words, even an inability to speak. This inability shows that we can always mistake the underlying motivations that hinder our need to say something. The kinship among secret, inhibition, resistance, disguise, lie, and hypocrisy is as close as it is hidden. The ipseity won from sameness at such a price on the conceptual plane is also the place for misunderstanding. Moreover, once again, what touches our personal identity also affects the whole fabric of our relations with others. We do not mistake ourselves without also being mistaken about others and our relations with them. If the essence of being mistaken is, as Pascal says, "not knowing," the misunder-standing of oneself does not avoid the risk of misunderstanding itself.

We cannot end this overview of the incapacities that cast a shadow over the attestation of my power to act without referring to those which affect memory and promises. On the one hand, forget-ting; on the other, perjury. Just as forgetting as the effacement of traces is an incapacity we undergo, its cunning forms contribute to misleading both oneself and others. As for perjury, it merits being called inability to keep one's word only as a kind of excuse, whether this excuse is acceptable or not. What is frightening about perjury is that it is a form of power, inseparable from the power to promise, the power not to keep one's word. By destroying the trustworthiness of the one who promises, this power of betrayal weakens the whole institution of language, insofar as it depends on our confidence in what others say.

It was in the third chapter that the dialectic between recognition and misrecognition first acquired its greatest visibility before taking on its forms of greatest dissimulation.

The investigation of mutual recognition can be summed up as a struggle against the misrecognition of others at the same time that it is a struggle for recognition of oneself by others. Hobbes's challenge, to which the theory of *Anerkennung* is meant to reply, is based on a fictitious description of the state of nature where distrust occupies the middle ground in the enumeration of the passions that lead to the war of all against all. However, we left room for the recognition at work in the expectation that each of the partners, in those contracts preceding the great contract of each with Leviathan, will at the proper time yield power along with everyone else.

Yet it is at the very heart of *Anerkennung* that the competition between recognition and misrecognition is revealed, both as regards self-recognition and as regards recognition of others. We have not forgotten the sequence on crime, the expression par excellence of the famous "work of the negative." The criminal makes himself recognized in his rebellious singularity vis-à-vis the law that refuses to recognize [*méconnaît*] him. In this way, misrecognition finds itself incorporated into the dynamic of recognition. This dialectic deploys its full resources in recent applications of the Hegelian theory. It is not surprising that it is negative feelings that motivate the conflicts that are at work in the successive models of recognition, on the level of emotions, then on the juridical and social levels. These negative feelings find their emblematic sense in the word *contempt*. In French we can place the word for contempt [*mépris*] lexically close to the one for mistake [*méprise*], the figure of misunderstanding we saw in the first chapter. From mistaking to contempt, we might say. This closeness on the verbal level gives us an occasion for comparing their respective roles in their contexts of usage. Given the threat of making errors, mistakes are something to avoid, and first of all to discover and condemn. It is only after the fact that mistakes show themselves to be a relevant part of the search for the truth. With contempt, the incorporation of the negative into the winning of recognition is complete. We may even dare to speak here of the work of misrecognition in the gaining of recognition. It is this involvement of misrecognition in recognition that leads to the expression "struggle for recognition"—where conflict is the soul of this process.

This inherence of misrecognition in recognition in the form of contempt sets us on the path toward a form of misrecognition that our last reflections devoted to the gift and the exchange of gifts give us a way of detecting. Recall that the transition from the theme of struggle to that of the gift was linked to a question having to do with the always incomplete nature of the struggle for recognition. It was as a truce at the heart of this endless conflict that the actual experience of a ceremonial exchange of gifts was invoked as a special form of states of peace.

It is precisely the promises contained in such states of peace that pose the problem of a concealed form of misrecognition that could not be uncovered until the idea of mutuality had been brought to term. We defended the idea of a mutuality exercised "between" the protagonists of such an exchange against its reduction to a form of reciprocity where the relation takes place at a transcendent level in relation to the transactions between those who give and those who receive.

It was then that the idea arose of a mutual recognition backed by the gift as something given. And we risked the complementary idea that this recognition did not recognize itself, to such a degree was it invested in the exchange of gifts that substitute for it even while securing it. Following Derrida, the question then arises whether there may not be, associated with this one, a more subtle form of misrecognition that misrecognizes itself.

What kind of misrecognition? That of the originary asymmetry between the self and the other, an asymmetry that mutual reciprocity does not eliminate. An asymmetry that would like to forget itself in the happiness of "each other." Even in the festivity of an exchange of gifts, the other remains inaccessible in his or her alterity as such. Misrecognized or recognized, the other remains unknown in terms of an originary apprehension of the mineness of selfhood.

This misrecognition is not that of misrecognizing someone, but rather that of misrecognizing the asymmetry in the relation between me and the other.

Here the discussion comes up again that I deliberately placed at the head of the second chapter, as a kind of anticipatory text held in reserve for the discussion of this final phase of the dialectic between recognition and misrecognition.

It is first as a hindrance, even a calling into question of the whole phenomenological enterprise, that there appears the difficulty that phenomenology encounters in trying to get beyond this originary asymmetry between the self and others, and in forming an idea of reciprocity that is just as essential to the idea of truth as that of justice. This hindrance is exacerbated by the fact of the opposition between two versions of this originary asymmetry—that of Husserl, which takes the ego as its pole of reference, and that of Levinas, which proceeds from the other person to the ego. It is as if there existed no higher point of view on this divergence in approaches, and as if one could take up the question of the passage from this asymmetry to reciprocity only in one of these two ways, something that renders the whole argument concerning the preeminence of one way over the other pointless and sterile.

We recall that for Husserl the egological stage of self-consciousness is attained at the price of what we can call a stunning response to the objection of solipsism. Adopted as a kind of ascetic discipline, this objection requires "constituting" the alterity of others "in" and "through" self-consciousness, with no other point of reference than the "sphere of belonging" that alone can be said to be originary. What belongs to the experience of others then arises through what Husserl calls an "analogizing grasp" and at best a "pairing." As for another person's experience of him- or herself, it remains forever closed to me in its innermost form, and is at best only analogical for me, even in the most favorable case of a confirmation of my presumptions drawn from the coherence of the other's gestures and verbal expressions, deciphered from his or her bodily appearance. I alone belong to myself as "presented"; the other, the presumed analogue, remains "appresented." I shall not dwell on the laborious character of the subsequent derivation of the idea of a common nature, within which I appear to myself as myself, one other among others, nor that of "communities" that can be called intermonadic. The closing paragraphs of the fifth *Cartesian Meditation* are devoted to this derivation. With great effort, some thinkers who take up the phenomenological heritage have undertaken to construct an "intentional sociology" on the basis of Husserl's fifth *Meditation*. The laborious character of this phenomenology of others, which counts against it, authorizes us at the end of our own undertaking to consider once again its meaning and to discern in it a powerful reminder, when praise of mutual recognition leads us to forget the originary asymmetry in the relation between the self and others, which even the experience of peaceful states does not manage to abolish. Forgetting this asymmetry, thanks to the success of analyses of mutual recognition, would constitute the ultimate misrecognition at the very heart of actual experiences of recognition.

For me, the same reproach can be directed at many readings of Levinas's *Totality and Infinity* and *Otherwise than Being or Beyond Essence.* We ought not to forget that the subtitle of the former work is "Essay on Exteriority." The first exteriority is that of the voice and its primordially ethical accent. The alterity of others is not perceptual, which would threaten to allow the other's difference to be absorbed into the dominion of the idea of totality, un-

262 · THE COURSE OF RECOGNITION

folded by ontologies with their idea of being. It is in the ethical mode of interpellation that the ego is called to responsibility by the other's voice. Levinas's second work radicalizes this idea of exteriority even further by that of the "Otherwise," by virtue of which the ethical "saying" constantly breaks away from the "said," which semantics and ontology articulate in their own ways. It is against the background of this primordial ethics which grants the first word to the Other that the difficulties relative to the theme of the third party, the agent of justice and truth, stand out. These difficulties, which are symmetrical with those encountered by Husserl in the fifth *Cartesian Meditation*, are the ones that are also easily placed on the debit side of a philosophy held to be incapable of moving from the dissymmetry between the self and the other to their reciprocity and mutuality.

Again, and beyond any quarrel over the preeminence of Husserl or Levinas, I want to turn the objections that each phenomenologist runs into along his own way into a warning addressed to every conception of the primacy of reciprocity over the alterity of the protagonists in an exchange with each other. Earlier, the problem was to overcome this dissymmetry in order to make sense of reciprocity and mutuality. Now it is just the opposite: How to integrate into mutuality the dissymmetry, in response to the suspicion that this dissymmetry is capable of undermining from within any confidence in the power of reconciliation attaching to the process of recognition? My thesis here is that the discovery of this forgetfulness about dissymmetry is beneficial to recognition in its mutual form.

What is at stake is the meaning of the "between" that we have so stressed over the course of the discussion that led us to distinguish mutuality on the plane of relations "between" protagonists of the exchange of gifts from reciprocity conceived of as a transcendent form of circulation of goods and values, where the individual actors are merely its bearers.

It is in the "between" of the expression "between the protagonists of the exchange" that is concentrated the dialectic of the dissymmetry between me and others and the mutuality of our relations. And it is to the full meaning of this "between" that the integration of this dissymmetry into mutuality in the exchange of gifts contributes.

Admitting the threat that lies in forgetting this dissymmetry first calls attention to the irreplaceable character of each of the partners in the exchange. The one is not the other. We exchange gifts, but not places. The second benefit of this admission is that it protects mutuality against the pitfalls of a fusional union, whether in love, friendship, or fraternity on a communal or a cosmopolitan scale. A just distance is maintained at the heart of mutuality, a just distance that integrates respect into intimacy.

Finally, gratitude, the last form of recognition considered in this work, receives from the dialectic between dissymmetry and mutuality a surplus of meaning. We have considered reception as the pivotal term between giving and giving in return. In receiving, the place of gratitude, the dissymmetry between the giver and the receiver is affirmed twice over: other is the one who gives and the one who receives; other is the one who receives and the one who gives in return. This twofold alterity is preserved in the act of receiving and in the gratitude it gives rise to.

Long before Simone Weil pleaded for distance in the proximity of love and friendship, Montaigne, mourning his friend La Boétie, wrote these lines in the chapter on friendship in book 1 of his *Essays:* "In the friendship I speak of, our souls mingle and blend with each other so completely that they efface the seam that joined them and cannot find it again. If you press me to tell why I loved him, I feel that it cannot be expressed, except by answering: Because it was he, because it was I."[3]

ACKNOWLEDGMENTS

Having completed the writing of this work, I want to address my thanks to the two institutions that welcomed the lectures from which it stems: the Institute for Human Sciences in Vienna and the Husserl Archives in Freiburg, Germany.

Also, I want to address my deepest feelings of gratitude to those friends who accompanied me through some difficult times and who contributed to the conception and execution of this book.

I especially want to acknowledge François Azouvi with whom we have shared so much over the decades and whom I wish to thank for including me in the series he edits.

NOTES

Introduction

1. Émile Littré, *Dictionnaire de la langue française* (Paris: Hachette, 1889); Alain Rey, ed., *Le grand Robert de la langue française,* 2nd ed. (Paris: Robert, 1985).

2. Antoine Furetière, *Dictionnaire universel françois et latin,* 3 vols. (Trévoux, 1704).

3. Littré gathers together at the end of his list those uses which in appearance do not differ from the grammar of the meanings already considered. "To recognize oneself" in the sense of "to find a resemblance in a portrait, a mirror" (which goes with sense 2: "to recognize someone by certain signs"). To this is added the reflexive movement toward oneself. This would be important if we were to take into account the recognition of a memory, not really emphasized by Littré. He came before Bergson, after all. Next comes an addition to the very first meaning, where recognition doubles knowing: "to call to mind the idea of a place one has known or in which one finds oneself once again." It is oneself that one recognizes, but thanks to the mark of a place: one recognizes oneself *there* [*on s'y reconnaît*]. "To recognize oneself in" adds nothing to recognizing a sign, unless it is oneself. Similarly, "to recognize oneself as" stems from avowal: it is to avow "something about oneself" (number 21). The next number follows from this, which underscores the admission of error: "22. To know that one has sinned, made a mistake."

4. Rudolf Hallig and Walter von Wartburg, *Begriffssystem als Grundlage*

für die Lexikographie: Versuch eines Ordnunngsschemas = Système raisonné des concepts pour servir de base à la lexiocographie: Essai d'un schéma de classement, 2nd ed. (Berlin: Akademie-Verlag, 1963); P. Boissière, *Le dictionnaire analogique de la langue française,* 9th ed. (Paris: Larousse, 1900).

5. Paul Imbs, ed. *Trésor de la langue française: Dictionnaire de la langue du XIXe et du XXe siècle,* 16 vols. (Paris: Éditions du Centre national de la recherché scientifique, 1971–1994).

1. Recognition as Identification

1. In the sense that Heidegger makes a distinction between general [*existenzial*] and concrete, individuated [*existentiell*] structures of existence.—Trans.

2. Thus *The Sophist* goes on to say that "change" (the first great kind considered) is other than "rest" or other than "being." This metacategory of the other, Plato says, "pervades all of them, since each of them is different from the others, not because of its own nature but because of sharing in the type of the different" (255e). This reiteration without any recourse to some subsequent kind, or to any other kind, on this enigmatic page of *The Sophist* makes the *other* as the *different* the fifth and final term of the series. Plato emphasizes the dignity of this "grand kind": "Because as applied to all of them the nature of the *different* makes each of them not to be, by making it different from that which it is" (256e). Thus, being is not the highest notion of philosophy in relation to change and permanence, if it accepts being supplemented by this difficult-to-grasp category. Being comes third, because there is a fifth, otherness, difference.

3. Auguste Diès, *La définition de l'être et la nature des idées dans le Sophiste de Platon* (Paris: Vrin, 1932).

4. *Discourse on Method,* in *The Philosophical Writings of Descartes,* 2 vols., trans. John Cottingham, Robert Stoothoff, and Dugald Murdoch (New York: Cambridge University Press, 1985), 1:112–113.

5. Not everything has been said about the idea and its relation to the definitions of *simple, clear,* and *distinct.* Ideas, let us not forget, are "ideas of things." Beyond their presence in the mind, they have a representative value that allows us to speak of the "idea of things." "Some of my thoughts are as it were the images of things, and it is only in these

cases that the term 'idea' is strictly appropriate—for example, when I think of a man, or a chimera, or the sky, or an angel, or God" (*Meditations on First Philosophy*, ibid., 2:25). What is more, attached to the idea of representation is that of an "objective reality," of "objective being," through which the idea takes on a noteworthy ontological status. This latter aspect is so essential that it serves as the premise for the argument in the third *Meditation*, where the existence of God is demonstrated starting from the idea that this "objective reality" presents degrees of perfection: "Undoubtedly, the ideas which represent substances to me amount to something more and, so to speak, contain within themselves more objective reality than the ideas which merely represent modes or accidents." For example, the idea of God "certainly has in it more objective reality than the ideas that represent finite substances" (ibid., 28). The argument that then follows, applying causal reasoning to this objective reality and leading to the conclusion that the idea I have of God cannot exhaustively have its origin in me alone, owing to my imperfections, but proceeds from God himself, is not at issue here. My point is that to affirm that the kind of perfection that attaches to the objective reality of the idea, as the idea of something, constitutes the *definiens* of the sought-for clear idea. In this way, the correlation between the pair *clear* and *distinct*, and the pair *define* and *distinguish*, which I am taking as the first approximation of an integral concept of recognition, is complete.

6. The French reads: "Je n'ai plus de peine à reconnaître."—Trans.
7. The French reads: "J'ai découvert une raison suffisante."—Trans.
8. The French reads: "Depuis que j'ai reconnu."—Trans.
9. There are other occurrences of the verb *recognize* in the *Meditations*. It occurs in the second *Meditation*, in a context comparable to that of the fourth one. Descartes has shown that for the soul, to exist is to think. But a scruple slips in: "What else am I? I will use my imagination. I am not that structure of limbs which is called a human body. I am not even some thin vapour which permeates the limbs—a wind, a fire, air, breath, or whatever I depict in my imagination; for these are things which I have supposed to be nothing. Let this supposition stand; for all that I am still something. And yet it may not be the case that these very things which I am supposing to be nothing, because they are unknown to me, are in reality identical with the 'I' of which I am aware [*que j'ai reconnu être*]?" *(novi me existere; quaero auis sim ego ille quem novi)*

(2:18). *Novi:* in the accomplished past. It is the situation of recognizing [*reconnaître*] in relation to knowing [*connaître*]. Elsewhere we find occurrences of the verb referring to the idea of a sign of recognition. In one reply to the second set of objections we read this: "So I thought I would be doing something worthwhile if I explained how the properties or qualities of the mind are to be distinguished from the qualities of the body [*et comment il faut les reconnaître*]" (94). And a bit further on, discussing the question whether an atheist can clearly know that the angles of a triangle are equal to two right angles, Descartes does not dispute this excessive suggestion, but maintains that he does not know them on the basis of a true, certain science. He will always be in danger of being deceived about things that seem quite evident to him and never will be "free of this doubt until he acknowledges [*reconnaître*] that God exists" (101). With these passages we rediscover uses of *recognition* from the lexicon of everyday language.

10. There "are two stems of human knowledge—namely, *sensibility* and *understanding,* which perhaps spring from a common, but to us unknown root. Through the former, objects are given to us; through the latter, they are thought." Immanuel Kant, *Critique of Pure Reason,* trans. Norman Kemp Smith (New York: St. Martin's, 1965), A15/B30.

11. Let us recall the quite special terminology of the *Critique:* "logic in general" is the name given to the science of the rules of understanding in general (A52). That logic is called transcendental which considers only the form in the relationship governing what is known, that is, "the form of thought in general" (A55). Speaking of truth, ordinarily defined as the conformity of knowledge to its object, for this strict framework it is only a question of the criteria for the conformity between the rules of understanding and the principles of sensibility, to the exclusion of the material truth of empirical propositions. This reduction of the field of truth to the transcendental plane has its counterpart in the dismantling of the empty allegations that the mind forges concerning what is beyond the limited field of the transcendental aesthetics, that is, reference to something in space and time. Therefore, a logic of appearances will parallel this transcendental logic. This will be divided between an analytic of concepts devoted to the division of the understanding into a number of formal principles, the categories, and an analytic of principles devoted to the faculty of judgment. The former makes sense only in relation to the latter, which returns judgment to the place of honor that belongs to it.

12. The French translation of Kant reads: "un art caché . . . nous aurons de la peine à arracher la nature des secrets."
13. I shall retain the German word *Vorstellung,* traditionally translated by "representation," in order not to compromise other uses of representation irreducible to the Kantian use, as is the case for my own works.
14. Edmund Husserl, *The Crisis of European Sciences and Transcendental Philosophy,* trans. David Carr (Evanston, Ill.: Northwestern University Press, 1970).
15. Emmanuel Levinas, *Discovering Existence with Husserl,* trans. Richard A. Cohen and Michael B. Smith (Evanston, Ill.: Northwestern University Press, 1998), 111–121.
16. Levinas is quoting from Husserl's *Cartesian Meditations,* trans. Dorian Cairns (The Hague: Martinus Nijhoff, 1973), 46.
17. Martin Heidegger, *Kant and the Problem of Metaphysics,* 5th ed., trans. Richard Taft (Bloomington: Indiana University Press, 1997).
18. "The Laying of the Ground for Metaphysics as 'Critique of Pure Reason.'"
19. Maurice Merleau-Ponty, *Phenomenology of Perception,* trans. Colin Smith (New York: Humanities Press, 1962), 299–345.
20. "It is . . . quite true that any perception . . . any perceptual constancy refers back to the positing of a world and of a system of experience in which my body is inescapably linked with phenomena" (ibid., 303–304).
21. Rainer Maria Rilke and Balthus, *Lettres à un jeune peintre* suivi de *Mitsou* (Paris: Payot et Rivages, 2002).
22. "A thing, then, will be affected by time, just as we are accustomed to say that time wastes things away, and that all things grow old through time, and that people forget owing to the lapse of time, but we do not say the same of getting to know or of becoming young or fair. For time is by its nature the cause rather of decay, since it is the number of change, and change removes what is." Aristotle, *Physics,* book IV, 221a30-b2.
23. Marcel Proust, *Time Regained,* trans. Andreas Mayor and Terence Kilmartin, ed. D. J. Enright (New York: Modern Library, 1993), 336.

2. Recognizing Oneself

1. Bernard Williams, *Shame and Necessity* (Berkeley: University of California Press, 1993).

2. "If people need a *thumos* to think or feel with, it is equally true that a *thumos* needs a person if any thinking or feeling is to go on" (ibid., 26–27).

3. In this regard, I do not share Williams's ironic skepticism concerning such a desire for more depth when, speaking for them, he says, "The Greeks were not involved in those attempts; this is one of the places at which we encounter their gift for being superficial out of profundity" (68).

4. Ricoeur cites the French translation of *L'Odyssée* by Victor Bérard (Paris: Belles Lettres, 1924).—Trans.

5. Ricoeur cites the French translation of Sophocles, *Oedipe à Colone,* trans. Paul Masqueray (Paris: Belles Lettres, 1934).—Trans.

6. Ricoeur cites the French translation of Aristotle, *Éthique à Nicomaque,* trans. René Antoine Gauthier and Jean-Yves Jolif (Paris: Béatrice-Nauwelaerts, 1958).—Trans.

7. "Wisdom has human goods as its object, that is, those which provide matter for deliberation. For as soon as we speak of a wise man, that is above all the task we attribute to him: to deliberate well. Now, no one deliberates about things that cannot be other than they are, nor about anything that is not directed to some end, and to an end that would be an object of action. Furthermore, the excellent deliberator, purely and simply, is the one who aims to attain the best of the objects offered to human beings and calculates so well that he hits the bull's-eye" (1441b8–13).

8. Hans-Georg Gadamer translates this *to hauto eidenai* as *Sichwisse* in his *Wahrheit und Methode,* 2nd ed. (Tübingen: Mohr, 1965), 298; *Truth and Method,* 2nd rev. ed., trans. Joel Weinsheimer and Donald G. Marshall (New York: Crossroad, 1991), 314: the object of the moral sciences is "man and what he knows of himself."

9. Jean Nabert, *Le désir de Dieu* (Paris: Cerf, 1996).

10. J. L. Austin, *How to Do Things with Words* (Cambridge, Mass.: Harvard University Press, 1963).

11. Elizabeth Anscombe, *Intention* (Oxford: Blackwell, 1957), 48.

12. Donald Davidson, *Essays on Actions and Events* (Oxford: Clarendon Press, 1980).

13. Vladimir Propp, *Morphology of the Folktale,* trans. Laurence Scott; 2nd rev. ed., ed. Louis A. Wagner (Austin: University of Texas Press, 1968).

14. A. J. Greimas, *Structural Semantics: An Attempt at a Method,* trans.

Deniel McDowell, Ronald Schleifer, and Alan Velie (Lincoln: University of Nebraska Press, 1983).

15. Hans Robert Jauss, *Toward an Aesthetic of Reception*, trans. Timothy Bahti (Minneapolis: University of Minnesota Press, 1982).

16. Wilhelm Schapp, *In Geschichten Verstrickt* (Wiesbaden: B. Heymann, 1976). Jean Greisch draws on Schapp to present an alternative to my theory of narrative in his *Paul Ricoeur: L'itinéraire du sens* (Paris: Millon, 2001), 147–173. To my "well-tempered" notion of plot Greisch opposes the "untamed" notion of "being entangled in," with the aim of outlining their complementarity on the phenomenological plane.

17. Immanuel Kant, *The Metaphysics of Morals*, trans. and ed. Mary Gregor (Cambridge: Cambridge University Press, 1996), 16.

18. Here I shall not go into the attempts that have been made to bring together the disparate causalities of this coherent model in order to account for phenomena like initiative or intervention, which consist in making an action correspond to what we are permitted to do and where occasions of intervention are related to a finite and relatively closed physical system.

19. Hans Jonas, *The Imperative of Responsibility: In Search of an Ethics for the Technological Age* (Chicago: University of Chicago Press, 1984).

20. This treatise is one of those in the collection titled *Parva naturalia*. "On Memory," in *The Complete Works of Aristotle*, 2 vols, ed. Jonathan Barnes (Princeton, N.J.: Princeton University Press, 1984), 1:714–720. There is an earlier translation by Richard Sorabji, *Aristotle on Memory* (Providence, R.I.: Brown University Press, 1972).

21. The enigma of the presence of an absent thing is posed forcefully in *Theatetus* 163.

22. *The Collected Works of Spinoza*, vol. 1, ed. and trans. Edwin Curley (Princeton, N.J.: Princeton University Press, 1985), 465.

23. Edmund Husserl, *Phantasie, Bildbewusstsein, Erinnerung (1898–1925)*, ed. Eduard Marbach (Dordrecht: Martinus Nijhoff, 1980).

24. In Edmund Husserl, *On the Phenomenology of the Consciousness of Internal Time (1893–1917)*, trans. John Barnett Brough (Dordrecht: Kluwer Academic, 1991), 3–103.

25. "It is I who remember, I who am mind." Saint Augustine, *Confessions*, trans. Henry Chadwick (Oxford: Oxford University Press, 1991), 193.

26. Charles Taylor, *Sources of the Self* (Cambridge, Mass.: Harvard University Press, 1989).

27. John Locke, *An Essay concerning Human Understanding*, 2 vols. (New York: Dover, 1959), 1:439.
28. Derrick Parfit, *Reasons and Persons* (Oxford: Oxford University Press, 1986).
29. Henri Bergson, *Matter and Memory*, trans. N. M. Paul and W. S. Palmer (New York: Zone Books, 1988).
30. Henri Bergson, *Mind-Energy*, trans. H. Wildon Carr (Westport, Conn.: Greenwood, 1975), 186–230.
31. Henri Bergson, *The Creative Mind: An Introduction to Metaphysics* (New York: Philosophical Library, 1946), 75.
32. Bergson, *Matter and Memory*, 155.
33. Daniel Vanderbeken, *Les actes de discours* (Paris: Éditions Pierre Mardage, 1998), 7.
34. Here is Vanderbeken's definition: To promise "is the verb of commitment par excellence. However, a promise is a speech act of a type of commitment endowed with some rather particular features. In the first place, when one promises, one commits himself to the other party to do or give him something in presupposing that this is good for him (the first special condition). In the second place, a promise is successful only if the speaker is able to place himself under a certain obligation to do what he says. This special aspect of accomplishment augments the degree of force involved" (ibid., 176).
35. Friedrich Nietzsche, *Human, All Too Human: A Book for Free Spirits,* trans. R. J. Hollingdale (New York: Cambridge University Press, 1996), 42, no. 58.
36. See, for example, Vanderbeken, *Les actes de discours,* 167ff.
37. Hannah Arendt, *The Human Condition* (Chicago: University of Chicago Press, 1958).
38. Friedrich Nietzsche, *On the Genealogy of Morals* and *Ecce Homo,* trans. Walter Kaufmann and R. J. Hollingdale (New York: Vintage Books, 1967), 57.
39. Geoffrey E. R. Lloyd presents a devastating critique in his *Demystifying Mentalities* (Cambridge: Cambridge University Press, 1990).
40. Bernard Lepetit, ed., *Les formes de l'expérience: Une autre histoire sociale* (Paris: Albin Michel, 1995).
41. See, for example, Jacques Revel, ed., *Jeux d'échelles: La micro-analyse de l'expérience* (Paris: Gallimard/Seuil, 1996).
42. Norbert Elias, *The Court Society,* trans. Edmund Jephcott (New York:

Pantheon, 1983); *The Civilizing Process: Sociogenetic and Psychogenetic Investigations,* trans. Edmund Jephcott; ed. Eric Dunning, Johan Doudsblom, and Stephen Mennell (Malden, Mass: Blackwell, 2000).

43. Jean-Marc Ferry, *Les puissances de l'expérience: Essai sur l'identité contemporaine* (Paris: Cerf, 1991). The first volume of this work is titled "Le sujet et le verbe." In the first part the question of acts of discernment (feeling, acting, speaking) is considered; in the second, forms of identity. I am referring here to this first part of volume 1. I shall return in my next chapter to Ferry's discussion in volume 2 of "orders of recognition."

44. Amartya Sen, *On Ethics and Economics* (Oxford: Basil Blackwell, 1987); *Commodities and Capabilities* (Amsterdam: North Holland, 1985).

45. Robert Nozick, *Anarchy, State and Utopia* (New York: Basic Books, 1974); Ronald Dworkin, *Taking Rights Seriously* (Cambridge, Mass.: Harvard University Press, 1978); J. L. Mackie, *Ethics: Inventing Right and Wrong* (New York: Penguin, 1977).

46. Isaiah Berlin, *Four Essays on Liberty* (New York: Oxford University Press, 1968).

47. Amartya Sen, *Poverty and Famine* (Oxford: Oxford University Press, 1981).

48. John Rawls, *A Theory of Justice,* rev. ed. (Cambridge, Mass.: Harvard University Press, 1999).

3. Mutual Recognition

1. Similarly, in his discussion of the schematism we find that "the community or reciprocity, the reciprocal causality of substances in respect of their accidents, is the co-existence, according to a universal rule, of the determinations of the one substance with those of the other" (A144/B183–184).

2. Emmanuel Levinas, *Totality and Infinity: An Essay on Exteriority,* trans. Alphonso Lingis (Pittsburgh: Duquesne University Press, 1969); *Otherwise than Being or Beyond Essence,* trans. Alphonso Lingis (Dordrecht: Kluwer, 1991).

3. Paul Ricoeur, "Otherwise: A Reading of Emmanuel Levinas's *Otherwise than Being or Beyond Essence,*" trans. Matthew Escobar, *Yale French Studies,* no. 104 (2004): 82–99.

4. "The *otherwise than being* that is stated in a saying that must also be unsaid in order thus to extract the *otherwise than being* from the said in which it already comes to signify but a *being otherwise*" (*Otherwise than Being or beyond Essence*, 7).

5. In my "Otherwise" I noted: "I do not know whether readers have measured the enormity of the paradox consisting in using malice to speak of the degree of extreme passivity of the ethical condition. It is 'outrage,' the height of injustice, that is asked to signify the appeal to benevolence: 'It is through the condition of the hostage that there can be pity, compassion, pardon, proximity in the world'" (*Otherwise than Being*, 117).

6. "Politics tends toward reciprocal recognition; that is, toward equality; it assures happiness" (*Totality and Infinity*, 64). "One should then also recall that proximity is not from the first a judgment of a tribunal of justice but first a responsibility for the other which turns into judgment only with the entry of the third party" (*Otherwise than Being*, 190, n.35). But who is the third party? The other of the other? The other than the other? Or, as I think, the place of truth rather than that of the state? The site of discourse about the same and the other? The place where kindness is spoken?

7. Leo Strauss, *The Political Philosophy of Hobbes: Its Basis and Its Genesis*, trans. Elsa M. Sinclair (Chicago: University of Chicago Press, 1952).

8. Thomas Hobbes, *Leviathan,* with selected variants from the Latin edition of 1668, ed. Edwin Curley (Indianapolis, Ind.: Hackett, 1994), 76.

9. I acknowledge my debt here to Y.-Ch. Zarka's *L'autre voie de la subjectivité* (Paris: Beauchène, 2000). With this title, Zarka means to refer to a non-Cartesian option, that of "the invention of the subject of the law from Grotius to Leibniz" (3).

10. Grotius' model, Suarez, with Thomas Aquinas in the background, insisted that justice includes equality. Things that are equal to each other, adjust to each other. Grotius himself does not fail to link this natural gift with the social nature of human beings. Otherwise, how are we to speak of respecting the other's property, of keeping our word, of making amends for harm done, of carrying out punishment? Third persons are implied in each such case. But what is a person? The upshot is that if the *jus naturalis* opens another way to subjectivity, this is immediately an intersubjective way in terms of the express mode of reciprocal action.

11. Axel Honneth, *The Struggle for Recognition,* trans. Joel Anderson (London: Polity, 1995).

12. Alexandre Kojève, *Introduction to the Reading of Hegel,* trans. James Nichols (New York: Basic Books, 1969).

13. G. W. F. Hegel, *Système de la Vie éthique,* trans. Jacques Taminiaux (Paris: Payot, 1976); Jacques Taminiaux, *Naissance de la philosophie hégélienne de l'État* (Paris: Payot, 1984).

14. G. W. F. Hegel, *System of Ethical Life (1802–1803)* and *First Philosophy of Spirit,* ed. and trans. H. S. Harris and T. M. Knox (Albany: State University of New York Press, 1979), 102.

15. Taminiaux, *Système de la Vie éthique,* 59.

16. Leo Rauch, *Hegel and the Human Spirit: A Translation of the Jena Lectures on the Philosophy of Spirit (1805–1806) with Commentary* (Detroit: Wayne State University Press, 1983).

17. "In order that I may have my *positive* Self in the common will, the being-recognized [as intelligence] is known by me, so that the will is posited by me, so that I therein have it *negatively,* as my power, as the universal, which is the negative of my own will, through the intuition of its necessity, i.e., through the externalization" (ibid., 153).

18. "A Systematic Renewal: The Structure of Social Relations of Recognition."

19. "It is assumed here that the task of reality-acceptance is never completed, that no human being is free from the strain of relating inner and outer reality, and that relief from this strain is provided by an intermediate area of experience . . . which is not challenged (arts, religion, etc.). This intermediate area is in direct continuity with the play area of the small child who is 'lost' in play" (103, citing Donald W. Winnicott, "Transitional Objects and Transitional Phenomena," in *Playing and Reality* [London: Tavistock, 1971], 13).

20. Simone Weil, "The Love of God and Affliction," in *The Simone Weil Reader,* ed. George A. Panichas (New York: David Berg, 1977), 445–446.

21. Françoise Héritier, *Masculin/Féminin: La pensée de la différence* (Paris: Odile Jacob, 1995).

22. I owe these comments to the fourth chapter of Pierre Legendre, *L'inestimable objet de la transmission: Étude sur le principe généalogique en Occident* (Paris: Fayard, 1985).

23. Arendt, *The Human Condition,* 247.

24. My first confrontation with this theme of birth was in *Freedom and*

Nature: The Voluntary and the Involuntary, trans. Erazim Kohak (Evanston, Ill.: Northwestern University Press, 1966), under the rubric of the absolute involuntary. It remained curiously confined within the limits of a reflection on the fact of being already born without any consideration of desire—whatever that might be—on the part of the parents. Hence I placed what I called the genetic antecedent, in other words, heredity, in the realm of alienating objectivity. One could also think, in regard to the origin that is not the beginning, of Angelus Silesius' "The rose is without why; it blooms because it blooms."

25. I shall leave aside the question of the ultimate ground of the genealogical principle on the symbolic plane: a single phallus for both sexes? The great Other? An original Father? This question torments Legendre, following in Lacan's footsteps. For my part, and within the limits of my own project, I shall confine myself within the boundaries of the genealogical principle as the invariant behind all the invariants that make up filiation. Already inscribed in the unbounded scale of ages, each rank is both instituted and instituting, none of them being the foundation. All the lineages are already double, both paternal and maternal. Female and male are already involved. This twofold condition, affecting every rank and lineage, suffices to establish a relationship of indebtedness in the ascending order and one of a heritage in the descending order. Even without taking on the problematic of the absolute foundation of the genealogical principle, the experience of recognizing oneself through filiation within the limits of its patrilineal and matrilineal lines is sufficient for confronting the fantasy of being all-powerful, as well as for revealing the mystery of birth and testifying to the objection that the genealogical principle makes against the incest drive as the bearer of nondistinction.

26. Honneth cites in this regard a passage from Hegel's *Encyclopedia* that clearly underscores the double intention of recognition: "In the state . . . man is recognized and treated as a *rational* being, as free, as a person; and the individual, on his side, makes himself worthy of this recognition by overcoming the natural state of his self-consciousness and obeying a universal, the will that is in essence and actuality will, the *law;* he behaves, therefore, toward others in a manner that is universally valid, recognizing them—as he wishes others to recognize him—as free, as persons" (*The Structure of Recognition,* 108).

27. Following Habermas on this point, Honneth strongly emphasizes the difference between postconventional morality characterized by the

conquest of such rights and conventional morality dominated by ties of allegiance to communities based on traditional forms of authority. I shall not make use of this opposition, which runs the risk of imposing an excessive simplification on the passage to modernity. The break between esteem at the stage of conventional morality and respect at the postconventional stage is not so great that the lexicon of esteem is prevented from returning with the third model of intersubjective recognition.

28. Robert Alexy, *A Theory of Legal Argumentation* (Oxford: Clarendon, 1989); Talcott Parsons, *The System of Modern Societies* (Englewood Cliffs, N.J.: Prentice Hall, 1971).

29. Joel Feinberg, *Rights, Justice, and the Bounds of Liberty: Essays in Social Philosophy* (Princeton, N.J.: Princeton University Press, 1980), 151, cited by Honneth, 120.

30. I have already given an echo of this structural analysis of the idea of identity in my reflections on "social capacities," at the end of the previous chapter.

31. "The question bears centrally on the conditions under which personal identities can be produced and maintained in a social context where the recognition of persons is highly mediated by systemic 'regulators,' such as monetary considerations and legal rules, and what in general constitutes the 'system' in its different—technical, monetary, fiscal, bureaucratic, legal, democratic, publicity, pedagogical, and scientific—aspects, along with all the 'signs' that correspond to them, which are all indicators of behavior meant to coordinate individual actions within collective undertakings on a large scale" (Ferry, 2:9).

32. Arnold Gehlen, *Anthropologie et psychologie sociale*, trans. J. L. Dbande (Paris: Presses Universitaires de France, 1990).

33. "Communication is *our* postindustrial ideology, but it contains another ideal of a morality that needs to be resuscitated and extended, through the recognition of those who could not speak of the injury done to them—those anonymous victims of whom Walter Benjamin speaks, who cannot even be quoted (see his third thesis on the concept of history). As with Benjamin, and unlike with Jonas, responsibility here is turned not toward the future, but toward the past. In this, the ethics of communication is close to religion, for it too is an ethics of redemption. As such, it is founded on *reconstructive* identity rather than on an *argumentative* identity" (Ferry, 2:156).

34. I shall say nothing here about the problems having to do with citizen-

ship. I shall return to this problem in discussing Charles Taylor's book dealing with the "politics of recognition." Ferry does take a stand on the discussion opened by Habermas on the relation between the national and the postnational, and more precisely on the question of the construction of Europe (2:161–222).

35. Luc Boltanski and Laurent Thévenot, *De la justification: Les économies de la grandeur* (Paris: Gallimard, 1991).

36. See Paul Ricoeur, *The Just,* trans. David Pellauer (Chicago: University of Chicago Press, 2000), 77–81.

37. The precedents here are numerous; for example, Adam Smith's *Theory of Moral Sentiments,* ed. D. D. Raphael and A. L. Macfie (Oxford: Oxford University Press, 1976). See here also A. Hirschman, *Les passions et les intérêts* (Paris: Presses Universitaires de France, 1980).

38. Jacques Bénigne Bossuet, *La politique tirée des Propres paroles de l'Écriture sainte* (Geneva: Droz, 1709).

39. Boltanski and Thévenot, *De la justification,* 61.

40. "We are indebted to A. Hirschman (1977) for having reconstructed, by means of an analysis of a sequence of intellectual elaborations on the ideas of desire, glory, amour propre and vanity, appetite, virtue, and so on, the history of the treatment of the notions of passion and interest preceding the construction of Adam Smith's system and, more generally, the arguments developed with regard to liberalism" (ibid., 68).

41. Boltanski and Thévenot do this in their seventh chapter, devoted to a "table of critiques" (291–334).

42. Marcel Détienne, *Comparer l'incomparable* (Paris: Seuil, 2000).

43. Boltanski and Thévenot, "Figures du compromis," 357ff.

44. Pascal, *Pensées,* trans. A. J. Krailsheimer (Baltimore: Penguin, 1966), no. 116, 59.

45. See my essay "Le paradoxe de l'authorité," in *Le juste 2* (Paris: Éditions Esprit, 2001), 107–123.

46. "The authority of persons is ultimately based not on subjection and abdication of reason but on an act of acknowledgement and knowledge—the knowledge, namely, that the other is superior to oneself in judgment and insight and that for this reason his judgment takes precedence—i.e., it has priority over one's own. This is connected with the fact that authority cannot actually be bestowed but is earned, and must be earned if someone is to lay claim to it. It reasons on acknowledgement and hence on an act of reason itself which, aware of its own limi-

tations, trusts to the better insight of others. Authority, in this sense, properly understood, has nothing to do with blind obedience to commands. Indeed, Authority has to do not with obedience but rather with knowledge." Hans-Georg Gadamer, *Truth and Method,* 2nd rev. edition, trans. Joel Weinsheimer and Donald G. Marshall (New York: Crossroad, 1991), 279.

47. I introduce the concept of enunciated authority, as distinguished from institutional authority, in *Le juste 2,* 119.

48. Charles Taylor, "The Politics of Recognition," in Amy Gutman, ed., *Multiculturalism* (Princeton, N.J.: Princeton University Press, 1994), 25–73.

49. "The claim is that the supposedly neutral set of difference-blind principles of the politics of equal dignity is in fact a reflection of one hegemonic culture" (ibid., 43).

50. *Hegel's Philosophy of Right,* trans. T. M. Knox (New York: Oxford University Press, 1967), §257, p. 155.

51. See "Should We Renounce Hegel," in my *Time and Narrative,* vol. 3, trans. Kathleen Blamey and David Pellauer (Chicago: University of Chicago Press, 1988), 193–206.

52. Marcel Hénaff, *Le prix de la vérité: Le don, l'argent, la philosophie* (Paris: Seuil, 2002). See, for example, Luc Boltanski, "Agapè: Une introduction aux états de paix," in *L'amour et la justice comme compétences* (Paris: Métaillé, 1990).

53. This maxim should be compared with the earlier theses in the book published with Laurent Thévenot, *Économies de la grandeur,* discussed above.

54. Søren Kierkegaard, *Works of Love,* trans. Edna and Howard Hong (Princeton, N.J.: Princeton University Press, 1993).

55. Franz Rosenzweig, *The Star of Redemption,* trans. William W. Hallo (New York: Holt, Rinehart and Winston, 1970).

56. In my essay "The Nuptial Metaphor" in André LaCocque and Paul Ricoeur, *Thinking Biblically,* trans. David Pellauer (Chicago: University of Chicago Press, 1998), 265–303, I discuss the Song of Songs as a garden of metaphors. This capacity to signify more than erotic love was underestimated by Anders Nygren when he opposed *eros* and *agape,* and by those who followed him in building on a dichotomy of *eros* and *agape.*

57. Pascal, *Pensées,* no. 308, pp. 123–125.

58. Fyodor Dostoevsky, *The Idiot*, trans. Constance Garnett (New York: Bantam Books, 1968).

59. Boltanski has attempted to describe this back-and-forth movement between these two realms, where we see the generous person driven to trying to justify him- or herself, if, for example, his or her gift is refused, and the litigious person is touched by the freedom and insouciance of the generous one and his or her apparently erratic character (230–242). We may ask ourselves if the juxtaposition in the Gospel of Luke (6:27–35) of the commandment to love our enemies, to which is added the condemnation of any expectation of a gift in return, and the repetition of the golden rule does not stem from this back-and-forth.

60. Marcel Mauss, *The Gift: Forms and Functions of Exchange in Archaic Societies*, trans. Ian Cunnison (New York: W. W. Norton, 1967).

61. Claude Lévi-Strauss, *Introduction to the Work of Marcel Mauss*, trans. Felicity Baker (London: Routledge and Kegan Paul, 1987).

62. Claude Lefort, "L'échange et la lutte des hommes" (1951), reprinted in his *Les formes de l'histoire: Essai d'anthropologie politique* (Paris: Gallimard, 1978).

63. Mark Rogin Anspach, *À charge de revanche: Figures élémentaires de la réciprocité* (Paris: Seuil, 2002).

64. François Tricaud, *L'accusation: Recherche sur les figures de l'agression éthique* (Paris: Dalloz, 1977); Raymond Verdier, *La vengeance* (Paris: Cujas, 1980–1984), vol. 4: *La vengeance dans la pensée occidentale*, ed. Gérard Courtois.

65. Jean-Pierre Dupuy, *Aux origines des sciences cognitives* (Paris: Découverte, 1994).

66. "The *hau*, in fact, is only a reification of the circulation of gifts themselves" (Anspach, *À charge de revanche*, 42).

67. Anspach runs into this use of recognition in a traditional formula for "recognizing what is not to be recognized" (52), which applies to the transmission of a message at the metalevel. This recognition-identification is already present in the formulation of the double bind: "In recognizing a present by giving one in return, does one not destroy the original gift as gift?" The two levels between which the theory tries to distinguish are merged in this "to recognize as" (53–54).

68. It would be another discussion to consider the phenomena of trust and loss of trust connected with the fiduciary dimension of monetary cases. In this regard, Anspach turns his back on Adam Smith's optimism as

symbolized by the metaphor of the invisible hand. He depicts people as "prisoners of the market" (68). In the face of this powerlessness, which recalls the theme of the vicious circle first illustrated by vengeance, Anspach calls for help from "a superhuman power, one situated at a metalevel." Luckily, he adds, such a power exists: it is the state. "With the state, individuals escape the vicious circle of the *hau*" (72). The only thing that is important to us here is the assurance that the fiduciary phenomena with which the state must in turn deal, in the economic sphere, are of another nature than the trust that marks the initial entry into the circle of exchanging gifts.

69. Michael Walzer, *Spheres of Justice: A Defense of Pluralism and Equality* (New York: Basic Books, 1983).
70. Hénaff, *Le prix de la vérité*. See especially the second part, "L'univers du don."
71. According to Émile Benveniste, the merchant was already absent from the list of the three functions at the basis of the Indo-European system. *Indo-European Language and Society,* trans. Elizabeth Palmer (London: Faber, 1973). See chap. 11: "A Nameless Profession: Commerce."
72. Hénaff, *Le prix de la vérité,* cites Flaubert as saying, "My service remains undefined and consequently unpayable" (142).
73. Natalie Zemon Davis, *The Gift in Sixteenth-Century France* (Madison: University of Wisconsin Press, 2000).
74. "I believe that one must live by law and authority, not by reward and grace. . . . I flee from submitting myself to any kind of obligation, especially one that attaches me by the duty of honor. I find nothing so costly as that which is given me, for then my will is mortgaged by a title of gratitude. I'd rather buy a [royal] office than be given one, for buying it, I just give money. In the other case, I give myself. The knot that ties me by the law of honor seems much tighter than the knot of civil constraint. I'm throttled more gently by a notary than by myself." Further: "From what I know of the science of benefit and gratitude, which is a subtle science and very much in use today, I don't see anyone more free and less indebted than I am up to now. What I owe, I owe to our common and natural obligations" (74). In fact, Davis notes, Montaigne was not so free from this world of favor as his self-portrait suggests. Speaking of the transactions that went with his offices as judge, then of mayor, she concludes: "Montaigne was writing about the public world of benefits and favors as a participant as well as an observer" (75).

75. Cited by Hénaff, *Le prix de la vérité,* 171.

76. The *Littré* dictionary lists this sense as "souvenir affectueux d'un bienfait reçu avec désir de s'acquitter en rendant en pareille" (a fond memory of some received kind deed along with the desire to pay one's debt by giving back something similar). The *Grand Robert* assigns the third of its three overall senses of the word to *reconnaissance-gratitude.* Attested to since the twelfth century, one century after the sense of taking as true, the confession characterizing the second sense, *to recognize* means "témoigner par de la gratitude que l'on est redevable envers quelqu'un de quelque chose, une action"—to testify through one's gratitude that one owes something to someone for something, for some action. We can see how the shift from the second to the third sense takes place though the unsaid of the *bienfait* as an "admitted," acknowledged value, hence as something taken "to be true."

77. Paul Ricoeur, *Memory, History, Forgetting,* trans. Kathleen Blamey and David Pellauer (Chicago: University of Chicago Press, 2004), 477.

Conclusion

1. Paul Ricoeur, "The Logic of Jesus, the Logic of God," in *Figuring the Sacred: Religion, Narrative, and Imagination,* trans. David Pellauer, ed. Mark I. Wallace (Minneapolis, Minn.: Fortress, 1995), 279–283.

2. Karl Jaspers, *Philosophy,* vol. 2, trans. E. B. Ashton (Chicago: University of Chicago Press, 1970).

3. *The Complete Essays of Montaigne,* trans. Donald M. Frame (Stanford, Calif.: Stanford University Press, 1957), 139.

WORKS CITED

Alexy, Robert. *A Theory of Legal Argumentation*. Oxford: Clarendon, 1989.

Anscombe, G. E. M. *Intentions*. Oxford: Blackwell, 1957.

Anspach, Mark Rogin. *À charge de revanche: Figures élémentaires de la réciprocité*. Paris: Seuil, 2002.

Arendt, Hannah. *The Human Condition*. Chicago: University of Chicago Press, 1958.

Aristotle. *Éthique à Nicomaque*. Trans. René Antoine Gauthier and Jean-Yves Jolif. Paris: Béatrice-Nauwelaerts, 1958.

———. *The Complete Works of Aristotle*, 2 vols. Edited by Jonathan Barnes. Princeton, N.J.: Princeton University Press, 1984.

Augustine. *Confessions*. Trans. Henry Chadwick. Oxford: Oxford University Press, 1991.

Austin, J. L. *How to Do Things with Words*. Cambridge, Mass.: Harvard University Press, 1963.

Benveniste, Émile. *Indo-European Language and Society*. Trans. Elizabeth Palmer. London: Faber, 1973.

Bergson, Henri. *The Creative Mind: An Introduction to Metaphysics*. Trans. Mabelle L. Andison. New York: Philosophical Library, 1946; Carol Publishing Group, 1992.

———. *Mind-Energy*. Trans. H. Wildon Carr. Westport, Conn.: Greenwood, 1975.

———. *Matter and Memory*. Trans. N. M. Paul and W. S. Palmer. New York: Zone Books, 1988.

Berlin, Isaiah. *Four Essays on Liberty*. Oxford University Press, 1968.

Boissière, P. *Le dictionnaire analogique de la langue française.* 9th ed. Paris: Larousse, 1900.

Boltanski, Luc. *L'amour et la justice comme compétences: Trois essais de sociologie de l'action.* Paris: Métaillé, 1990.

Bossuet, Jacques Bénigne. *La politique tirée des Propres paroles de l'Écriture sainte.* Geneva: Droz, 1709.

Davidson, Donald. *Essays on Actions and Events.* Oxford: Clarendon Press, 1980.

Davis, Natalie Zemon. *The Gift in Sixteenth-Century France.* Madison: University of Wisconsin Press, 2000.

Descartes, René. *The Philosophical Writings of Descartes,* 2 vols. Trans. John Cottingham, Robert Stoothoff, and Dugald Murdoch. New York: Cambridge University Press, 1985.

Détienne, Marcel. *Comparer l'incomparable.* Paris: Seuil, 2000.

Diès, Auguste. *La définition de l'être et la nature des idées dans le* Sophiste *de Platon.* Paris: Vrin, 1932.

Dostoevsky, Fyodor. *The Idiot.* Trans. Constance Garnett. New York: Bantam, 1968.

Dupuy, Jean-Pierre. *Aux origines des sciences cognitives.* Paris: La Découverte, 1994.

Dworkin, Ronald. *Taking Rights Seriously.* Cambridge, Mass.: Harvard University Press, 1978.

Elias, Norbert. *The Court Society.* Trans. Edmund Jephcott. New York: Pantheon, 1983.

———. *The Civilizing Process: Sociogenetic and Psychogenetic Investigations.* Trans. Edmund Jephcott with some notes and corrections by the author; ed. Eric Dunning, Johan Doudsblom, and Stephen Mennell. Malden, Mass: Blackwell, 2000.

Feinberg, Joel. *Rights, Justice, and the Bounds of Liberty: Essays in Social Philosophy.* Princeton, N.J.: Princeton University Press, 1980.

Ferry, Jean-Marc. *Les puissances de l'expérience: Essai sur l'identité contemporaine.* Paris: Cerf, 1991.

Furetière, Antoine. *Dictionnaire universel françois et latin,* 3 vols. Trévoux, 1704.

Gadamer, Hans-Georg. *Wahrheit und Methode.* 2nd ed. Tübingen: Mohr, 1965.

———. *Truth and Method,* 2nd rev. ed. Trans. Joel Weinsheimer and Donald G. Marshall. New York: Crossroad, 1991.

Gehlen, Arnold. *Anthropologie et psychologie sociale.* Trans. J. L. Dbande. Paris: Presses Universitaires de France, 1990.

Greimas, A.-J. *Structural Semantics: An Attempt at a Method.* Trans. Deniel McDowell, Ronald Schleifer, and Alan Velie. Lincoln: University of Nebraska Press, 1983.

Greisch, Jean. *Paul Ricoeur: L'itinéraire de sens.* Paris: Millon, 2001.

Hallig, Rudolf, and Walter von Wartburg. *Begriffssystem als Grundlage für die Lexikographie: Versuch eines Ordnunngsschemas = Système raisonné des concepts pour servir de base à la lexicographie: Essai d'un schéma de classement,* 2nd ed. Berlin: Akademie-Verlag, 1963.

Hegel, G. W. F. *Hegel's Philosophy of Right.* Trans. T. M. Knox. New York: Oxford University Press, 1967.

———. *Système de la vie éthique.* Trans. Jacques Taminiaux. Paris: Payot, 1976.

———. *System of Ethical Life (1802–1803)* and *First Philosophy of Spirit.* Ed. and trans. H. S. Harris and T. M. Knox. Albany: State University of New York Press, 1979.

Heidegger, Martin. *Kant and the Problem of Metaphysics,* 5th ed., enlarged. Trans. Richard Taft. Bloomington: Indiana University Press, 1997.

Hénaff, Marcel. *Le prix de la vérité: Le don, l'argent, la philosophie.* Paris: Seuil, 2002.

Héritier, Françoise. *Masculin/Féminin.* Paris: Odile Jacob, 1995.

Hirschman, A. *Les passions et les interêts.* Paris: Presses Universitaires de France, 1980.

Hobbes, Thomas. *Leviathan,* with selected variants from the Latin edition of 1668. Ed. Edwin Curley. Indianapolis, Ind.: Hackett, 1994.

Homer. *L'Odyssée,* trans. Victor Bérard. Paris: Les Belles Lettres, 1924.

Honneth, Alex. *The Struggle for Recognition.* Trans. Joel Anderson. London: Polity, 1995.

Husserl, Edmund. *The Crisis of European Sciences and Transcendental Philosophy.* Trans. David Carr. Evanston, Ill.: Northwestern University Press, 1970.

———. *Cartesian Meditations.* Trans. Dorian Cairns. The Hague: Martinus Nijhoff, 1973.

———. *Phantasie, Bildbewusstsein, Erinnerung (1898–1925).* Ed. Eduard Marbach. Dordrecht: Martinus Nijhoff, 1980.

———. *On the Phenomenology of the Consciousness of Internal Time*

(1893–1917). Trans. John Barnett Brough. Dordrecht: Kluwer Academic, 1991.

Imbs, Paul, ed. *Trésor de la langue française: Dictionnaire de la langue du XIXe et du XXe siècle*, 16 vols. Paris: Éditions du Centre national de la recherche scientifique, 1971–1994.

Jaspers, Karl. *Philosophy*, vol. 2. Trans. E. B. Ashton. Chicago: University of Chicago Press, 1970.

Jauss, Hans Robert. *Toward an Aesthetic of Reception*. Trans. Timothy Bahti. Minneapolis: University of Minnesota Press, 1982.

Jonas, Hans. *The Imperative of Responsibility: In Search of an Ethics for the Technological Age*. Chicago: University of Chicago Press, 1984.

Kant, Immanuel. *Critique of Pure Reason*. Trans. Norman Kemp Smith. New York: St. Martin's, 1965.

———. *The Metaphysics of Morals*. Trans. and ed. Mary Gregor. Cambridge: Cambridge University Press, 1996.

Kierkegaard, Søren. *Works of Love*. Trans. Edna and Howard Hong. Princeton, N.J.: Princeton University Press, 1993.

Kojève, Alexandre. *Introduction to the Reading of Hegel*. Trans. James Nichols. New York: Basic, 1969.

LaCocque, André, and Paul Ricoeur. *Thinking Biblically*. Trans. David Pellauer. Chicago: University of Chicago Press, 1998.

Lefort, Claude. *Les formes de l'histoire: Essai d'anthropologie politique*. Paris: Gallimard, 1978.

Legendre, Pierre. *L'inestimable objet de la transmission: Étude sur le principe généalogique en Occident*. Paris: Fayard, 1985.

Lepetit, Bernard, ed. *Les formes de l'expérience: Une autre histoire sociale*. Paris: Albin Michel, 1995.

Levinas, Emmanuel. *Totality and Infinity: An Essay on Exteriority*. Trans. Alphonso Lingis. Pittsburgh, Pa.: Duquesne University Press, 1969.

———. *Otherwise than Being or Beyond Essence*. Trans. Alphonso Lingis. Dordrecht: Kluwer, 1991.

———. *Discovering Existence with Husserl*. Trans. Richard A. Cohen and Michael B. Smith. Evanston, Ill.: Northwestern University Press, 1998.

Lévi-Strauss, Claude. *Introduction to the Work of Marcel Mauss*. Trans. Felicity Baker. London: Routledge and Kegan Paul, 1987.

Littré, Émile. *Dictionnaire de la langue française*. Paris: Hachette, 1889.

Lloyd, Geoffrey E. R. *Demystifying Mentalities.* Cambridge: Cambridge University Press, 1990.

Locke, John. *An Essay Concerning Human Understanding,* 2 vols. New York: Dover, 1959.

Mackie, J. L. *Ethics: Inventing Right and Wrong.* New York: Penguin, 1978.

Mauss, Marcel. *The Gift: Forms and Functions of Exchange in Archaic Societies.* Trans. Ian Cunnison. New York: W. W. Norton, 1967.

Merleau-Ponty, Maurice. *Phenomenology of Perception.* Trans. Colin Smith. New York: Humanities Press, 1962.

Montaigne, Michel de. *The Complete Essays of Montaigne.* Trans. Donald M. Frame. Stanford, Calif.: Stanford University Press, 1957.

Nabert, Jean. *Le désir de Dieu.* Paris: Cerf, 1996.

Nicole, Pierre. *De l'éducation d'un prince.* (Paris: chez la veuve Charles Savreux, 1670).

Nietzsche, Friedrich. *On the Genealogy of Morals* and *Ecce Homo.* Trans. Walter Kaufmann and R. J. Hollindale. New York: Vintage, 1967.

———. *Human, All Too Human: A Book for Free Spirits.* Trans. R. J. Hollingdale. Cambridge: Cambridge University Press, 1996.

Nozick, Robert. *Anarchy, State and Utopia.* New York: Basic, 1974.

Parfit, Derrick. *Reasons and Persons.* Oxford: Oxford University Press, 1986.

Parsons, Talcott. *The System of Modern Societies.* Englewood Cliffs, N.J.: Prentice-Hall, 1971.

Pascal, Blaise. *Entretien avec M. de Saci sur Épictète et Montaigne.* Aix-en-Provence, France: Éditions Provençales, 1946.

———. *Pensées.* Trans. A. J. Krailsheimer. Baltimore, Md.: Penguin, 1966.

Plato. *Plato: Complete Works.* Ed. John M. Cooper. Indianapolis, Ind.: Hackett, 1997.

Propp, Vladimir. *Morphology of the Folktale.* Trans. Laurence Scott; 2nd rev. ed., ed. Louis A. Wagner. Austin: University of Texas Press, 1968.

Proust, Marcel. *Time Regained.* Trans. Andreas Mayor and Terence Kilmartin, rev. D. J. Enright. New York: Modern Library, 1993.

Rauch, Leo. *Hegel and the Human Spirit: A Translation of the Jena Lectures on the Philosophy of Spirit (1805–1806) with Commentary.* Detroit: Wayne State University Press, 1983.

Rawls, John. *A Theory of Justice*, rev. ed. Cambridge, Mass.: Harvard University Press, 1999.

Revel, Jacques, ed. *Jeux d'échelles: La micro-analyse à l'expérience.* Paris: Gallimard/Seuil, 1996.

Rey, Alain, ed. *Le grand Robert de la langue française*, 2nd ed. Paris: Le Robert, 1985.

Ricoeur, Paul. *Freedom and Nature: The Voluntary and the Involuntary.* Trans. Erazim Kohak. Evanston, Ill.: Northwestern University Press, 1966.

———. *Time and Narrative*, 3 vols. Trans. Kathleen Blamey and David Pellauer. Chicago: University of Chicago Press, 1984–1988.

———. "The Logic of Jesus, the Logic of God." In *Figuring the Sacred: Religion, Narrative, and Imagination*, trans. David Pellauer, ed. Mark I. Wallace. Minneapolis, Minn.: Fortress, 1995.

———. *The Just.* Trans. David Pellauer. Chicago: University of Chicago Press, 2000.

———. *Le juste 2.* Paris: Esprit, 2001.

———. *Memory, History, Forgetting.* Trans. Kathleen Blamey and David Pellauer. Chicago: University of Chicago Press, 2004.

———. "Otherwise: A Reading of Emmanuel Levinas's *Otherwise than Being or Beyond Essence*." Trans. Matthew Escobar. *Yale French Studies*, no. 104 (2004): 82–99.

Rilke, Rainer Maria, and Balthus, *Lettres à un jeune peintre suivi de Mitsou.* Paris: Payot et Rivages, 2002.

Rosenzweig, Franz. *The Star of Redemption.* Trans. William W. Hallo. New York: Holt, Rinehart and Winston, 1970.

Schapp, Wilhelm. *In Geschichten Verstrickt.* Wiesbaden, Germany: Heymann, 1976.

Sen, Amartya. *Poverty and Famine.* Oxford: Oxford University Press, 1981.

———. *Commodities and Capabilities.* Amsterdam: North Holland, 1985.

———. *On Ethics and Economics.* Oxford: Blackwell, 1987.

Smith, Adam. *Theory of Moral Sentiments.* Ed. D. D. Raphael and A. L. Macfie, Oxford: Oxford University Press, 1976.

———. *Inquiry into the Nature and Cause of the Wealth of Nations.* (New York: Oxford University Press, 1993).

Sophocles. *Oedipe à Colonne.* Trans. Paul Masqueray. Paris: Les Belles Lettres, 1934.

Spinoza, Baruch. *The Collected Works of Spinoza,* vol. 1. Ed. and trans. Edwin Curley. Princeton, N.J.: Princeton University Press, 1985.

Strauss, Leo. *The Political Philosophy of Hobbes: Its Basis and Its Genesis.* Trans. Elsa M. Sinclair. Chicago: University of Chicago Press, 1952.

Taminiaux, Jacques. *Naissance de la philosophe hégélienne de l'État.* Paris: Payot, 1984.

Taylor, Charles. *Sources of the Self.* Cambridge, Mass.: Harvard University Press, 1989.

———. "The Politics of Recognition." In Amy Gutman, ed., *Multiculturalism.* Princeton, N.J.: Princeton University Press, 1994, 25–73.

Tricaud, François. *L'accusation: Recherche sur les figures de l'agression éthique.* Paris: Dalloz, 1977.

Vanderbeken, Daniel. *Les actes de discours.* Paris: Éditions Pierre Mardage, 1998.

Verdier, Raymond. *La vengeance,* 4 vols. Ed. Gérard Courtois. Paris: Cujas, 1980–1984.

Walzer, Michael. *Spheres of Justice: A Defense of Pluralism and Equality.* New York: Basic, 1983.

Weil, Simone. "The Love of God and Affliction." In *The Simone Weil Reader.* Ed. George A. Panichas. New York: David Berg, 1977.

Williams, Bernard. *Shame and Necessity.* Berkeley: University of California Press, 1993.

Winnicott, Donald W. *Playing and Reality.* London: Tavistock, 1971.

Zarka, Y.-Ch. *L'autre voie de la subjectivité.* Paris: Beauchène, 2000.

INDEX

Abraham, 134
Action, 71, 81, 87, 88, 90, 92, 93, 96–99, 105, 131, 140, 146, 147, 149, 218, 225, 231, 253; analogy of, 94; rational, 80, 83, 85, 87; reciprocal, 149; social, 88; sociology of, 220, 225, 227; symbolic, 104
Agape, 219, 220, 222–225, 227, 228, 231, 232, 242, 243, 251
Agency, 72, 75, 79, 96, 125; social, 138–139, 142, 145, 248, 252
Alexy, Robert, 199
Alterity, 93, 103, 154, 155, 262; dialectic of, 93, 152, 170–171, 251, 252, 254
Anscombe, G. E. M., 96
Anspach, Mark Rogin, 227, 229, 231
Approbation, 14, 96, 191, 255
Appropriation, 98, 101, 122
Aquinas, Thomas, 166n10
Arendt, Hannah, 131, 132, 162, 194, 221, 250, 253
Aristotle, 1, 66, 70, 71, 75, 76, 79–89, 92, 94, 98, 100, 111, 113, 119, 126, 130, 147, 162, 172, 190, 198, 221, 225, 234
Aron, Raymond, 213
Ascription, 98, 105, 106, 149

Attestation, 30, 91–92, 148, 149, 151, 250, 254
Augustine, Saint, 70, 112, 118–119, 120, 122, 127, 130, 207, 212
Austin, J. L., 94, 95, 128
Authority, 7, 15, 16, 169, 210–212
Autonomy, 90, 174, 189

Bacon, Francis, 163
Balthus, 64
Baudelaire, Charles, 234
Being-in-the-world, 41–42, 61, 62
Benveniste, Émile, 234n71
Bergson, Henri, 14, 17, 18, 19, 21, 45, 70, 110–111, 113, 123, 124, 125, 126
Berkeley, George, 47
Berlin, Isaiah, 143
Boltanski, Luc, 204–212, 220, 222, 224, 225, 226, 251
Bossuet, Jacques Bénigne, 9, 207
Breton, Stanislas, 26
Braudel, Fernand, 135, 138

Capable human being, 69, 89, 91, 94, 128, 134, 141, 147, 151, 187, 217, 248, 249, 251, 252, 253; hermeneutics of the, 95
Change, 62, 64, 65